FROM CHAOS TO COOPERATION

FROM CHAOS TO COOPERATION:

TOWARD REGIONAL ORDER IN THE MIDDLE EAST

ROSS HARRISON, PAUL SALEM, EDS.

 Middle East Institute

THE MIDDLE EAST INSTITUTE
1761 N STREET NW
WASHINGTON, D.C. 20036

Follow MEI:

 @MiddleEastInst

 /MiddleEastInstitute

 /user/middleastinstitute

CONTENTS

CONTRIBUTORS

ROSS HARRISON
Ross Harrison is a scholar at The Middle East Institute and is on the faculty of the School of Foreign Service at Georgetown University, and the University of Pittsburgh.

PAUL SALEM
Paul Salem is vice president for policy and research at The Middle East Institute.

SHAHROKH FARDOUST
Shahrokh Fardoust is a research professor at the Institute of the Theory and Practice of International Relations at the College of William and Mary.

JEAN-FRANCOIS SEZNEC
Jean-Francois Seznec is an adjunct professor at the McDonough Schoool of Business at Georgetown, as well as at Johns Hopkins' School of Advanced International Studies.

BERNARD HOEKMAN
Bernard Hoekman is a professor and director of the Global Economics program at the Robert Schuman Centre for Advanced Studies, European University Institute in Florence, Italy.

HEDI LARBI
Hedi Larbi, a former Tunisian minister, is an Associate Scholar at the Kennedy School of Government, Harvard University.

GERALD STANG
Gerald Stang is a Senior Associate Analyst with the European Union Institute for Security Studies where he primarily works on energy, climate change and other emerging security challenges.

AYSEGÜL KIBAROGLU
Aysegül Kibaroglu is professor and faculty member in the Department of Political Science and International Relations at MEF University Istanbul, Turkey.

ANTHONY H. CORDESMAN
Anthony H. Cordesman is the holder of the Arleigh A. Burke Chair in Strategy at the Center for Strategic and International Studies.

QUERINE HANLON
Querine Hanlon is the founding president of Strategic Capacity Group (S.C.G.), a nonprofit institution created to enhance security sector capacity in the United States and its key security partners.

ACKNOWLEDGEMENTS

A ll books are a collective effort. First and foremost, we would like to thank Antoun Issa, senior editor at the Middle East Institute, for his excellent and tireless work in helping turn first and second drafts into finished and polished chapters, and then helping corral the various chapters into book form. Thanks are due also to Charlotte Lathrop, MEI's graphic designer, and Aliya Iftikhar, an intern at MEI, for their creative work in the design and layout of the book. We also thank Mark Scheland, director of programs and government relations at MEI, for organizing the conference on Advancing Regional Cooperation for Stability and Growth in the Middle East on December 7, 2016 in Washington, D.C.

We would also like to extend our sincerest thanks to all the contributors to this volume, who bore patiently with us from the early gestation of this project, all the way through to its fruition; and who gave generously of their time, energy, expertise, and advice.

This book is dedicated to the youth of the Middle East. We hope that this book will help ensure that they reap the rewards of cooperation, rather than the whirlwind of conflict and chaos.

PREFACE

Ross Harrison and Paul Salem

It might seem confounding to explore the pathways and prospects for regional cooperation in a Middle East currently mired in proxy conflict, civil war, and terrorism. But the Middle East is not the first region in the world to pass through a period of intense conflict—take Europe or East Asia just a few decades ago—and exit on a path toward regional cooperation. Indeed, it is exactly the immense toll that regional conflict is taking on states, societies, and economies of the region that makes developing a vision toward defusing regional conflict and building stability all the more urgent. Societies at war are those that urgently need an alternative vision of regional order and a roadmap for getting there.

Part of the violent confusion of the current Middle East disorder is the absence of a collective long-term vision. As a wry wit once remarked, "If you don't know where you're going, you're probably going to end up somewhere else." For five centuries before the 20th century, much of the Middle East was simply part of the Ottoman Empire. After the two world wars, the Arab states developed an Arabist version of regional order, while the non-Arab states of Turkey, Iran, and Israel decidedly looked westward.

With the Islamic revolution in Iran in 1979 and the rise of the Islamist-leaning Justice and Development Party in Turkey, those two countries turned back toward the region—albeit with Israel remaining isolated and aloof. And with the dismantling of the Iraqi state in 2003, and the disintegration of the Syrian state in 2012-2013, what was left of the old Arab order collapsed. Iran and Turkey have since been drawn deep into the region in proxy conflicts with each other and other Arab powers, Saudi Arabia specifically.

The current regional disorder serves none of the security or economic interests of the main regional states, but is a conflict trap that has ensnared all. Current conflicts are seen by protagonists in zero-sum terms, and a systemic shift from a regional conflict system to a regional cooperation system is a paradigm shift that few leaders can even imagine in theory, let alone work toward in practice. Global powers like the United States and Russia haven't helped either, providing no broader incentive structure for regional de-escalation and cooperation, but rather injecting themselves on one or another side of regional fault lines.

It should be quite commonplace to assert that a regional order in which the states of the region abide by the rules of international law; respect the security, sovereignty, and territorial integrity of each other; commit to peaceful resolution of disputes; and work toward building on common economic interests would benefit all the region's states and peoples. Unfortunately, current conditions in the region present an exactly opposite reality.

Despite—or perhaps because of—the conflicted realities of today's Middle East, this volume takes on the issue of regional cooperation head-on. In total, it attempts to provide a balanced approach—neither falling into the traps of naïve optimism nor cynical pessimism. It does, however, approach the topic from the belief that the only way to move the Middle East from its current state of instability, destruction, and despair is through eventual cooperation between the major regional powers, as remote as the prospects for this appear today.

Our angle of attack into the question of regional cooperation is to be both general and specific. The three chapters by Harrison and Salem look at the question of regional cooperation more broadly, while the other authors each tackled a specific sector of cooperation in either the politics and security or economics and environmental spheres. Each of the authors approached the topic of regional cooperation asking the same set of questions, with a long-term view of the region: what will the region look like in 2030 if the current levels of conflict and non-cooperation continued and what would an alternative future look like in 2030 if the path of cooperation and coordination was taken? They addressed the question of the current state of cooperation (or lack thereof) in their particular domains. They also grappled with the question of what the implications of 'muddling through' at the current state of cooperation would be. They then discussed what cooperation might look like in their specific sector, what obstacles stand in the way of this, and what positive impact cooperation could have should it materialize.

There is a danger of reductionism in this approach. The challenge is that it is easy to wrongly conclude that incremental progress in a number of these sectors leads to a tipping point toward more general cooperation. This is not our premise and we sought to avoid this trap by treating incremental progress in the various sectors, not as movement toward a tipping point, but rather as fuel awaiting the spark of political will necessary for broader cooperation. In fact, each author either explicitly or implicitly argues that the biggest impediment to connecting these sector specific nodes of cooperation to broader forms of cooperation is the absence of political will.

Additionally, there are answers to several different questions about cooperation that can be teased out of the chapters. First, what is the regional and international context for cooperation? Regional cooperation in the Middle East doesn't take place in a vacuum, but rather within the context of regional and international dynamics. In this spirit, Salem addresses questions about the Middle East regional order, specifically discussing the role international powers have played in shaping that order, and what steps can be taken for moving the region closer to cooperation. Harrison focuses less on the notion of a regional order and more on the questions around regionalization in the Middle East, the lack of positive interdependencies between states, and what role regional institutions can play in fostering cooperation.

Second, what are the specific issues around which cooperation may be possible? Given the mega trends of climate change, drought, and water shortages, two authors weighed in on this topic. Stang argues that there are plans on the shelf for cooperating on environmental issues, with only a lack of will impeding progress. Kibarlou looks at failures, but also opportunities for dealing with water management, arguing that cooperation on this issue could create opportunities for cooperation in other critical economic and political areas. Seznec and Larbi each argues that while cooperation on energy and infrastructure, respectively, may be a long way off, there are assets in place that could be deployed toward cooperation once there is sufficient political will. The machinery of cooperation is already in place in many of these areas; it just needs to be plugged in.

Third, what are the underlying conditions that affect the prospects for cooperation? Cordesman is skeptical about regional conditions being supportive of cooperation and doesn't go as far as either Salem or Harrison in viewing the international community as playing a supportive role. Instead, he sees the United States as the primary actor, though acknowledges the emerging role of Russia. Hanlon suggests that regional capacity-building measures in the areas of security sector reform can pay dividends in other areas of cooperation by creating a foundation of stability. On the economic front, Fardoust argues that state-based reform is a sine qua non for cooperation. But he sees this as a necessary, but insufficient condition for cooperation, arguing that given the state of affairs in the region today, a mini-Marshall plan involving international and regional actors will also be necessary.

Fourth, what could be specific accelerants to cooperation? All authors see little progress possible in the absence of political will, but Hoekman isn't completely pessimistic, suggesting that in the absence of state-to-state cooperation, bottom-up measures by businesses interested in building regional value chains are possible starting points in the march toward economic cooperation. Harrison points to existing sub-regional institutions like the Gulf Cooperation Council, the Arab League, and the Arab Maghreb Union as possible assets in fostering cooperation. He also sees regionalization and the eventual creation of even more robust regional institutions as a pre-condition for cooperation.

This book as a whole should be thought of as providing different possible pathways toward cooperation, some involving back-door approaches and some more direct methods. This volume should be a useful guide for anyone wanting to understand the complexities, difficulties, and opportunities this region has as it moves toward 2030.

CHAPTER ONE

THE ROAD LESS TRAVELED:

POTENTIAL PATHWAYS FROM DISORDER TO ORDER IN THE MIDDLE EAST

PAUL SALEM

THE EVOLUTION OF A BROKEN REGIONAL ORDER[1]

The Middle East today has no regional order in any positive sense. It is the least ordered or governed regional sub-system in the world, and is contested by Iran, the Gulf states, Turkey, Egypt, and Israel. This chapter examines the elements of today's unstable Middle East, and suggests a path toward building a more stable and prosperous order. Building a stable regional order is key to ending civil wars and rebuilding failed states. And reconstituting states is key to reclaiming ungoverned space from terrorist groups, and denying ungoverned space to them in the future.

Other regions around the world have made the difficult transition from conflict to some measure of regional stability and cooperation. The Middle East has the potential to do so as well. Fifty years ago, Saudi Arabia and Egypt were engaged in a fierce struggle for dominance over the region, which led to direct war in Yemen and the toppling of governments in Iraq, Syria, Libya, and Sudan. Yet, the two states have moved past their differences. Israel and the Arab states engaged in multiple wars between the 1950s and 1970s, but Egypt, Jordan, and Israel found peace, albeit at times a cold one, and the Arab states proposed a comprehensive peace initiative in 2002. The current proxy conflict between Iran, Turkey, and the G.C.C. might seem unstoppable today, but an understanding of both the converging and diverging interests of the states involved, and the potential for strategic vision and effective leadership to bring about change, indicates that there is an alternative future available.

The region is not completely bereft of mechanisms for cooperation. The Gulf states have evolved a regional architecture among themselves under the Gulf Cooperation Council; and the Gulf states, Egypt, and other Arab countries are grouped within the weak Arab League. The countries of North Africa similarly established the Arab Maghreb Union, but that has been stymied by continued Algerian-Moroccan tension over Western Sahara, and the collapse of Libya. The Organization of Islamic Cooperation includes the Arab countries with Turkey, Iran, and other Muslim majority countries in Asia, but it has been more an arena of tension between the Sunni powers and Iran than one of cooperation. OPEC includes the Gulf States and Iran, and has seen periods of cooperation on oil production and pricing as well as competition. The Madrid peace process was designed to lead to the development of a regional security and economic cooperation architecture between Israel and the Arab countries, but the process failed. Most recently, the International Syria Support Group has been one of the only venues where Saudi, Turkish, and Iranian leaders have met in a political context.

Unlike in East Asia, Africa, the Americas, or Western Europe, there is no dedicated forum or institutionalized mechanism for the main regional powers to communicate, identify concerns, defuse conflicts, build on common interests, and work toward establishing a set of principles for regional interaction other than direct or proxy war. Working toward establishing such a functioning order is essential to rebuilding regional stability and a fundamental necessity in the broader campaign to deny space to terrorist organizations.

The challenge of building a stable regional order in the modern Middle East is not a new one. An historical look at both the erection and collapse of regional orders will also help us think ahead as to the prospects for cooperation. For five centuries the Ottoman Empire was the regional order, as it governed— directly or indirectly—the bulk of Arab lands. The interwar period postponed the question of regional order, as it was managed from Europe, but created precarious new Arab states—particularly in the Levant—with fresh borders and no recent legacy of indigenous government. World War II brought independence from European control and the establishment of the League of

Arab States.

The idea of an Arab order took deeper root after the Arab-Israeli war of 1948, and subsequent wars in 1967 and 1973. It had a strong Arab nationalist ethos. The Arab order had its own cold war between Saudi Arabia and Nasser's Egypt that raged from the late 1950s to the late 1960s. After the death of Nasser, Egypt and Saudi Arabia came together around the 1973 war against Israel. Between the end of World War II and the late 1970s, both Iran and Turkey were oriented westward with little interest in getting greatly involved in the Arab Middle East.

The global U.S.-Soviet Cold War impinged upon this Arab order from the 1950s onward, with Arab states aligning with one global power or another. The West tried to create an anti-Soviet regional order through the Baghdad Pact of 1955, which included Iraq, Turkey, Iran, and Pakistan, and with the hope that other Arab states would follow. Iraq withdrew from the pact after the overthrow of the monarchy there in 1958, and Nasser opposed it vehemently. The Soviet Union meanwhile made rapid headway, establishing strong political and military relations with Egypt, Iraq, Syria, Libya, Somalia, and the People's Democratic Republic of Yemen. Nasser built strong relations with the USSR, but tried to keep Egypt and his Arab allies away from direct Cold War alignments. Nasser was a founding member of the Non-Aligned Movement.

RISE OF THE IRANIAN-SAUDI RIVALRY

1973 and 1979 were watershed years in regional power patterns. The 1973 War set Egypt and Israel on the path to an eventual peace treaty that effectively ended the inter-state Arab-Israeli conflict. Peace with Israel also isolated Egypt and ended its leadership position in the Arab world. The 1973 War and the Saudi-led oil embargo against the United States and other countries triggered an enormous oil price surge: prices climbed from $3 per barrel at the beginning of 1973 to $38 per barrel by the end of the decade. With this, regional power decidedly shifted away from Egypt to the petro-states of Saudi Arabia and Iran. They are still the beneficiaries of that power shift.

Until 1979, Iran and Saudi Arabia were on the same general strategic page: two conservative monarchies aligned with the United States against Communist expansion and revolutionary change. The Islamic Revolution in Iran 1979 changed that. It pitted the two petro-states against each other for the ensuing decades and helped bring about the regional conflict system that persists until today.

Revolutionary Iran challenged the regional order at several levels: it proclaimed that it was a pan-Islamic revolutionary movement, not a strictly Iranian one, whose goals included the overthrow of conservative monarchies, the overthrow of regimes aligned with the United States, the championing of Islamist causes, and the bringing about of an Islamic regional order effectively under Iranian leadership. And it organized its religious, political, and military institutions to turn outward, identify potential proxies around the region, and proceed to organize, indoctrinate, arm, and train them.

Iraq responded immediately by invading Iran. The eight-year war was effectively the first Arab-Iranian war of modern times, as Saudi Arabia and the majority of Arab states backed Iraq; only Syria sided with Iran, an alliance that still stands today. The war ended inconclusively in 1988. The Saddam regime that prosecuted it is no more, but a generation of Iranians—and the majority of Iran's current leadership—were shaped by the events of that war. It underlies the deep hostility, anxiety, and distrust with which most of Iran's current leaders regard the Arab and Sunni states to their south.

Saudi Arabia responded to Ayatollah Khomeini's attempt to claim the mantle of pan-Islamic leadership and use it against them, by pivoting to a much more Islamic profile of the monarchy (the King was re-titled "Custodian of the Two Holy Mosques"), emphasizing the centrality of Mecca and Medina in the annual Hajj and Islamic gatherings, and using their resources to spread the influence of their own Wahhabi religious establishment throughout the Muslim world.

The Saudi pivot toward a more religious profile was also motivated by the 1979 armed takeover of the Grand Mosque in Mecca by Islamist extremists calling for the overthrow of the ruling family. During the 1950s and 1960s, the Saudis faced challenges from Arab nationalists and various secular leftists and communists; from 1979 onwards, the main challenges would come from both Shiite and Sunni Islamists. The kingdom adopted a more religious profile in both its domestic and foreign policy to shore up its legitimacy.

While Iran proceeded to 'weaponize' its religious foreign policy by creating the radical Shiite non-state actor Hezbollah in the early 1980s, and reaching out to other groups in the region, Saudi Arabia and the United States proceeded to weaponize radical Sunni non-state actors in the war against the 1979 Soviet invasion of Afghanistan. The conditions unleashed by the momentous events of 1979 are still with us today: conflict between Iran and its neighbors; the instrumentalization and weaponization of sectarian proxy groups; and the empowerment of armed non-state actors.

The Middle East today is locked in deep conflict between a revolutionary and interventionist Iran and its allies on one side, and a loose alignment—not strictly an alliance—including Saudi Arabia, Turkey, and other Gulf states struggling to contain and pushback on Iran. The conflict has helped rip Syria, Iraq, and Yemen apart, and has provided ideal conditions for sectarian radicalization and the spread of armed non-state actors and transnational terrorist groups. Defusing this region-wide conflict system, which could rage on for decades more, and replacing it with a more stable regional order, needs to be a top priority.

The Challenges Posed by a Revisionist Iran and the Paradox of Threat Perceptions

Iran, Turkey, and the G.C.C. actually have many core interests in common. These potentially include regime and state security, regional stability, economic cooperation, and regional prosperity. But so far this potential positive interdependence has been overshadowed by the negative interdependence of security fears, conflict, and sectarian violence. These fears and perceptions are exacerbated by internal politics in these states that discourage rather than encourage cooperation. While all the region's states and societies would benefit from a stable and cooperative regional order, they are stuck in what might be best described as a 'violence trap.' Part of the problem are patterns of threat perception that fuel the ongoing conflict, which need to be unpacked and disentangled.

Iran's conflictual approach to dealing with its region is perhaps the linchpin of the current violence trap. Its foreign policy is a toxic mix of haughty ambition linked to lofty revolutionary goals, the proud history of imperial grandeur, the paranoia of a regime that was attacked at birth, and a country with a long history of foreign intervention and invasion from the Anglo-Russian invasion of 1941 to the U.S.-engineered overthrow of Mossadegh in 1953. Its mix of ambition and paranoia have driven it to challenge the prevailing state order in the region, seek out sectarian allies, and build up armed non-state actors. This policy triggered a mirror response from some of the G.C.C. countries, and recently Turkey as well. Seeking to change Iranian policy in the region will be central in defusing the current violence trap, and rebuilding stability and order in the region.

In the section on foreign policy in the Iranian constitution, Article 154 states that the Islamic Republic "supports the just struggles of the oppressed against the oppressors in every corner of the globe." The same article tries impossibly to square the circle by stating that this will be pursued "while scrupulously refraining from all forms of interference in the internal affairs of other nations." This contradiction illustrates Henry Kissinger's view that "Iran has to decide whether it is a nation or a cause;" and "If Iran thinks of itself as a nation or can be brought to do so, it can be accorded a respected place in the international system."[2] No doubt, getting Iranian leaders to emphasize the former over the latter will be key to stabilizing the region.

But in addition to Iran's constitution and its ideological rhetoric, a significant portion of Iran's regional policy is driven by traditional concerns for regime and national security. The Iranian leadership might be described as paranoid, but even paranoiacs sometimes have cause for their fears. Most Iranians cannot forget that the Gulf states backed Iraq in its long and devastating war against Iran, or, more recently, Wikileaks' revelations of some Gulf leaders privately urging Washington to bomb Iran.[3] And they interpret firebrand pronouncements from some Saudi Wahhabi preachers against Shiites as an existential threat.

Further afield, both Washington and Moscow backed Baghdad in the Iran-Iraq war, and regime change has been—on and off—part of official U.S. policy, even under the Clinton administration. The Bush administration invaded Iran's two neighbors, declared Iran a member of the Axis of Evil, and made no secret of their preference for regime change in Tehran.[4] The Obama administration changed that narrative with the nuclear deal, but the new Trump administration has many Iran hardliners who consider Iran a principal foe. Of course, Iran and Israel are also locked in confrontation, with Iran occasionally threatening to wipe Israel off the map, and Israel occasionally threatening to bomb Iran.

Under sanctions for several decades and lacking the conventional capacities of the United States and Israel, Iran invested in asymmetric warfare. It built up Hezbollah as the equivalent of a powerful aircraft carrier parked off Israel's northern border, to deter a potential Israeli or U.S. attack against Iran. It built up relations with Iraqi anti-Saddam groups to weaken Saddam and neutralize the threat from it western neighbor. It rushed to the support of Bashar al-Assad after the uprising in Syria in 2011 for fear that if Damascus fell to what they perceived as an American-Sunni alliance, Hezbollah would fall soon after, the friendly regime in Baghdad would be vulnerable, and the threat would directly reach Tehran itself. The opportunity to exploit the Houthi rebellion in Yemen was seized to weaken Saudi Arabia on its vulnerable flank and deter them from progress in Syria and the Levant.

The Iranian regime not only feels vulnerable from regional and international enemies, it also feels internally vulnerable. Like other Middle Eastern autocracies, it sits uneasily over a young and restive population that revolted once already in 2009, and might do so again.

Iranian fears are matched by G.C.C. fears, which underpin the current violence trap. While Iran sees existential enemies everywhere, Gulf leaders see an Iranian quest for regional hegemony everywhere. And Iranian actions in Lebanon, Syria, Iraq, and Yemen have triggered strong reactions from Gulf States. Like two boxers in a darkened ring, the two sides are bloodying each other to no benefit for either side.

Restoring a balance of power in the region and pursuing negotiations toward a state-based regional order have to go hand-in-hand. Power and politics have to be used concomitantly and intelligently. Currently, there is a destabilizing imbalance of power between Iran and its neighbors. Iran has successfully expanded its influence, consolidating its hold on the Levant from Basra and Baghdad, through Mosul, Aleppo, Hama, Homs, Damascus, and Beirut, as well as a strong influence in Yemen. Under these conditions of imbalance, any chance of regional stability will be lost to decades more of regional and sectarian war. Only if there is a serious strategy to pushback against Iran's external ambitions—while negotiating with it to acknowledge the legitimate national security concerns of Tehran and all other states—can a regional order be achieved. As during the nuclear negotiations, a robust sanctions regime was necessary to bring Iran to the table and to get it to accept international norms and limits on its nuclear program. Similar pressure will have to be brought to bear to get Iran to accept international norms of interstate behavior.

Power balancing is necessary, but the desired end point is not an open war for the Middle East that leaves more societies in ruins and more communities radicalized. It would instead entail a diplomatic process in which all countries, including Iran, Saudi Arabia, Turkey, and others, agree on the need to rebuild a state-based order, defuse regional conflict, end proxy wars, build on common interests of security and economic development, and coexist in the region on the basis of respect for international law, and non-interference in the affairs of other states.

OUTLINES OF A TRANSFORMATIVE POLICY

The point of robust and intelligent diplomacy is to disentangle the legitimate concerns of regime and national security among all sides. The proxy wars are not enhancing any state's regime or national security. Quite the contrary, they are devastating the region and draining valuable resources.

A robust diplomatic effort would have to be sustained over several years. It would require some leadership from global players such as the United States and Russia, but much of the work and hard choices would have to be made by regional states and leaders themselves. It is not necessarily a costly strategy as it does not involve military or economic outlays, but rather intelligent and sustained political and diplomatic effort. Nor is it a risky strategy per se, in that even if attempts at regional cooperation move slowly—or fail—we would be no worse off than we already are today.

When the time is right, such an initiative could proceed along three tracks. These tracks are not sequential and could be pursued simultaneously. The first track would focus on the macro issue of working toward an agreement of principles on a regional order and gradually building a regional institutional framework. The second track would focus on disentangling current proxy wars in a phased approach. The third would work on boosting cooperation on economic development, trade, investment, labor movement, water, energy, cultural exchange, and some form of a Marshall Plan for the region.

Track One: Regional Contact Group

Track one could begin with establishing a regional contact group or consultation forum including officials from the G.C.C., Egypt, Turkey, and Iran. This could be chaired by the U.N., but facilitated and backed by the United States and Russia, with support from the E.U. and China. This group would not grapple directly with the ongoing conflicts in the region, but would work to build agreement among regional states on a core set of long-term common principles for regional order.

Learning from the experience of other regions, this declaration of principles could include something along the lines of the following points:

➤ Affirmation of the Westphalian principles of respect for the sovereignty and territorial integrity of signatory states
➤ Respect for the national security of signatory states and refraining from the threat or use of force against each other
➤ De-escalation and de-militarization of relations
➤ Commitment to the eradication of armed non-state actors
➤ Commitment to helping failed and failing states reach internal political agreement and rebuild state sovereignty
➤ Commitment to regular consultation and discussion

A more ambitious set of core principles might also include points related to the following:

➤ Shift from conflict management to conflict prevention and peace-building
➤ Confidence-building measures and pilot initiatives for security cooperation
➤ Acceptance of cultural, religious, and ethnic diversity
➤ Phasing out of religious and sectarian proselytization and propaganda as a tool of foreign policy
➤ Building social and cultural interchange and ties
➤ Encouraging economic relations, trade, investment, and joint projects
➤ Exploring the establishment of a more permanent and structured cooperation framework

Saudi Foreign Minister Adel Jubeir declared that the region needed an agreement among regional powers, including Iran, to—in his words—"abide by the good neighborhood principle and to refrain from interfering into the affairs" of neighboring states.

Iranian Foreign Minister Javad Zarif proposed something along these lines in an op-ed in the New York Times in April 2015[5], where he called for "regional dialogue … based on generally recognized principles and shared objectives, notably respect for sovereignty, territorial integrity and political independence of all states; inviolability of international boundaries; noninterference in internal affairs; peaceful settlement of disputes; impermissibility of threat or use of force; and promotion of peace, stability, progress and prosperity in the region." The problem is, unfortunately, Zarif does not control Iran's foreign policy in the Middle East, and those who do—led by Gen. Qasim Suleimani and the Islamic Revolutionary Guards Corps—regularly violate almost every one of these necessary principles.

Nevertheless, Zarif's position along with Jubeir's position creates an important opening for such a regional contact group. Turkey has proposed such frameworks for the Caucasus and the Black Sea areas, and had established the outlines of a cooperative economic framework that included Turkey, Syria, Jordan, and Lebanon, prior to the Syrian uprising.

The U.N. can bring to the table the experiences of other regions around the world in transforming regional conflict systems toward more stable and cooperative regions with some form of institutional regional architecture. The experience of Europe turning from continent-wide wars that killed over 80 million to a cooperative framework is uppermost in most minds. There, the path from the Treaty of Paris of 1951 that created the European Coal and Steel Community to the Treaties of Rome in 1957 that established the European Economic Community is instructive. So too might be the experience of the Organization of Security and Cooperation in Europe that emerged from the Helsinki talks and created a platform in the mid-1970s that brought together eastern and western bloc countries, including the Soviet Union and the United States. The experience of the creation of ASEAN, the Organization of American States, the African Union, the Arctic Council, Mercosur, the Southern African Development Community, and other regional and sub-regional frameworks also provide important guides.

The goal of this track would be to seek an agreement on principles by the main Arab countries, Turkey and Iran; and the beginning of discussions on some form of regional communication and cooperation architecture. It should be clear that this trilateral Arab-Turkish-Iran forum would not supplant or necessarily run counter to other regional forums and frameworks that the various countries are part of. The Arab League would remain the principle forum among Arab states. Turkey and Iran are part of various other regional forums.

This framework would also be separate from any eventual or potential Arab-Israeli peace. Currently, the prospects for Israeli-Palestinian peace appear dim. However, if that were to happen, the Arab states and Israel could find agreement based on the Arab Peace Initiative of 2002. And Israel and the Arab countries could establish a regional framework such as that proposed during the Madrid peace process. Turkey could possibly be included in such a framework; but it is hard to imagine Israel and Iran in any joint forum in the foreseeable future.

TRACK TWO: DE-CONFLICTION AND DE-ESCALATION

The second track should be a behind-the-scenes diplomatic track that tries to disentangle the regional players from the ongoing proxy arenas in the region. This track would concern itself with the regional involvements in Syria, Yemen, Iraq, and Lebanon.

Moving forward in Syria will still hinge on the regime and the opposition negotiating an end to the conflict and some form—even if minimal—of political transition. If and when that happens, this track would focus on getting the commitment of regional players to support the new government and help it reestablish authority over Syria. More importantly, this track would have to manage and phase the withdrawal of Iranian, Hezbollah, and other Shiite militias from Syria; the withdrawal of support by Turkey and the G.C.C. from armed opposition groups; and the transfer of that support to the new authorities and their reconstituted security forces.

In Yemen, the challenge might be not as complex as in Syria. Although it supports the Houthis, Iran has no significant direct or proxy forces imported to Yemen from other countries. There are ongoing U.N.-led Yemeni peace talks among the main parties. If and when they reach agreement, the regional players must be brought to commit to supporting the new government and its state institutions. This track would also need to ensure the withdrawal of support by Iran to the Houthi rebel movement, withdrawal of Saudi and coalition forces, and the transfer of support to the new authorities.

In Iraq, there already is a constitutional and state structure—albeit somewhat dysfunctional—to support. However, there are two regionally problematic challenges. First, the Arab Sunni community continues to feel excluded from representation and power sharing in the new order, and the rise of the Iranian-dominated Popular Mobilization Units is a cause of great concern. This track would need to get regional players to help the Iraqi government and the Arab Sunni leadership in Iraq to find an inclusive way forward in government, and get regional players to transfer their support from the P.M.U. or other irregular armed groups to support for the Iraqi armed forces.

The issue of Hezbollah in Lebanon might be the hardest of all. Its existence predates the current crises in the other three countries. Although it was born in the midst of civil and regional conflict in the 1980s, it remains a permanent fixture in Lebanon 26 years after the end of the civil war and 16 years after the end of the Israeli occupation. It violates the simplest principles of Westphalia, as one state, Iran, openly and officially supports and maintains the world's largest non-state army, Hezbollah, in another country, Lebanon. In the long run, if no solution is found for Hezbollah, there can be no agreement on regional order and little hope for regional stability.

The challenge on this issue will be complex. Some phases of the work would include ensuring Hezbollah's withdrawal from Syria—if and when a transition deal is reached—and the withdrawal of its trainers and support from other arenas such as those in Yemen and Iraq. A second phase is dealing with its presence in Lebanon. This might initially include a gradual diminution of its forces and deployments in the country, but will have to eventually broach the subject of its integration into the armed forces of the Lebanese state. In Iraq, the fear is that the P.M.U. will become a permanent non-state army like Hezbollah in Lebanon. The hope is, rather, that the P.M.U. and Hezbollah could be integrated into the armed forces of their inclusive state structures.

What this track would also have to grapple with in this area is the explosively high tension between Israel, Hezbollah, and Iran. Hezbollah does not want to start another war with Israel, and does Israel want to get into one; but the tension on both sides could easily lead to another major conflagration. U.N., U.S., and Russian diplomacy could do more to reinforce the U.N. Security Council Resolution 1701 that maintains the precarious peace after the 2006 war, but also to resolve the remaining and fairly minor dispute over the Shebaa farms.

More importantly, if the direct threat of Iranian nuclear weapons program remains managed within the P5+1 nuclear deal with Iran—at least for the next 10-15 years—there should be renewed back channel efforts to de-escalate tension between Iran and Israel, perhaps to reach some form of detente. If Iran is not moving toward a nuclear weapon, Israel has no existential urgency to attack Iran. And if Iran does not fear an attack from Israel, it has less reason to maintain a large proxy army on Israel's northern border. Russia has good relations with both Israel and Iran, perhaps it could play a role in a gradual back channel escalation.

TRACK THREE: REGIONAL ECONOMIC INTEGRATION

The third track should focus on building intraregional economic ties and interdependence. Levels of intraregional trade and economic exchange remain low by international standards. Intelligent country level reforms and better intraregional economic integration could boost national G.D.P.s from the 3.0–4.5 percent a year range to the 5–8 percent a year range (similar to the performance of developing countries in Asia).[6] This is a valuable job-creating and stabilizing goal in itself, but creating common economic interests will also raise the cost of conflict and encourage governments in a cooperative direction. The reference point here is not the 1648 Treaty of Westphalia, but the 1951 Treaty of Paris which created the European Coal and Steel Community between long-time regional enemies, France and (West) Germany, as well as Belgium, Italy, the Netherlands, and Luxembourg. Its aim was to build on the deep common economic interests within the European region and make war less attractive and more costly.

This track could encourage a piecemeal cumulative bottom-up approach as well as a region-wide top-down approach. In the former category, the track could encourage sectoral cooperation among two or more countries in the region. This could be in the realm of building better cooperation over energy, water, trade, labor, investment, IT, or any number of other sectors. As sectoral and bilateral ties grow among regional states, this should help boost region-wide economic interdependence. Bottom-up initiatives could be taken by governments, but other economic actors in the private sector, chambers of commerce, sector-specific interest groups, could work to boost economic cooperation between two or more countries in the region.

The more formal top-down approach implies working toward region-wide economic agreements. It will not be easy. Attempts at economic integration even among the Arab countries have met with resistance from entrenched government and business interests. It will require a patient and phased approach, beginning with an agreement on principles, then moving toward pilot projects and establishing sector-specific working groups.

In addition, given the magnitude of the region's humanitarian, post-conflict, and economic challenges, many observers have rightly suggested launching something akin to the Marshall Plan for the Middle East.[7] This is all the more relevant as many of the problems of today's Middle East stem from underlying factors of high unemployment, and strained land and water resources. If present trends continue, and if one also factors in the likely effects of climate change,[8] these problems are only likely to get significantly worse.

Within this track there is need to bring together regional and international players behind the establishment of something akin to a Middle East refugee, reconstruction, and development fund. Regional players such as the G.C.C., Iran, and Turkey should be principal contributors, but there would also need to be important roles for the United States, Europe, Russia, China, and Japan, among others. The fund will have to move quickly to respond to the urgent needs of Syrian and other refugees in the region. It also would have to organize policies and resources for reconstruction in Yemen, Syria, parts of Iraq, and Libya. On the development side, it should focus its investments on infrastructure and connectivity that would assist strained economies like Egypt, Tunisia, Jordan, Yemen, and Lebanon, but would also lay the emphasis on building intraregional connectivity and interdependence. Such an initiative could build strong positive linkages with the ambitious Chinese One Belt, One Road program announced in 2013 and the Asian Infrastructure Investment Bank that started operations in January 2016. Importantly, Turkey, Iran, Saudi Arabia, and other G.C.C. states are all founding members of the AIIB.

In Closing

This chapter sought to grapple with the underlying regional conflict system that fuels much of the instability of the Middle East that has brought down states, and created the conditions for the rise of major terrorist groups. It proposes a broad direction aimed at defusing regional conflict and building a more stable and sustainable regional state order.

It is a long-term vision whose enabling conditions are perhaps not ripe today, but it is important to be aware of the alternative future that is available to the Middle East if regional and international players work cooperatively in that direction. The long-term goal must be to work toward a sustainable, stable, and inclusive state-based regional order. Only by finding a way to reaffirm and rebuild a balanced, rules-based, Westphalian state order in the Middle East can stability and security be restored, and armed non-state actors and terrorist groups be decisively disenfranchised and defeated.

ENDNOTES

1. This chapter is a revised version of my article, "Working Toward a Stable Regional Order," that appeared in The Annals of the American Academy of Political and Social Sciences 668 (2016): 36-52.

2. Stephen Graubard, "Lunch with the FT: Henry Kissinger," *Financial Times,* May 24/25, 2008, http://www.henryakissinger.com/interviews/FinancialTimes240508.html

3. Ian Black and Simon Tisdall, "Saudi Arabia urges US attack on Iran to stop nuclear programme," *The Guardian,* November 28, 2010, http://www.theguardian.com/world/2010/nov/28/us-embassy-cables-saudis-iran

4. John Barry and Dan Ephron, "War-Gaming the Mullahs," *TruthOut,* September 20, 2004, http://www.truth-out.org/archive/item/49827-wargaming-the-mullahs

5. Mohammad Javaad Zarif, "Mohammad Javad Zarif: A Message From Iran," *New York Times,* April 20, 2015, http://www.nytimes.com/2015/04/20/opinion/mohammad-javad-zarif-a-message-from-iran.html?_r=0

6. Shahrokh Fardoust, "Economic Prospects for the Middle East through 2030: From Chaos to Growth with Stability through Reform and Regional Cooperation", *Middle East Institute,* June 29, 2016, http://www.mei.edu/sites/default/files/publications/PP5_Fardoust_RCS_economic_web.pdf

7. Mona Yacoubian, "Middle East 'Marshall Plan' will sustain Arab Spring," *The Hill,* January 11, 2012, http://thehill.com/blogs/congress-blog/foreign-policy/203639-middle-east-marshall-plan-will-sustain-arab-spring; Karoun Demirjian, "Lindsey Graham wants a new Marshall Plan for the Middle East," *Washington Post,* April 8, 2016, https://www.washingtonpost.com/news/powerpost/wp/2016/04/08/lindsey-graham-wants-a-new-marshall-plan-for-the-middle-east/; Franco Frattini, "Marshall Plan for the Arab world," *Global Europe,* 18 (2011): http://europesworld.org/2011/06/01/marshall-plan-for-the-arab-world/#.VwPFAsdiDSw;

8. Gerald Stang, "Climate Challenges in the Middle East: Rethinking Environmental Cooperation," *Middle East Institute,* May 03, 2016, http://www.mei.edu/content/climate-challenges-middle-east-rethinking-environmental-cooperation

CHAPTER TWO

DEFYING GRAVITY:

WORKING TOWARD A REGIONAL STRATEGY FOR A STABLE MIDDLE EAST

ROSS HARRISON

INTRODUCTION

A French philosopher once said that "no problem can withstand the assault of sustained thinking."[1] This bold claim might never have been made had he encountered the challenges of the modern Middle East, where solutions to problems have stumped some of the best strategic minds.

Finding opportunities to solve the problems of the Middle East and eventually transition from chaos to stability requires looking in the right places. Currently the right place to find robust opportunities is not at the ground level, where the civil wars in Iraq, Syria, Libya, and Yemen are raging, but rather at the regional level, where a new order is emerging out of these conflicts. The pillars of this regional order are Saudi Arabia, Turkey, Iran, and Egypt. Whether the future of the Middle East will be a continuation of the current chaos and destruction or a more positive transition toward stability and prosperity will heavily depend on the relationships among these four regional titans. The United States and other global powers, namely Russia, China, and the European Union (E.U.), should concentrate their strategic efforts on creating conditions conducive to cooperation among these regional powers. Enhancing their cooperation is necessary, not just to help this troubled region but also to protect the global system from the destabilizing effects of a continued downward spiral in the Middle East.

There is a reason why raising our gaze to the regional level reveals opportunities, while the ground level conflicts appear impervious to strategy. Two essential preconditions for strategy are absent in the ground level conflicts of the Middle East. One is leaders' ability to see the strategic environment clearly enough to calculate whether the actions they are considering taking have a reasonable probability of producing their desired effects. Amidst the chaos in the region today, it is almost impossible to get the relationship between cause and effect right. The second missing element is actors' ability to accurately assess how their interests are affected by events. In an environment so dynamic and unstable, it is easy for parties involved in the conflicts to lose their strategic compass and resort to groping in the dark.

But this chaos that makes strategic opportunities so scarce at the ground level is already creating a new order at the regional level, where the necessary preconditions for strategy are more abundant. While at this level there is still uncertainty, peering beyond the fog of the current chaos and focusing on the four relatively stable regional powers yields a clearer picture of the strategic environment. This clearer perspective reveals more precisely where the interests of the various parties conflict and overlap within the evolving regional structure, and thus highlights strategic opportunities for solving some of the region's most vexing problems through cooperation.

How is the suggestion that the regional level is the right place to look for strategic opportunities realistic, given the immediacy of crises faced by policymakers? No doubt fighting gravity in the political world is just as difficult as it is in the physical world. The gravitational tug of day-to-day crises might make chasing a regional approach seem quixotic and naive. However, the response to those who dismiss a longer-term regional approach is that without one, any gains made in managing conflicts on the ground today are likely to be fleeting. In the absence of a healthier regional context, policymakers will likely continue playing a game of whack-a-mole in which just as traction is created in addressing one problem, new crises emerge that erase previous gains.

THINKING IN REGIONAL TERMS

Hasn't any notion of a regional system been destroyed with the implosion of the Arab world and the proliferation of political vacuums in the Middle East? The answer is both yes and no. Yes, the old Arab state system has been hollowed out by the civil wars and the inroads made by ISIS.[2] But no, the notion of a regional system itself has not been destroyed. Out of these deadly conflicts a new regional order is emerging, dominated by Saudi Arabia, Iran, Turkey, and Egypt, all of which are relatively stable states that retain the capacity to withstand challenges from insurgency movements like ISIS. Think of these four states as pillars of a structure that remain after a building has burned to the ground. Any strategy aimed at creating a better future for the Middle East must be built atop these pillars.

Why these four powers? First, they are already projecting significant influence into the region through their involvement in the conflicts in Libya, Syria, Iraq, and Yemen. While up to this point the interactions among them have created a dysfunctional regional system, it is these same four powers that have the potential to form a more positive system that takes on the region's most pressing problems. Second, collectively these four countries have the greatest capacity to impact the economic health of the region, since together they represent more than 70 percent of its G.D.P..

Identifying these four powers as the regional pillars is not meant to minimize the influence other Gulf Cooperation Council (G.C.C.) countries or Israel can have on the health of the region. Any initiatives by Saudi Arabia and Egypt to create a new Arab political order that becomes part of a larger Arab-Turkish-Iranian regional system will certainly include the other G.C.C. countries. Israel's impact on the current negotiations with Iran, plus the recent convergence of Israeli geopolitical interests with those of Egypt and Saudi Arabia, will be critical variables in the region's stability equation. And whether future Israeli governments commit to a peaceful process that resolves the dispute with the beleaguered Palestinians will also be a significant factor affecting stability. But given the nature of the threats to the regional order today, the most influential states in shaping the future will be Iran, Turkey, Egypt, and Saudi Arabia.

GRAVITATIONAL PULL: OBSTACLES TO COOPERATION

With Saudi Arabia, Turkey, and Egypt engaged in yet another proxy war against Iran in Yemen, and Turkey and Iran having recently traded barbs, it is hard to fathom regional cooperation. But the fact that these countries jockey for influence in—and even inflame—the region's conflicts should not cause us to lose sight of their significant common interests.

The principal common interest is the need for a more stable and cooperative regional context, without which none of these countries will be able to reach their full potential in the coming decades.[3] The economic vibrancy of each country depends on increased levels of intraregional trade and the peace dividend that would accrue should the region stabilize (estimated at 2.4 percent of the combined G.D.P. of the four countries).[4] Another common political and security interest is the defeat of groups like ISIS, al-Qaʻida, and their affiliates, which unless checked could challenge the sovereignty of more states in the region. Pursuing these common interests does not just have long-term payoffs but also produces immediate economic security benefits for all four countries.

The four regional powers' significant common interests notwithstanding, there are several factors that could reinforce the current pattern of rivalry and pose obstacles to any significant regional cooperation. First, old animosities and distrust die hard, particularly with regimes that have made rivalries with other states central themes of their political narratives and legitimacy formulas. Historically this has been particularly true in the case of Saudi Arabia and Iran, and a similar dynamic is increasingly evident today between Egypt and Turkey. Modern Turkish, Iranian, and Arab nationalisms, strains of wistfulness for former Persian and Ottoman empires, as well as Sunni-Shiʻi sectarian identities tend to affirm these narratives and perpetuate rivalries.

Second, the acceleration of events in the conflict zones of the Arab world makes deliberative calculations of interests difficult for leaders. This increases the likelihood of reflexive reactions rather than careful consideration of the available options. While Saudi Arabia and Iran have fueled the civil wars in Syria, Iraq, and now in Yemen, the spiraling nature of these proxy conflicts makes it politically difficult for leaders in Riyadh and Tehran to escape them, even if the benefits of continuing these battles become less clear over time.

A third factor that could undermine cooperation arises from the likely effects of social and economic megatrends. The real story, however, is not the individual trends themselves but rather how they are converging to create an even more powerfully disruptive trend, namely a rapid acceleration in the rate of political and economic change that is likely to stress the capacity of regimes in the future. This can be conceptualized as a "speeding up" of history, with leaders challenged by potentially disruptive changes occurring at a faster clip than will be their ability to cope.[5]

Social megatrends such as the empowerment of individuals, particularly women and minority groups—fueled to a large degree by technological innovations, and political trends such as a diffusion of power away from traditional sources of authority and toward networks and non-state actors— will challenge leaders in all four countries. Simultaneously, leaders will have to contend with the demographic trend of an expanding youth bulge. This will challenge governments unable to create economic opportunities for the deluge of youth rushing toward job markets.

Adequate responses to these social, political, and demographic trends will be made more difficult by environmental trends like climate change, desertification, and water and food shortages.[6] The combined effect of these trends will be faster social change, greater difficulty in creating economic traction, and more challenges to governments by citizens. The risk is that these trends create legitimacy issues for governments that draw them inward toward shoring up their power base rather than propelling them outward toward regional cooperation efforts. Or, if they do project outward, the risk is that they will use hostility toward their neighbors to cover up their domestic legitimacy issues.

Of course, these risks will be different for each of the four countries. Egypt, which suffers from both severe economic problems and deep political divisions, is the most vulnerable in this regard. Water shortages, desertification, the effects of the youth bulge, and rising inequality will hit Egypt hard in the years to come. Egyptian President Abdel Fattah el-Sisi's current social contract, which imposes a strong security crackdown and restrictions on human rights in exchange for the promise of greater economic growth and neutralization of terrorist threats, will be particularly fragile because of these trends. One thing seems certain. Given the accelerating pace of change in the post-Arab Spring era, Sisi and his successors will have a limited time frame for showing results. This is in contrast to former President Mubarak, who ruled for 30 years before societal pressures boiled over. This means that if the Sisi administration is unable to deliver on the economic part of its social contract, it will likely further emphasize terrorism threats and continue using the Muslim Brotherhood as a scapegoat. This could push Egypt away from cooperation and toward a more confrontational posture vis-à-vis Turkey. And should the Egyptian government expand its crackdown to other Islamic groups, this could trouble the country's currently warm relations with Saudi Arabia.

Iran's leaders in the years ahead will also be under great internal pressure to deliver economically and politically. Up until now the regime has had the luxury of pointing to international sanctions as the source of economic hardship. Now that the nuclear negotiations with the P5+1 culminated in a deal, and some international sanctions have been lifted, pressure will likely build on the regime to improve economic performance. The youth bulge trend is one of Iran's biggest time bombs, causing a rise in the number of unemployed and underemployed college graduates clamoring for economic opportunities. Moreover, if oil prices remain low for several more years and water shortage problems become more acute, the combination of these trends could cause a rapid downturn in the economy.[7] Thus, even in the wake of the nuclear deal, Iran could use a more adversarial foreign policy as a distraction from economic issues, despite the fact that most Iranian youth yearn for improvement in the country's international standing.

Both Saudi Arabia and Turkey have stronger economic capabilities today than either Iran or Egypt, giving them greater shock absorbers for coping with these megatrends and therefore posing fewer roadblocks to regional cooperation. Largely fueled by the relatively high oil prices, Saudi Arabia's economy grew more than 5 percent annually over the past decade, which has led to large account surpluses.[8] Moreover, the Saudi leadership is already responding to water issues by building desalination plants. But on the other side of the ledger, economic diversification is not happening fast enough to absorb the high levels of unemployment, particularly among the country's increasingly restive youth.[9]

Also, if the recent oil price collapse lasts for more than a couple of years, this will introduce major downside risks to the Saudi social welfare system, with possible destabilizing effects. Turkey has the most diversified and advanced economy of the four powers, but it is currently undergoing deceleration in its G.D.P. growth, having slowed from 9.2 percent in 2010 to 4.1 percent in 2013 and 3.1 percent in 2014.[10] If this continues, its government will also be under pressure to reform, which could lead to internal political dislocations.[11] This, combined with how the individual empowerment trend could raise the temperature of Turkey's Kurdish issue, might work against regional cooperation.

DEFYING GRAVITY: TOWARD A REGIONAL STRATEGY

If these impediments to regional cooperation among Egypt, Saudi Arabia, Iran, and Turkey are not dealt with, the probability that the Middle East will remain one of the most unstable, least integrated, and most economically underperforming regions of the world for decades to come is high. Of course, the ultimate burden for dealing with these issues and for building regional cooperation rests with the four regional powers themselves. They have the most at stake in a more stable and prosperous region, and collectively they have the capability, if not currently the will, to jointly pursue shared objectives. But the international community can play a role in helping to remove some of the impediments to cooperation these countries will face. That role consists of working toward a regional strategy in the following three ways:

1) Do No Harm: Abandon the "Great Game"

The future role of the international community in the Middle East cannot be accurately discussed without acknowledgement of an unpleasant reality. International powers, including the United States, bear some responsibility for the rivalry among states in the region. The Middle East has long been one of the regions of the world most heavily penetrated by outside powers. The Sykes-Picot Agreement between the French and British initially set the boundaries of several states in the region. And since then the politics of the

Middle East have to a large degree reflected the divisions in the international system. During the Cold War, the United States and the Soviet Union foisted their superpower conflict onto the Middle East, polarizing the region. After the Iranian Revolution in 1979, the United States backed Iraq in its war against Iran and encouraged its regional allies to deepen their hostility toward Iran.

Later, the U.S. invasion of Iraq in 2003 led to new regional power imbalances. The toppling of Saddam Hussein and the collapse of the Iraqi state as a counterweight to Iran gave Iran opportunities to project its power into the Arab world. Facing this unintended consequence of the invasion, the United States began encouraging Saudi Arabia (along with other G.C.C. countries) to act as the main bulwark against Iran, further exacerbating historical tensions and suspicions between these two powers. The United States certainly is not alone in this regard. Russia's role in the Middle East has to a certain degree been that of spoiler, motivated by its own interest in undermining U.S. influence rather than by any concern for regional cooperation and stability.

If the international powers are going to play a constructive role in this critical region, they need to send signals that this "great game" is over.[12] The P5+1 negotiations with Iran reflect an acknowledgement among the major powers that a zero-sum game approach produces no long-term winners, and that cooperation can yield significant mutual benefits. There seems to be recognition that without a stable and prosperous Middle East, the entire international system is likely to be fraught with economic and political risk. No longer is the Middle East only on the receiving end of international politics. Shocks and risks in the region can be globalized very quickly, as we have seen with recent terrorist attacks. If the objective is for Egypt, Iran, Saudi Arabia, and Turkey to shed old patterns of behavior, the international powers need to do the same.

But it is naive to think that an end of "great game" behavior on the part of the international powers would alone translate into cooperation among the regional powers. The power dynamics in the region need to be such that leaders conclude that confrontation is not winnable, and that the best option to avoid losing is negotiation and cooperation. This is most likely to come about in a balance-of-power system in which the only pathway to gaining security and winning is not one-upmanship, but cooperation.[13]

The international powers will inevitably play a role in the balance-of-power equation in the Middle East. The presence of the U.S. military in the Gulf alone can play a balancing role by reassuring the Saudis and other G.C.C. countries that Washington will not abandon them or disregard their security concerns following the nuclear deal with Iran. Coupled with effective diplomacy, this military presence can help compensate for real or perceived power imbalances. But in the spirit of "do no harm," the United States must do this subtly, refraining from active involvement in the conflicts among the big four regional powers. Trying to correct a power imbalance through direct involvement runs the risk of overcompensating and inadvertently tipping the balance, possibly triggering unwanted aggression instead of cooperation. Active U.S. backing for the Saudi campaign in Yemen, which could be justified by the need to allay Saudi concerns that the power balance has tipped toward Iran, runs the risk of making matters worse by reinforcing Iran's fears that a nuclear deal with the United States is just the first step in an attempt to subjugate it. Given the unstable power dynamics in this proxy war in Yemen, U.S. intervention could inadvertently contribute to a power imbalance, precipitating more aggression by either Iran or Saudi Arabia, thereby pushing any prospects for regional cooperation further down the road. The now moribund Saudi- and Egyptian-led initiative to create a new Arab League Defense Force was an example of a more constructive mechanism for correcting a perceived regional power imbalance.[14] The international community needs to recognize the current volatility in the relationship between the regional powers and refrain from actions that could jeopardize ultimate cooperation.

2) Help the Big Four Powers Build a Regional Security and Economic Framework

Advocating restraint among the international powers in the Middle East does not mean disengagement, but rather a new form of engagement. The United States and others need to shift the emphasis from on-the-ground involvement to working at the regional level with Saudi Arabia, Iran, Turkey, and Egypt to develop a new security and economic framework for the Middle East. While the international community cannot own the process, it can provide good offices by helping the regional powers come up with the right institutional mechanisms for cooperation. The P5+1 arrangement for dealing with the Iranian nuclear issue could be something of a model, provided that the regional powers assume the primary roles while the international powers limit themselves to providing needed support.

The regional powers are not neophytes when it comes to cooperation within the context of institutional frameworks. Iran and Saudi Arabia are members of OPEC, while Turkey and Saudi Arabia are part of the G20. And each of the four powers is party to one or more existing regional frameworks (such as the Arab League, the G.C.C., the Arab Maghreb Union, or non-Arab organizations like the Economic Cooperation Organization (ECO), to which Iran and Turkey belong). A new regional security and economic framework would not replace any of these existing institutional arrangements. The idea instead would be for the regional powers to tap into the capacity of these existing organizations, coordinate their efforts, and perhaps reenergize older, creakier institutions to better serve the purpose of regional cooperation.

While a new overarching regional security arrangement would ultimately need to be open to all states in the region and embody norms like the sanctity of borders, given the current turmoil the big four countries would lead the process at the onset.[15] The security framework's mandate should have two tracks. The first would deal with common issues related to the megatrends, such as trade, water, energy, food, climate, and counterterrorism. It would also address economic issues, such as the facilitation of intraregional trade. The second track would create working groups for grappling with the more difficult issues tied to conflict resolution in Syria, Iraq, Yemen, and Libya. Syria would be the first priority given the scale of its humanitarian disaster. While all of the major regional powers will need to cooperate through the framework to tamp down these conflicts and push back ISIS, when it comes to post-conflict reconstruction efforts in the Arab world, Saudi Arabia (with the other G.C.C. countries) will likely play the lead role, with help from the international community and multilateral institutions like the World Bank.

Such arrangements have worked for other regions. In fact, the Middle East is late to the regionalism game. Other regions where erstwhile adversaries have transitioned into healthy competitors through stronger regional institutions could serve as models. In Latin America (through the Rio Pact and Mercosur) and Asia (through ASEAN), region-wide economic and political integration has occurred over the past decades, despite tensions among the member states of these organizations. Parts of Africa have become more integrated under the African Union (AU) and the Common Market for Eastern and Southern Africa (COMESA).[16] And of course in Europe former blood enemies came together after World War II under new institutional arrangements such as NATO and the European Union.

The assumption is not that a regional framework will eliminate conflicts between states, only that it will recognize and build on common interests and provide mechanisms for more peaceful dispute resolution.[17] Unlike earlier regional efforts like the Baghdad Pact (later CENTO) of the 1950s, which included Great Britain and was oriented toward confronting what was perceived to be an external Communist threat, this framework would include only members from the region and be oriented more toward mitigating intraregional conflicts. The biggest security and economic challenges for the Middle East now and in the future will likely come from within the region, not from without.

Skeptics will likely assert that this kind of a broad regional framework is pie-in-the-sky. But there are several reasons why the timing is right for this to happen. First, there are few good alternatives to cooperation given the dystopian state of the Middle East today. In order to battle common foes like ISIS and find a way out of the current civil wars, the only real option is for cooperation among the four regional powers. While the obstacles may appear insuperable and should not be underestimated, it must be kept in mind that these civil wars and the rise of ISIS are as much a symptom of a toxic regional climate as they are a cause of it. While creating a healthier regional context would not be a panacea for these conflicts, it could go a long way in helping to defuse them.

Second, times of crisis can be the most opportune moments for introducing new institutional structures because at these moments awareness of the need for change is often the greatest. Out of the crucible of the current crises new arrangements have already started to emerge. A baby step in this regard was the Egypt Economic Development Conference convened in Sharm el-Sheikh in March 2015. The conference yielded $12-15 billion in pledges from regional and international donors, providing President Sisi the support he needs to attempt a serious development surge.[18] There have been other efforts, mostly ad hoc, to cooperate in fortifying the region against ISIS. Iran nudged former Prime Minister Nuri al-Maliki out of power in 2014, an outcome the Saudis lauded, and both countries welcomed incoming President Haider al-Abadi.[19] Also, both Iran and Saudi Arabia offered subsidies to the Lebanese Army in order to strengthen the country's defenses against ISIS. While the Lebanese declined the Iranian offer, the convergence of the two feuding powers' interests was nonetheless significant.[20] A broader security pact would formalize cooperation, minimizing reliance on only ad hoc measures.

Third, the precedent of the agreement between Iran and the P5+1 on the nuclear issue makes this kind of arrangement more viable. While Arab angst that Iran will use its rehabilitation in the international system to more aggressively pursue regional ambitions may increase tensions in the near term, effective bilateral diplomacy coupled with reassurances from the international community should allay some of these fears and shift the attention to other pressing regional issues.

3) Role for the United States: Lead Diplomat

Any transition from chaos to stability in the Middle East will require involvement from a number of international powers and institutions. But the U.S. role in helping to create a new security framework will be pivotal due to its strong diplomatic capabilities and its power to convene. The United States will also need to take a lead role in coordinating efforts between the E.U. countries, Russia, China, and the four regional titans, much like it has done in the P5+1 negotiations with Iran. In playing this role, the United States needs to be careful that regional stability efforts do not lead to a new Pax Americana, but instead transition to a new "Pax Regionis," in which regional powers contribute constructively to their own security concerns and economic future.

Aside from assisting in the establishment of a regional security and economic framework, the United States should also help the four regional titans deal with their most vexing internal issues. The purpose would be to address the most challenging effects of the megatrends that could impede cooperation. The priority should be Egypt, since among the four countries it is the most economically and politically vulnerable. While the G.C.C. countries have thrown Egypt an economic lifeline, long-term stability will require more sustainable measures. The United States can help Egypt in its private sector development and foreign direct investment initiatives. These need to be fundamental elements of Egypt's strategy for absorbing the droves of educated youth into the workforce and creating sustainable economic growth.

Also, the United States should not underestimate its diplomatic capacity to foster intraregional cooperation. The United States continues to exert a strong influence on the behavior of the regional powers, as evidenced by the fact that U.S. decisions to abstain from action on critical issues rattle the region as much as U.S. decisions to intervene. For example, Saudi Arabia threatened a policy shift in 2013 due to what was perceived by Riyadh to be a U.S. failure to act on Syria.[21] The United States' formidable diplomatic capability was also on display as it assembled a coalition of international and regional powers to fight ISIS. In the future, this diplomatic power can be repurposed to nudge the regional powers toward cooperation on issues of common interest.

The United States has much to gain by embracing a regional approach, aside from the obvious benefits that derive from a more stable Middle East. One upside to such an approach is that it would give the Trump administration the ability to focus on Asia in a way that sounds like a new form of engagement, not disengagement, something the Obama administration has been charged with. Additionally, it is consistent with Obama's national security strategy of 2015, which specifies that cooperating with regional actors, rather than intervening in the region directly, is the best way to work toward long-term stability in the Middle East.[22]

CONCLUSION

The multiple crises afflicting the Middle East have now reached a critical inflection point. The region is undergoing the proverbial perfect storm, with more states descending into civil war and a proliferation of failed states now being exploited by ISIS.

Regional cooperation led by Egypt, Iran, Saudi Arabia, and Turkey represents the best means for resolving these problems and avoiding catastrophic scenarios for the Middle East in the decades ahead.[23] But the risk that the four powers will just muddle through and not cooperate is high given the "speeding train" effects of the megatrends and the momentum of the current conflicts.[24]

Assuming the international community, especially the United States, can rise to the occasion, it can help manage some of these risks. But this requires having a strategic vision at the level of the region and avoiding the gravitational tug of crisis politics. This will not be easy for either the international or the regional powers, but it is not an impossible feat. The current crises represent a potential opportunity to shape a better future for the region and avoid the global instability that could result from a continuation of the status quo. While relations between the United States and Iran in the early days of the Trump administration are tense, the Iran nuclear deal creates an additional opportunity for eventual regional cooperation. If this moment is to be seized, the international community—along with Egypt, Iran, Saudi Arabia, and Turkey—needs to start laying the foundation for a better future. As crises multiply in the Middle East, time is working against the region; thus it is critical that efforts toward a regional strategy begin now.

ENDNOTES

1. This quote is attributed to François-Marie Arouet, also known as Voltaire.

2. For a voice from the past on an Arab state system, see Michael C. Hudson, *The Middle East Dilemma: The Politics and Economics of Arab Integration* (New York: Columbia University Press, 1999). Also see Florence Gaub and Alexandra Laban, "Arab Futures: Three Scenarios for 2025," *Issue*, Report No. 22, E.U. Institute for Security Studies, February 2015, which only includes the Arab system, and Magdi Amin et al., *After the Spring: Economic Transitions in the Arab World* (New York: Oxford University Press, 2012), which also has a focus limited to the Arab world.

3. Walter Mattli, *The Logic of Regional Integration: Europe and Beyond* (New York: Columbia University Press, 1999) and Katarzanyna Krokowska, "Cooperation among Adversaries: Regionalism in the Middle East," Centre International de Formation Européenne, Paris, 2010.

4. Stockholm International Peace Research Institute's (SIPRI) Military Expenditure Database, http://www.sipri.org/research/armaments/milex/milex_database. I thank my friend and colleague, Shahrokh Fardoust, research professor at the Institute of the Theory and Practice of International Relations at the College of William and Mary and (from 2008 to 2011) director of strategy and operations, development economics at the World Bank, for pointing me to and interpreting this data.

5. I thank my friend and colleague, Chester Crocker, James R. Schlesinger Professor of Strategic Studies at Georgetown University and former assistant secretary of state for African affairs. This language of "history speeding up" was a metaphor he used in our discussions.

6. I thank Shahrokh Fardoust for his contribution on megatrends. See also "Global Trends 2030: Alternative Worlds," The National Intelligence Council, December 2012, http://www.dni.gov/index.php/about/organization/global-trends-2030, for its analysis of megatrends, and Gaub and Laban, "Arab Futures: Three Scenarios for 2025," 11-18.

7. Jason Rezaian, "Iran's Water Crisis the Product of Decades of Bad Planning," *Washington Post*, July 2, 2014.

8. Ross Harrison and Shahrokh Fardoust, "The Middle East in 2030: What Kind of Future?" unpublished working paper for The Middle East Institute, March 2015.

9. Julia Glum, "Saudi Arabia's Youth Unemployment Problem among King Salman's Many New Challenges after Abdullah's Death," *International Business Times*, January 23, 2015.

10. The World Bank, "World Bank Lowers 2014 G.D.P. Growth Estimate for Turkey to 3.1%, Maintains 2015 Forecast," December 23, 2014, http://www.worldbank.org/en/news/press-release/2014/12/23/world-bank-lowers-2014-growth-estimate-for-turkey.

11. I acknowledge my friend and colleague, Shahrokh Fardoust, who through his unpublished draft of a paper, "A Glimpse into the Future of the Middle East: Scenarios for the Middle East and North Africa in 2030," February 28, 2015, contributed much of the thinking on megatrends represented in this chapter.

12. David Fromkin, "The Great Game in Asia," *Foreign Affairs* (Spring 1980) and Hugh Wilford, *America's Great Game: The CIA's Secret Arabists and the Shaping of the Modern Middle East* (New York: Basic Books, 2013).

13. T.V. Paul, James J. Wirtz, and Michel Fortmann, *Balance of Power: Theory and Practice in the 21st Century* (Stanford, CA: Stanford University Press, 2004) and George Friedman, "The Middle East Balance of Power Matures," Stratfor Global Intelligence, March 31, 2015. I also thank my colleague, Paul Salem, vice president for policy and research at The Middle East Institute, for his insights on the role that a balance-of-power system can have in regional cooperation.

14. Hamza Handawi, "Arab League Unveils Joint Military Force amid Yemen Crisis," ABC News, March 29, 2015.

15. For an analysis of options for a new security

framework in the Middle East, see Stockholm International Peace Research Institute (SIPRI), "Towards a Regional Security Regime for the Middle East: Issues and Options," October 2011.

16. Woodrow Wilson International Center for Scholars: Africa Program, "African Regional and Sub-Regional Organizations: Assessing their Contributions to Economic Integration and Conflict Management," October 2008.

17. For an examination of the logic behind a regional security framework, see Sam Sasan Shoamanesh, "It's Time for a Regional Security Framework for the Middle East," Al Jazeera, January 26, 2012. Also see SIPRI, "Towards a Regional Security Regime for the Middle East."

18. Leslie Wroughton, "Kerry Pledges Support for Egypt Economic Reforms, Urges Investment," Reuters, March 13, 2015.

19. Ahmed Rasheed and Alan Raybould, "Saudi Arabia Invites Iraq's Abadi to Visit in Big Sign of Thaw," Reuters, March 23, 2015.

20. Anne Barnard, "Saudi's Grant to Lebanon is Seen as Message to U.S.," *New York Times*, January 6, 2014; "Iran to Give Military Grant to Lebanese Army: Official," Reuters, September 30, 2014; and Ross Harrison, "Towards a Regional Strategy Contra ISIS," *Parameters* (U.S. Army War College Quarterly) 44, 3 (Autumn 2014).

21. Amena Bakr and Warren Strobel, "Saudi Arabia Warns a Shift Away from U.S. over Syria, Iran," Reuters, October 22, 2013.

22. President Barack Obama, "National Security Strategy," February 2015, 26.

23. For the "Arab implosion" scenario, see Gaub and Laban, "Arab Futures: Three Scenarios for 2025," 30-39.

24. For the "muddling through" scenario, see Harrison and Fardoust, "The Middle East in 2030: What Kind of Future?"

CHAPTER THREE

ECONOMIC INTEGRATION IN THE MIDDLE EAST:

PROSPECTS FOR DEVELOPMENT AND STABILITY

SHAHROKH FARDOUST

INTRODUCTION

The global economic slowdown, and the macroeconomic and financial challenges it has wrought, as well as key regional megatrends, create daunting policy challenges for governments across the Middle East and North Africa (MENA). An inhospitable business climate, weak governance, and lack of sufficient economic integration have stifled the region's ability to tap its significant potential for economic growth and job creation to address high youth unemployment and very low female labor force participation. The region's limited integration into the global economy, the lack of diversification of its production base, and its low productivity growth will make it difficult to accelerate economic growth at a time when commodity prices have declined sharply and there is little room for accommodating fiscal or monetary policies.

This chapter highlights the important role the largest and most powerful players in the region—Saudi Arabia, Egypt, Iran, and Turkey—could play in spearheading stabilization of the political and economic situation in the region and addressing root problems. It argues that instead of continuing to incur huge losses from poor economic performance and costly conflicts, which have required massive military outlays, the region should use its substantial human, natural, and financial assets more efficiently, adopting economic and social policies that would lead to rapid and inclusive economic growth for the entire region.

Given the region's massive economic needs and resource constraints and the fact that political unrest and the civil wars in Syria, Iraq, and Yemen must be quieted as economic remedies are implemented, a regional development and reconstruction program is urgently needed. World powers, led by the United States and including Europe, China, and Russia, as well as the regional powers (Egypt, Iran, Turkey, Saudi Arabia, and the other G.C.C. countries) should bring together the international donor community to lay out the basis for a mini–Marshall Plan for the region.

BACKGROUND

Political and economic crises have engulfed large segments of the MENA region since 2011, with disastrous human and economic consequences. A crescent of instability now extends from Libya into the Sinai, the Occupied Palestinian Territories, through Syria, Iraq, and Yemen. The region as a whole continues to experience low economic growth, as a result of regional conflict and the adverse effects of lower oil prices on the oil exporters within the region. As a consequence, real G.D.P. growth for the region, which had averaged about 4 percent a year over the last two decades—compared with 5.5 percent for emerging economies and developing countries as a whole—has grown by only about 2.8 percent a year (about 1 percent a year in per capita terms) since 2012.[1] The slowdown has weakened the region's already fragile economic structure and increased poverty and youth unemployment.

To date the region has "muddled through" these problems. Given the political instability and weak economic performance of much of the region, continuing to do so could quickly deteriorate into deeper economic stagnation and eventually to chaos and destruction, as has already happened in parts of the region, with adverse global consequences.

PURPOSE AND SCOPE OF THE CHAPTER

This chapter, which focuses on the economic aspects of the region's long-term prospects, poses three important questions and identifies policies and conditions that would address them in ways that would help stabilize the region and put it on a sustainable and inclusive growth path:

> ➤ What are the key economic and social dimensions of the current situation in MENA?
> ➤ What fundamental factors and policies led to the region's economic and social deficits despite its massive resources and financial wealth?
> ➤ What steps do the leading countries in the region need to take in terms of economic and institutional reforms to address regional challenges and provide substantially better outcomes for the region's citizens?

The approach emphasizes the important role that the largest and most powerful players in the region—Egypt, Saudi Arabia, Turkey, and Iran, which together account for about 70 percent of the region's $4 trillion economy and are home to about 285 million of its 485 million inhabitants[2] —could play in spearheading the stabilization of the situation and addressing root problems.[3] Global and regional megatrends, ranging from demographic and climatic changes to disruptive technologies, are likely to intensify the challenges faced by MENA governments, further weakening them unless they decide to act jointly in addressing them.[4]

A key message of this chapter is that the most serious downside risks to long-term stability will continue to arise from poor governance and weak institutions; the weak business climate; inadequate infrastructure; low economic growth; high unemployment rates, particularly among educated youth; growing disparity in income and wealth; and shortages of water and emerging food insecurity across much of the region.

Two major interrelated initiatives could spur growth:

> ➤ Undertaking internal economic and institutional reforms to accelerate growth and job creation - while enhancing productivity and competitiveness, and introducing well-targeted polices in each country that reinforce the reforms by addressing the most binding constraints on private sector–led growth. These constraints have caused serious distortions, leading to high unemployment rates among educated youth, very low labor participation rates among educated women, high defense budgets in response to perceived and largely self-generated internal threats and pointless intra-regional rivalries, and the creation of the least economically integrated region in the world.
> ➤ Implementing major regional infrastructure projects in energy, water, and transport (ground and air transport) to substantially improve links among the major countries in the region and deepen trade integration within the region and with the rest of the world.[5] Doing so could yield large direct gains from higher exports and productivity-enhancing F.D.I. and catalyze reforms in other areas that help countries compete, such as

improved access to markets in advanced economies, reductions in tariffs and nontariff trade barriers in the region, and the increasingly important areas of trade facilitation and export promotion.

Domestic reforms, together with a few win-win regional projects, could proceed even without a comprehensive regional political and security agreement. But these initiatives are more likely to be implemented and bear fruit if the region's big players act in unison, through diplomacy and with the support of the international community, to put an end to regional conflicts and substantially reduce tensions. By reducing risks and uncertainty, a well-coordinated regional strategy is likely to substantially raise the pace of growth, leading to a gradual but steady decline in the rate of unemployment, the increased productivity and competitiveness of the regional economy, and greater social and political stability.

THE GLOBAL CONTEXT AND THE CURRENT ECONOMIC SITUATION IN THE REGION

The pace of growth of the world economy remains modest and fraught with downside risks, as the latest forecasts by the I.M.F. and the World Bank indicate.[6] Recovery in the advanced economies is expected to continue to be slow and uneven. In many emerging economies and developing countries, the economic situation is becoming increasingly diverse and challenging, as a result of falling exports, massive capital outflows, depreciating currencies, and high and rising public and private debt, which taken together will continue to reduce their growth prospects over the medium term. The slowdown of the Chinese economy, the second largest in the world, has been an important factor in the plummeting of commodity prices, including oil prices. The sharp decline in commodity prices and capital outflows has had a severe adverse effect on the economic performance of many countries that rely on commodity exports, particularly the oil and gas exporters in MENA.

Growth could pick up in the next two-to-three years, mainly as a result of the lifting of the nuclear-related sanctions against Iran, the region's third-largest economy (after Saudi Arabia and Turkey), but new waves of political and economic shocks could frustrate even a modest recovery. Indeed, major risks to the global economic outlook, as well as to the region's economy, remain tilted toward the downside. They emanate mainly from a generalized slowdown in emerging market economies, China's rebalancing, further declines in oil and other commodity prices, the likely end of extraordinarily accommodative monetary conditions in the United States, and continued conflict in MENA.

Politically, economically, and socially, MENA has changed dramatically since the 1970s. Forty years ago, much of the region was growing relatively rapidly, and the locus of tension and change was limited largely to the Arab-Israeli conflict, the Soviet occupation of Afghanistan, and the beginnings of internal political turmoil in Iran. Today, much of the region is engulfed in what seems to be open-ended chaos, with the real possibility of changing borders, collapsing states, and spillovers into neighboring regions. The chaos is fueled primarily by intra-regional political rivalries among the larger regional players and an army of unemployed and disgruntled youth. Disruption on such a scale has not been seen since the fall of the Ottoman Empire a century ago. It has been argued that pressures were mounting in several Arab countries and that it was only a matter of time before an unravelling of the regional order occurred. But the following factors contributed to the speed with which the protests spread across the region:

➤ The pace of economic growth (and the non-inclusive nature of that growth) in most regional countries was insufficient to generate enough jobs in the private sector to absorb the rising number of entrants into the labor force.[7]

➤ A youth bulge resulted in high rates of unemployment among the 15–25 age group, and employment prospects weakened, as the state-dominated growth machine began to slow.

➤ Wages stagnated or fell in terms of their purchasing power, as food and fuel prices rose rapidly.

➤ Income and wealth disparities grew and became increasingly visible.

➤ The Great Recession of 2008–09 exacerbated feelings of insecurity.

➤ Social media and television networks like Al Jazeera increased awareness of political and economic realities across the region and elsewhere in the world.

➤ Regimes were repressive and corrupt.

The domino-like fall of Arab regimes that swept away Ben Ali in Tunisia, Mubarak in Egypt, Qaddafi in Libya, and Saleh in Yemen was perhaps too hastily dubbed the Arab Spring.

GLOBAL AND REGIONAL MEGATRENDS
THROUGH 2030

In the course of the 21st century, the world economy will be transformed beyond recognition, driven by forces that are only now beginning to be understood.[8] Some of these forces will be of direct relevance to current conditions and the future of citizens of MENA:

➢ Over the next two decades, demographic changes and fundamental forces of convergence and competition are likely to bring about massive shifts in both the sectoral and geographical composition of global output and employment.[9] The center of gravity of the global economy is already moving toward Asia.

MENA's share of exports to Asia more than doubled, to 38 percent, over the past decade.

➢ Developing countries will face stronger headwinds in terms of growth and employment generation in the decades ahead, both because the global economy is likely to be significantly less buoyant than in recent decades and because technological changes are rendering manufacturing (and some services) more capital- and skill-intensive. Ultimately, growth will depend primarily on what happens at home in almost all economies.

The economic future will be particularly challenging for MENA, because the manufacturing sector in most of the region was not able to take advantage of global markets in the last two decades. Indeed, the share of manufacturing in G.D.P. fell in nearly all of the region's major economies.

➢ Recent unprecedented changes in the quantity, quality, and mobility of the population will continue to affect the world throughout the 21st century, with important differences across countries, depending on the stage of the demographic transition and the level of economic development. The world's population is projected to grow by 1.5 billion (and the working-age population by 900 million) between 2010 and 2030, to 8.5 billion. It will be increasingly concentrated in Asia and Africa, and population mobility is likely to lead to substantial urbanization.

The population of MENA and Turkey is projected to increase by 125 million people—to 610 million—by 2030.

➢ The open, rules-based global trading system has delivered immense benefits—for the world, for individual countries, and for average citizens in these countries. It can continue to do so, helping today's low-income countries make the transition to middle-income status. Rich countries must sustain the social consensus in favor of open markets and globalization at a time of considerable economic uncertainty and weakness. The rising powers, especially China and increasingly India, will have a key role to play in resuscitating multilateralism.

Total trade in goods as a percent of G.D.P. has been hovering around 60 percent in MENA, indicating a relatively open regional economy (the figures are 48.5 percent for all developing countries and 50 percent for advanced economies).[10] There is substantial variation in the extent of openness of the economy to international trade within the region, however, with the ratio of trade to G.D.P. ranging from 35 percent in Egypt and Iran to about 100 percent in a number of G.C.C. countries. The region as a whole has not been successful in exporting manufactures, is only minimally involved directly in global supply chains, and is the least integrated region in the world. Some G.C.C. countries have been more successful than the rest of the region in exporting services, however.

> Finance has been, and will continue to be, beneficial for economic growth. But excessive finance can retard growth, by incubating economic booms and asset price bubbles that end in financial crises, followed by low rates of economic growth. Reform of the global financial architecture and the rapid growth of inclusive finance are among the most important requirements of a more stable and inclusive future financial system.

Many countries in MENA implemented financial reforms to strengthen their banking systems and promote financial development over the past decade, but the reforms were inadequate. Except in some G.C.C. countries, the region's financial systems remain excessively bank-based and uncompetitive. Inadequate access to finance, particularly by small and medium-size enterprises (SMEs), has contributed to the low rate of economic growth and high rate of unemployment in much of the region.

> Current patterns of energy and natural resource use, agricultural practices, and urbanization appear to be largely unsustainable and require urgent remediation. Left unchecked, they will lead to dangerous climate change and reduced economic growth, as a result of higher economic, social, and environmental costs and lower productivity. The good news is that raising energy and resource efficiency can lead to relatively large win-win gains. Smart policies combining carbon pricing and directed investment in research can increase investment, growth, and competitiveness. Providing long-term policy confidence about the price of carbon and the associated risks of stranded assets can increase investment. A variety of policies—including removing subsidies on fossil fuels, pricing carbon, and facilitating citizens' voice through the marketplace—will play important roles in putting economic processes on a more sustainable footing.

MENA's high and poorly targeted fuel subsidies and inadequate environmental regulations have led to serious environmental problems across the region. The decline in oil prices and the resulting budgetary pressures have resulted in the removal of some subsidies, but much more needs to be done. Massive investments in clean energy and infrastructure are needed. The region is facing serious water shortages: by 2040, 19 of the 33 most water-stressed countries in the world will be in MENA.[11] Most of them are already heavily dependent on food imports.

➤ The politics, rules, and institutions of cooperation among countries have not kept up with the demands from global citizens for changes in the global political order. A billion people moved out of extreme poverty in the past quarter century, social indicators improved in many emerging economies and developing countries, and world income inequality stabilized or declined as a result of the relatively rapid growth of large emerging economies such as China and India. Nevertheless, the challenges remain enormous. Whether norms and policies can make the politics of managing the global economy more effective, legitimate, and responsive to the needs of the bottom half of the world's population remains to be seen. But the time has come to think seriously about how improvements in official global governance, coupled with and reinforced by rising activism of 'global citizens,' can lead to welfare-enhancing and equitable results for global citizens through better national and international policies.[12]

Over the past decade, sharply rising oil revenues enabled the major oil producers in MENA, particularly the G.C.C. members, to become far more influential on the global scene, through their massive financial resources (international reserves and Soverign Wealth Funds). However, because of weak political institutions and serious governance and human rights issues, their elevated role in the international economy has not yet translated into empowerment of their citizens or led to increased cooperation at the regional level outside the G.C.C.

Longer-term megatrends, ranging from demographic and climatic changes to disruptive technologies, compound the region's short-term economic, social, and political challenges, further weakening the governments in the region unless they act jointly in addressing them through regional cooperation, coupled with deep domestic reforms.

To assess the impact of the above-mentioned megatrends on the MENA region, it would be useful to divide them into four sets of issues.

Issues Set 1: The New Demographic Reality

➤ The key trend for the region is the large cohort of people 15–24 combined with rapid urbanization. Very high unemployment rates among the region's youth (about 30 percent in 2014)—a key force behind the "Arab Spring"—are fomenting radicalization and violence. If enough private sector jobs could be created to absorb all new entrants into the labor force, the youth bulge could become a strong positive force, as it was in East Asia a decade ago, in support of higher economic growth: the "demographic dividend" could potentially raise economic growth by 1–2 percentage points a year. If the economic stagnation that has engulfed much of the region continues for several more years, the demographic dividend could turn into even more massive youth unemployment and social and political instability. However the youth bulge is handled, it will eventually give way to an aging population, imposing economic and social costs. By 2030, the window of opportunity for higher growth through the demographic dividend will already have started to close for most countries in the region.

➢ The number of unemployed university graduates is rising, with important political and social implications. This issue is a particularly serious one for the larger countries in the region. There are also a serious mismatch of skills and quality issues that compound the employment problem, including a lack of available talent, as a result of an insufficient number of qualified students coming out of the education system.[13] The quality of education is another serious issue confronting nearly all regional states. [14]

➢ In nearly all MENA countries, female labor force participation remains extremely low (10–20 percent) by developing country standards. The MENA region's real G.D.P. losses from economic gender gaps could be as much as 25–35 percent for several countries in the region.[15]

➢ Weak health, social security, and pension systems are under pressure, and there is a risk of further fiscal deterioration and a decline in the quality and coverage of the services provided, particularly in the region's more populous and poorer countries.

ISSUES SET 2: GROWING INEQUALITY AND WEAK PER CAPITA INCOME GROWTH

➢ Globally, income inequality is decreasing between countries, but increasing within countries. In MENA, both between- and within-county inequalities—as well as strong perceptions of inequity—are projected to continue to rise, possibly creating further social and political instability.[16]

➢ Higher-income groups in the region are likely to continue to benefit disproportionately from global, regional, and national income growth, increasing the concentration of wealth and power, because most countries in the region, particularly its oil exporters, lack effective and progressive systems of taxation and well-targeted social welfare spending.

➢ Under the current set of policies (the muddling-through scenario), per capita income growth is likely to continue to remain very low and lag the world average. As a result, the growth of the middle class in MENA is likely to be slower than elsewhere.

ISSUES SET 3: THE ENVIRONMENT, CLIMATE CHANGE, WATER SHORTAGES, AND EMERGING FOOD SHORTAGES

➢ MENA is the most water-scarce region in the world. Environmental pollution and lack of water will increasingly become severe constraints to health and socioeconomic development in all countries in the region by 2030.

➢ Groundwater and desalination are the only viable sources of water in the region. Both require huge amounts of energy and massive investments in infrastructure, which only the richest countries can afford.

➢ Simmering discontent over high food prices boiled over in some of the poorest and most unequal countries in the region in 2010–11. Water shortage was one of the key factors triggering widespread revolt in Syria. With increasingly volatile weather affecting harvests and global inventories set for further declines, the situation is not expected to improve soon; high volatility in agricultural commodity prices is here to stay.

➢ Increases in the world's population and the growth of the middle class could strain demand for food and natural resources. Given that MENA is already the world's largest net food importer and most of the countries in the region face water shortages, more severe shortages and price spikes could occur, disproportionately hurting the lower and middle classes.

ISSUES SET 4: WEAK GOVERNANCE, POLITICAL AND SOCIAL PRESSURES, AND THE EMERGENCE OF SOCIAL MEDIA

➢ Governance and institutions are weak in many MENA states. Trust in institutions has declined and their legitimacy challenged in nearly every country in the region.

➢ Social and political pressures on the lower and middle classes are likely to result in further alienation from the current economic and political system, particularly by youth.

➢ New technologies and social media are having transformative impacts on individual empowerment in parts of the region where individual freedom, particularly for women and ethnic and religious minorities, is severely limited. The Internet has become a proxy for freedom of opinion and even political parties. In general, there is a positive correlation between Internet penetration and democratic reform. Although it is not clear whether online activism in the region has translated into offline participation, the potential for it to do so is there.

Table 1 summarizes some key economic and social development indicators, as well as the currently projected real per capita income growth trajectories of the major economies in the MENA region over the medium- to long-term. The projections assume the continuation of current country-level policies (that is, no deep reforms and limited regional cooperation and trade integration). The projection figures are based on the assumption that the region or the global economy does not experience any major, long-lasting adverse shock over the next decade or so.

TABLE 1. SELECTED ECONOMIC AND SOCIAL INDICATORS FOR THE MIDDLE EAST AND NORTH AFRICA

	POP. 2014 (M)	PROJECTED POP. 2030 (M)	YOUTH LITERACY RATE (%)	YOUTH UNEMPLOYMENT RATE, MALES, 2014 (%)	FEMALE LABOR-FORCE PARTICIPATION RATE 2014 (%)	MILITARY EXPENDITURES % OF G.D.P. 2014	G.D.P. PPP 2014 ($BN)	G.D.P. PPP 2014 ($ PER CAPITA)	G.D.P. PER CAPITA GROWTH (% PER YEAR 2012-15)	PROJECTED G.D.P. PER CAPITA GROWTH (% PER YEAR 2015-2030)
MIDDLE EAST AND NORTH AFRICA	485.0	610.0	91	27	20	6.0	7,800.0	16,080	1.1	1.2-2.0B
EGYPT	89.6	117.0	92	33	24	1.8	919.2	10,280	0.7	1.7-2.6C
IRAN	78.1	88.5	98	26	17	2.2	1,280.2	16,580	-2.0	2.0-4.0C
SAUDI ARABIA	30.9	39.1	99	22	20	10.8	1,549.8	51,320	1.7	0.5-1.5C
TURKEY	75.9	87.7	100	17	29	2.2	1,441.0	18,980	2.0	2.6-2.5C
G.C.C.	51.6	65.7	98	12	35	7.2	2,939.2	57,410	1.7	1.0-1.5C
MAGHREB	90.1	108.2	92	28	32	3.7	1,013.3	11,246	2.4	2.2-3.7C
ALL DEVELOPING COUNTRIES	5,861.9	6,873.5	89	13	50	1.9	51,651.0	8,811	3.7	3.0-4.0C

SOURCE: : DATA FROM WORLD BANK, WORLD DEVELOPMENT INDICATORS, 2015; AND UNITED NATIONS, WORLD POPULATION PROSPECTS: THE 2015 REVISION, NEW YORK; CONFERENCE BOARD (JANUARY 2016); U.S. ENERGY INFORMATION, AGENCY (INTERNATIONAL ENERGY OUTLOOK, 2014); PwC, WORLD IN 2050(FEBRUARY 2015); OECD, LOOKING TO 2060: LONG-TERM GLOBAL GROWTH PROSPECTS (NOVEMBER 2012); SHORT- TO MEDIUM-TERM PROJECTIONS ARE BASED ON SEVERAL SOURCES, INCLUDING WORLD BANK, GLOBAL ECONOMIC PROSPECTS (JANUARY 2016); I.M.F., WORLD ECONOMIC OUTLOOK (APRIL 2016); AND OECD OUTLOOK (DECEMBER 2015); AND AUTHOR'S CALCULATIONS.

A. MIDDLE EAST AND NORTH AFRICA INCLUDES HIGH-INCOME COUNTRIES IN THE REGION (MEMBERS OF THE G.C.C.) AND TURKEY.

B. THIS IS EQUIVALENT TO 3.2-4.5 PERCENT FOR AVERAGE REAL G.D.P. GROWTH IN 2015-2030; LONG-TERM PROJECTIONS ARE BASED ON THE FOLLOWING SOURCES: THE CONFERENCE BOARD (JANUARY 2016); THE U.S. ENERGY INFORMATION AGENCY (INTERNATIONAL ENERGY OUTLOOK, 2014); PwC, WORLD IN 2050 (FEBRUARY 2015); OECD, LOOKING TO 2060: LONG-TERM GLOBAL GROWTH PROSPECTS (NOVEMBER 2012).

C. THE LOWER BOUND FIGURES ARE THE PROJECTED AVERAGE PER CAPITA G.D.P. GROWTH IN 2015-16; THE UPPER BOUND FIGURES ARE THE PROJECTED AVERAGE PER CAPITA G.D.P. GROWTH IN 2016 TO 2018/20 PERIOD; PROJECTIONS ARE BASED ON SEVERAL SOURCES, INCLUDING MEDIUM-TERM FORECASTS PUBLISHED IN THE WORLD BANK, GLOBAL ECONOMIC PROSPECTS (JANUARY 2016); I.M.F., WORLD ECONOMIC OUTLOOK (OCTOBER, 2015); AND O.E.C.D., OUTLOOK (DECEMBER, 2015). PROJECTIONS FOR MAGHREB'S G.D.P. PER CAPITA GROWTH EXCLUDE LIBYA.

D. ALGERIA, LIBYA, MOROCCO, TUNISIA.

THE POTENTIALLY DISASTROUS CONSEQUENCES OF DELAYING REFORMS AND COOPERATION

Low economic growth, combined with intensifying conflict across the region, is weakening the already fragile economic structure and leading to increased poverty and youth unemployment in MENA. Ongoing conflicts created more than 9 million refugees (about 62 percent of the world's total) as of early 2016. Nearly 60 percent of them have fled from Syria to neighboring countries, imposing huge economic and social costs, particularly on Lebanon and Jordan, where refugees now account for about 25 percent of the population.

Violent conflicts have had a devastating effect on macroeconomic performance. In MENA countries that have been in conflict during the past five years, output declined by about 2.25 percentage points a year, according to recent estimates by the I.M.F.[17]

As chaos and conflict spread throughout the region, defense and security expenditures in the region—already among the highest in the world—are likely to rise, just as oil revenues, tourism receipts, and worker remittances decline. Despite the drop in revenues, MENA governments are unlikely to cut back substantially on social programs or various subsidy schemes out of fear of the social and political ramifications of doing so. The result is larger fiscal and balance of payments deficits and the accumulation of debt, even in countries that traditionally maintained high levels of reserves and operate large sovereign wealth funds.

Nevertheless, the impact of the sharp decline in the price of oil on the region is likely to be significant, given large remittance and foreign aid flows, investments in infrastructure, and the banking and financial ties of the rich energy oil and gas exporters to the rest of the region.[18] Addressing these challenges, as well as security concerns and spreading violence, calls for dialogue and cooperation at the regional level rather than further increases in the region's already skyrocketing military budgets.

Military expenditure in MENA plus Turkey represented about 6 percent of the region's G.D.P. (at market prices) in 2014 (about $215 billion), a far higher share than the 2.5 percent in advanced economies or the 1.9 percent in emerging economies and developing countries as a whole. If the region's internal conflicts and tensions could be resolved diplomatically and military expenditures reduced to no more than 2.5 percent of G.D.P., the savings could be diverted to more productive and job creating domestic and regional projects.[19]

Box 1 provides the key economic issues and reform agenda the four major

BOX 1: REFORMS NEEDED IN SAUDI ARABIA, EGYPT, IRAN AND TURKEY

SAUDI ARABIA

Saudi Arabia's economy grew more than 5 percent a year over the past decade. The sharp drop in oil prices caused growth to slow, to about 3 percent a year in 2014-15. Depletion of the government's fiscal and balance of payments buffers has already adversely affected non-oil growth and bank balance sheets and required downward adjustments in fiscal spending. If the budget were put on a consolidation path, fiscal buffers could be used to smooth spending in the event of a temporary decline in oil prices. Targeting a positive structural balance over time would allow the accumulation of savings for future generations. The ambitious reform agenda in Vision 2030 with the overarching objective of diversifying the economy away from oil is an attempt to improve the country's performance.

EGYPT

Egypt's economy grew about 5 percent a year between 1990 and 2010, and good progress was made in the social sectors. Growth did little to reduce persistently high unemployment, however, which averaged about 10 percent during the 2000s (with youth unemployment approaching 40 percent in recent years). Although Egypt liberalized key segments of the economy in the 2000s, policies failed to ignite significant structural change, leaving the medium-term outlook uncertain. Between 2004 and 2013, growth was driven mainly by capital, followed by labor, and the contribution of T.F.P. to growth was barely positive (compared with 2-3 percentage points a year in high-performing countries in Asia). Macroeconomic adjustment and deep structural reforms are desperately needed to create conditions for higher, more sustainable, and more inclusive growth and to make public debt, which currently exceeds G.D.P., sustainable.

IRAN

The recent nuclear agreement improved Iran's economic outlook, but the medium- to long-term outlook remains highly uncertain and sensitive to Iran's domestic political situation. Most experts expect annual growth of no more than 1 percent in 2015/16, accelerating to 5-6 percent over the next three to five years—provided that Iran begins implementing badly needed reforms. The productivity shortfall is related largely to Iran's relatively low level of T.F.P. growth, a reflection of deep-seated structural problems. If Iran's economy is to grow at 6-8 percent a year on a sustained basis, T.F.P. needs to be increased substantially, through reforms, and there needs to be more efficient use of human capital, and technological upgrading of key industries. Three time bombs threaten Iran's future: vulnerability of its banking and financial sector to adverse shocks; the sustained rise in unemployment and underemployment of university graduates, and the deteriorating environment and severe water shortage.

TURKEY

Turkey has the largest, most advanced, and most diversified economy in the region (excluding Israel). Without a change in policies, Turkey's performance is likely to be weaker than in the recent past. Prudence would call for a tighter fiscal stance. In the short run, expenditure growth should be curbed. For the 2015-17 medium-term plan, the I.M.F. has recommended a cumulative fiscal adjustment of 2 percent of G.D.P. relative to its baseline. Productivity growth in Turkey contracted by 0.6 percent in 2013, after declining 0.8 percent in 2012. Underlying these estimates was a slightly better improvement in output growth than employment growth, but Turkey's T.F.P. growth continues to be negative and its labor productivity level is just 37 percent of the U.S. level. Macroeconomic policies can support rebalancing and preserve financial stability in the near-term, but improved medium-term growth will depend on progress with structural reforms that enhance Turkey's economic potential.

economic powers of the region need to consider in order to help break the vicious cycle of poor outcomes and social tension.

The four largest economies in the region—Saudi Arabia, Egypt, Iran, and Turkey—account for about 70 percent of the region's $4 trillion economy and are home to about 285 million of its 450 million current inhabitants. [20] All four countries are among the 25 largest economies in the world. Their performance over the next two decades will be critical to the economic prospects of the region and the global economy.

THE URGENT NEED FOR REFORMS AND REGIONAL COOPERATION TO BOOST GROWTH AND CREATE EMPLOYMENT

Limited integration has stifled MENA's ability to tap its significant potential for economic growth and job creation.[21] Although home to 6.5 percent of the world's population and 5.1 percent of the world's G.D.P., the region accounts for less than 2 percent of nonoil world trade (including oil and gas trade raises the figure to more than 7 percent).[22] By contrast, countries that opted for a liberal trade and investment regime—most notably in East Asia—have high levels of trade, employment, and per capita income.

Several economic and integration blocs include one or more MENA countries, but the region lacks an overarching cooperation and integration agreement.[23] Some schemes extend beyond the Greater Middle East.

Given the lack of economic dynamism in the region outside the G.C.C. and the low level of regional cooperation, it is not surprising that some countries have sought trade agreements outside the region. The most important are the Euro-Mediterranean agreements and a number of bilateral agreements between the United States and selected MENA countries. These agreements are useful starting points and provide a framework for cooperation, but they do not encourage competition and the development of regional value chains. Indeed, the proliferation of regional agreements has inadvertently hindered deeper integration within the region. Firms in MENA also face relatively high tariffs and restrictive nontariff measures on intermediate inputs, which prevents them from participating in global value chains.

Intra-MENA trade is below its potential. It represents about 9 percent of MENA's total exports—a smaller share than nearly all other regions, and a fraction of the region's trade with Europe and East Asia.

The region's links to the rest of the world remain strong. Merchandise exports of MENA plus Turkey to the rest of the world exceeded $1.4 trillion in 2014, and exports of commercial services (mainly travel and transport) amounted to

BOX 2: TYPES OF REGIONAL COOPERATION AND INTEGRATION

REGIONAL ECONOMIC INTEGRATION CAN TAKE FIVE FORMS:

1. A free trade area is the most basic form of economic cooperation. Members agree to remove all barriers to trade within the area, but are free to independently determine trade policies with nonmember nations. An example is the North American Free Trade Agreement (NAFTA).

2. A customs union provides for economic cooperation as in a free trade area and removes trade barriers among members. The primary difference between a customs union and a free trade area is that members in a customs union agree to treat trade with nonmember countries in a similar manner.

3. A common market allows for the creation of economically integrated markets among member countries. It removes trade barriers and restrictions on the movement of labor and capital among members.

4. An economic union is created when countries enter into an economic agreement to both remove barriers to trade and adopt common economic policies.

5. A mega-regional trade and investment agreement, such as the Trans-Pacific Partnership (T.P.P.) and Transatlantic Trade and Investment Partnership (T.T.I.P.), which mark the first time the largest and richest countries are negotiating preferential trade agreements with one another.

LESSONS FROM REGIONAL TRADE AGREEMENTS THAT MAY BE RELEVANT FOR THE MENA REGION INCLUDE THE FOLLOWING:

♦ Building effective regional institutions is a difficult, lengthy, process that requires incremental, gradual, and flexible implementation with visible payoffs.

♦ It is preferable to keep the number of members in sub-regional and regional organizations manageable; membership should be based on shared geography and common regional interests.

♦ Adequate funding mechanisms for regional investments are essential.

♦ Successful cooperation requires leadership at the country, institutional, and individual levels.

♦ External assistance can be helpful in establishing and sustaining sub-regional institutions, but it cannot substitute for ownership of the process from within the region.

♦ Open regionalism- the creation of institutions that are open to extra-regional participation and do not discriminate against non-regional economies in the long-term-is the most successful strategy, as demonstrated in East and Southeast Asia.

♦ Regional economic cooperation agreements that involve ministries of finance or economy and central banks tend to be more effective than agreements that rely on the leadership of line ministries or foreign affairs.

♦ Transparency and the engagement of the business community and civil society strengthen the mechanisms for regional cooperation.

♦ Monitoring and evaluating the performance of countries under regional agreements is important, as are incentives for better compliance.

about $175 billion, 3.8 percent of the world total. In 2014, the region's global share of F.D.I. outflows was 11 percent ($52 billion), and its share of workers' remittances outflows was about 20 percent ($92 billion). About $86 billion of remittances were sent from Kuwait, Qatar, Saudi Arabia, and the United Arab Emirates to the rest of the world. Egypt and Lebanon together received about $30 billion.

The regional schemes with the greatest potential are the Pan Arab Free Trade Area (PAFTA), which has 18 members, including all of the Arab Middle East and North Africa plus Sudan; the G.C.C.; and the Economic Cooperation Organization (ECO), founded by Iran, Pakistan, and Turkey in 1985 as a platform to discuss ways to enhance growth and development and promote trade and investment. Its current membership now includes seven Central Asian countries.[24]

A recent assessment of MENA's trade agreements concluded that trade in the region is well below its potential and the level of diversification is low.[25] It also finds that the overall impact of preferential trade agreements (P.T.A.s) has been negligible, with agreements failing to stimulate trade.[26] However, the findings also indicate that the Agadir agreement, as well as the U.S.-Jordan agreement, appear to have had a positive impact on trade, similar to the effects expected from standard P.T.A.[27] It concludes that for the regional preferential agreements to have a significant effect on trade and economic growth, they need to be deeper—involving improved governance, regulatory harmonization, labor mobility, and services trade.

With the exception of the G.C.C., MENA's regional schemes face serious challenges, because of inadequate infrastructure, policy distortions in domestic economies, and political friction among some members.[28] The ECO may have a promising future, provided that it addresses the sub-region's formidable trade facilitation challenges and is able to act as a bridge between East Asia and MENA.

Despite several reform efforts in recent years, MENA continues to face binding constraints on economic competitiveness in general and trade in particular. Of critical importance is the need to improve trade-related infrastructure and strengthen trade facilitation activities. P.T.A.s within the region, though helpful in many respects, have not led to significant expansion of nonoil exports, except perhaps in Turkey, which has a dynamic and diversified export sector. The focus in MENA must therefore be on opening up to the rest of the world, which may require that individual countries aggressively pursue unilateral liberalization policies as part of their national reform programs. Trade in services is a major untapped source of trade growth within the region and between the region and the rest of the world. Regional cooperation and integration can bring benefits, but these efforts can also impose significant costs if not carried out in a manner that is compatible with broader global integration trends. Box 2 identifies some of the benefits and costs of regional trade agreements.

MENA leaders appear to be sensitive to calls for reform and to accelerating measures to stimulate job growth, make the economic growth process more inclusive, and foster popular participation in the development process. Political economy issues, such as resistance to reforms by groups that fear losing their favorable position to greater competition, tend to slow the pace of reforms. Economic cooperation among the major economies in the region, coupled with regional trade and investment initiatives, could help address these challenges by further boosting growth and stimulating employment. More importantly, regional cooperation could help attract the private investment needed to generate more and better jobs by removing barriers to capital inflows and creating a better enabling environment for both domestic and foreign investment.

Regional cooperation and global economic integration are complementary processes. Regional integration contributes to global integration by allowing countries to reap the benefits of geographical proximity, promoting learning by doing, and fostering efforts to build competitiveness. Global integration can place added pressure on countries to improve intra-regional integration. In many respects, regional cooperation and integration can be understood as stepping stones to wider global market cooperation, with regional infrastructure investment and trade in goods, services, and factors within MENA boosting competitiveness and encouraging the development of the institutions necessary for integration on a wider scale. While many reforms can and should be implemented unilaterally, regional cooperation is needed to bolster trade in services, create regional markets to generate scale economies, cooperate on customs and the creation of joint border posts to lower trade costs, and improve connectivity through networked infrastructure.

Tapping Trade Potential through Regional Cooperation and Reform

MENA is not tapping its potential for exports, because the region is not competitive in producing goods it can export to the rest of the world. To become competitive, the region needs to consider a number of reforms, including reform of trade policy. MENA countries should lower tariffs and nontariff barriers, while improving productivity growth, the business environment, and the quality and skill base of their workforces.

DIVERSIFYING EXPORTS

MENA exports mainly primary commodities, largely oil and gas (65 percent of all exports in 2014). Manufactured goods accounted for just 21 percent of exports, with other sectors accounting for the remaining 14 percent. Exports are highly concentrated and undiversified. Egypt, Jordan, Lebanon, Morocco, and Tunisia fare better than the rest of the region on both indicators.

Although most countries have made some improvements in diversifying their exports over the past 15 years, the level of diversification remains low by international standards. Moreover, exports are generally produced with low levels of skill: less than 7 percent of the region's exports are classified as high technology, compared with about 25 percent in East Asian developing economies. This combination of limited export diversification and low-technology industry hampers productivity growth, which is already low relative to national income levels.

MENA's share of world exports of non-oil goods remained below 1 percent for years, gradually increasing over the past decade to about 2 percent in 2014. Within MENA, the U.A.E., Qatar, Kuwait, Egypt, Oman, Turkey, and Iran witnessed relatively rapid growth in non-fuel exports. Among oil importers, Egypt and Jordan made significant progress in diversifying exports. A number of countries in the region, including most G.C.C. countries, reduced their dependence on crude exports in favor of processed industrial goods, including chemicals, fertilizers, and other processed petroleum products.

INCREASING INTRA-REGIONAL INTEGRATION

Greater regional cooperation and economic or trade integration have been shown to yield significant economic gains to member countries. They can help alleviate shortages of energy and other resources, remove barriers to growth and job creation, and reduce prices of critical products, particularly in countries with limited access to markets. The long delay in concluding the W.T.O.'s Doha Development Agenda has been a key driver of regional trade agreements and the creation of free trade areas in the last two decades. According to the W.T.O., regional trade agreements can support the W.T.O.'s multilateral trading system. W.T.O. agreements recognize that regional arrangements and closer economic integration can benefit countries.[29]

Most agreements and new negotiations are bilateral, although some recent negotiations involved multiple W.T.O. members. The Trans-Pacific Partnership (T.P.P.) Agreement involved 12 parties, which joined the massive regional partnership in the hopes of getting around the impasse on a multilateral trade agreement. Similar agreement is under consideration between the United States and the European Union under the Transatlantic Trade and Investment

Partnership (T.T.I.P.), which aims to promote trade and multilateral economic growth. Except for Turkey, countries in MENA are not directly involved in either of these mega-regional agreements, but the agreements will affect them. Not having an effectively functioning regional trade agreement encompassing all four of the region's largest economies has weakened MENA's bargaining position with respect to the other regional agreements already in place or under negotiation.

Though rising, integration within the MENA region remains low, particularly compared with other middle- and high-income regions. In 2014, intra-regional exports of goods averaged less than 9 percent of total exports in MENA, compared with 59 percent in ASEAN and 63 percent in the European Union. The countries that trade the most within MENA are oil importers, led by Jordan (54 percent of total exports in 2013), Lebanon (54 percent), Egypt (33 percent), and Turkey (26 percent). Maghreb countries export within the region least (5–11 percent), with much of their exports going to Europe.

REDUCING TRADE BARRIERS

Significant progress has been made in reducing barriers to trade in goods within the region and, to some extent, between MENA and the rest of the world. Over the last decade, reductions in most favored nation tariffs complemented preferential liberalization under PAFTA and other P.T.A.s. Indeed, MENA was the region in which tariffs decreased the most during the global financial crisis, especially on manufactured goods. The average uniform tariff equivalent of all tariffs (ad valorem and specific) for the region fell from nearly 15 percent in 2002 to 5 percent in 2011.

Wide variations in trade restrictions exist across countries and sub-regions, however. The G.C.C. has brought common external tariff down to 5 percent on most imported merchandise and to zero on essential goods, but restrictions elsewhere in the region—and in the region as a whole—remain high. According to the tariff-only Overall Trade Restrictiveness Index, only South Asia had greater tariff restrictiveness than MENA in 2011. MENA compares unfavorably with its main competitors in Europe and Central Asia, Latin America and the Caribbean, and East Asia and Pacific.

Barriers to trade and investment in services are significant: the services trade restrictiveness index, which measures the extent of barriers to trade and investment in services, is twice as high in MENA as in Europe and Central Asia.[30] Although MENA doubled its exports of services over the past decade, their share has stagnated at just 2–3 percent of total trade for the past two decades. Services exports remain dominated by tourism-related travel of low value added. Travel and transport together made up about 80 percent of total MENA service exports in 2014. This profile contrasts sharply with that of South

Asia, driven by India, where information and communications technology (I.C.T.) and finance are the leading export services, making up 55 percent of service exports.

Opportunities to expand trade in services vastly exceed opportunities to expand trade in goods—and the gains could be enormous. Studies suggest that comprehensive reforms to strengthen competition and streamline regulatory frameworks would yield benefits two-to-three times greater than those achieved through tariff removal. Opening up services trade would facilitate trade in parts and components and contribute to the emergence of regional production networks.

IMPROVING INFRASTRUCTURE AND CROSS-BORDER TRADE FACILITATION

Trade costs constitute as much as 30 percent of the final delivered price of MENA's nonoil exports—about twice their share in Western Europe. Maghreb countries actually face lower costs trading with Europe than trading among themselves. Trade costs are high partly because backbone services, such as telecommunications, transport, and power, are not competitively priced. Opening these sectors to competition and trade would help reduce production costs, increase F.D.I., promote knowledge spillovers, and expand markets.

Trade facilitation and transport impediments impose greater losses than formal trade tariffs and quota restrictions. Logistics and trade facilitation indicators such as the Logistics Performance Index and the Liner Shipping Connectivity Index show that MENA fares better in terms of connectivity than in facilitation and logistics.[31] Although some countries, such as the U.A.E., have excellent logistics facilities, most MENA countries need to substantially improve logistics and trade facilitation to bring down the high costs of trade. [32]

Efficient ports and maritime and aviation services are crucial for the competitive export of goods. Most MENA countries have extensive road networks, modern facilities for air and sea transport, and, in many countries, well-developed rail networks. The quality of transport infrastructure is often deficient, however, unable to support growing modern economies.

Progress is being made in improving transport infrastructure. Implementation of the Mashreq Corridor Program, which aims to remove cross-border constraints, is expected to increase trade by about $25 billion a year by 2030. It will also create a large number of permanent jobs, mostly in export-oriented light manufacturing industries, which typically have a higher than average female share of employment.

Economic integration in the power sector is at an early stage of development. Major initiatives, such as the North Africa–Middle East–Europe Mediterranean Power Pool, are taking shape, though much remains to be done to introduce competition in the sector.

Considerable progress has been made in regional integration of mobile telephony, but many important cross-border issues still need to be tackled, particularly with regard to fixed and mobile broadband infrastructure. However, the infrastructure linking Arab countries to the potential growth poles in the region over the medium-term—Iran and Turkey—remain inadequate.

EFFECTS OF PREFERENTIAL TRADE AGREEMENTS

Over the past 15 years, there has been an unprecedented global increase in the number, breadth, and depth of P.T.A.s.[33] The number of P.T.A.s doubled during this period, to more than 250. MENA states have signed many P.T.A.s, both within the region and outside. This proliferation of P.T.A.s, with their varying sector and product coverage, rules of origin, and implementation requirements, constitutes a formidable implementation challenge for capacity-constrained institutions.

P.T.A.s have had mixed effects in MENA. They significantly reduced trade and investment barriers, provided an impetus for behind-the-border economic reforms, and helped spur trade. They also encouraged participating countries to improve their trade infrastructure, harmonize border policies and procedures, and improve their supply chains and logistics facilities. There is little evidence regarding causality between P.T.A.s and policy reforms, however, as countries such as Egypt, Jordan, Morocco, and Tunisia embarked on major reforms on their own.

The P.T.A.s that MENA countries signed gave rise to a far more rapid expansion in imports than exports. The findings from a gravity panel model prepared for this study suggest that trade preferences granted to MENA countries by the United States, the European Union, and Turkey did not have an additional effect on exports compared with P.T.A.s in general, which increased trade by an average of about 21 percent. In fact, the additional effect is negative in the case of the P.T.A.s with the European Union, not significant in the case of the P.T.A.s with Turkey, and largely accounted for by Jordan's Qualifying Industrial Zone in the case of the P.T.A.s with the United States. In contrast, PAFTA and the Agadir Agreement for the Establishment of a Free Trade Zone between Egypt, Jordan, Morocco, and Tunisia expanded exports by their members, albeit from a low intra-regional trade base.[34]

There is also no evidence that P.T.A.s contributed to investment flows into the region. Total F.D.I. rose sharply in MENA over the past decade, but the bulk of it came from within the region, essentially from the G.C.C. Relatively little F.D.I. has come from the European Union or the United States.

STEPPING UP POLICY REFORMS AND POLITICAL COMMITMENT

INCREASING REGIONAL AND GLOBAL ECONOMIC INTEGRATION

Regional integration and global economic integration should move hand-in-hand. There are tremendous opportunities to strengthen the linkages between MENA countries and wider and deeper global markets, including through vertical integration of global production chains.

Although progress has been made overall, albeit with wide country variations, substantial scope remains for further regional and global economic integration. To strengthen trade in goods, MENA countries could continue to unilaterally reduce their most favored nation tariffs, with an emphasis on reducing tariff peaks to the level of the most competitive regions of the world. Efforts could also be made to roll back nontariff barriers to trade, by reviewing nontariff measures, reducing their scope, and phasing out measures that are not deemed essential for national security purposes.

STRENGTHENING TRADE IN SERVICES

Reforms to strengthen trade in services include easing entry and licensing restrictions for both domestic and foreign firms in the services sectors, promoting competition, harmonizing and strengthening regulatory practices and arrangements, and lowering restrictions on the mobility of foreign workers residing in the region. Continued public ownership in the services sectors represents a potential hurdle to increased regional cooperation, given the caution with which countries of the region have moved toward privatization. Addressing these issues would have a direct impact on employment, the overriding problem in MENA, as services sectors are labor intensive and thus critical for reducing unemployment.

REDUCING THE COSTS OF TRADE

MENA countries need to reduce the costs associated with trading across borders. Doing so will require improving the efficiency of border-crossing points, including the harmonization of customs procedures. Logistics systems need to be vastly improved by abolishing policies that reserve activities for specific categories of domestic firms.

IMPROVING INFRASTRUCTURE AND MAKING IT MORE COMPETITIVE

Transport networks need to be strengthened to improve the efficiency of ports and make better use of regional rail potential. In the power sector, institutional prerequisites for cross-border power trade need to be put in place alongside strategic investments in regional distribution and transmission networks. Opening up backbone telecommunications infrastructure to competition and encouraging inward investment in broadband services could bring I.C.T. costs down and make Internet services more readily available. This broad reform agenda needs to be tailored to each country's circumstances, binding constraints on development and growth, and stage of reform.

SETTING REGIONAL AND INTRA-REGIONAL PRIORITIES

Strong political commitment and leadership will be required if regional economic cooperation and integration are to make meaningful contributions to growth and employment in MENA. It is critical that Iran be admitted to the W.T.O., a focal point for much needed economic reforms and better governance. Its admission would lead to improved trade competitiveness through the reduction of uncertainty and related risk perceptions, allowing Iran to also play an active role in intra-regional trade and in setting the region's trade policy agenda. The ongoing political change sweeping through the Arab world, combined with the Iran nuclear deal, provide an extraordinary opportunity for the region to accelerate economic integration efforts.

The G.C.C. has made substantial progress in reducing tariffs and nontariff measures and improving trade logistics and infrastructure, but reforms are needed in services. In the Mashreq countries, which have strong links to the G.C.C., good infrastructure and cross-border trade facilitation should be prioritized. In the Maghreb, which has strong links to the European Union, reducing tariffs and nontariff measures and improving cross-border trade facilitation should be high on the reform agenda.

WHAT SHOULD BE DONE? POLICY RECOMMENDATIONS

Analysis of conditions in the region as well as regional and global megatrends yields several recommendations for MENA.

ADOPT A FOUR-PRONGED STRATEGY

1. For each of the major players in the region, a strategy could include four prongs:

2. Reduce regional tensions and end conflicts through diplomacy, recognizing that current approaches are impeding investment and economic growth, and will result in lose-lose outcomes.
3. Undertake significant economic and institutional reforms at home to remove binding constraints on growth and development, particularly in manufacturing and services; reform the banking and financial sector and improve access to funds by the private sector and citizens; and improve the quality of education.
4. Focus on well-targeted policies and structural reforms that would lead to significant reductions in youth employment and increased female labor force participation, introduce cuts in military expenditures as regional tensions subside, and reallocate the savings to clean energy and infrastructure investments to crowd in private investment and boost growth.
5. Increase cooperation and trade, both within the region and with major global growth poles. Initiate regional projects (in partnership with the private sector) with high payoffs for all countries in the region and their citizens—in areas such as tourism, air and ground transport, regional energy and water, regional health and education, and research hubs—to increase trade in goods and services (within the region and globally), build confidence and good will, and create positive spillover effects within the region over the medium term.

Taken together, these country-based reforms and regional initiatives could boost the region's long-term growth potential from the 3.0–4.5 percent a year range to the 5–8 percent a year range, similar to the performance of developing countries in Asia. Significant contributions would come from the more efficient use of factor inputs, particularly human capital with improved skills, and technological progress, in the form of more rapid growth of total factor productivity, which has been low and declining in all major economies of the region.

Craft and Implement Significant National-Level Reforms

National reforms to boost inclusive and sustainable growth, through increases in investments and acceleration of total factor productivity growth, would likely involve the following measures:

➤ Adopt a bold economic reform agenda to propel private sector activity and foster a more dynamic, competitive, innovation-driven, and inclusive economy. To achieve broad-based and sustainable growth, countries need to gradually move away from state-dominated to private investment, from protected and rent-seeking enterprises to export-led growth and value creation.

➤ Craft policies that improve the business climate, revive private sector confidence, and lay the foundations for higher growth. Gradually transform the public sector from a system that provides privileges— public employment, subsidies, economic rents, tax exemptions—to one that provides basic economic services, adequate social protection, better governance, a level playing field for all economic actors, and a competitive environment for the private sector.

➤ Deepen trade integration. In addition to the large potential direct gains of boosting exports and attracting productivity-enhancing F.D.I., trade integration can catalyze reforms in other areas that help countries compete. Deeper trade integration will require better access to markets in advanced economies, reductions in tariffs and nontariff trade barriers, and a focus on the increasingly important areas of trade facilitation and export promotion.

➤ Simplify complex and burdensome business regulation in order to unleash entrepreneurial activity and private investment. Reforms must streamline business regulation, reduce the scope for discretion, increase transparency, and strengthen institutional autonomy and accountability.

➤ Adopt labor market reforms that provide incentives for hiring and boost employment in the formal private sector labor market, and eliminate regulations that discourage hiring women.

➤ Create social safety nets that protect the poor in cost-effective ways. To transition from costly generalized subsidies to targeted forms of social protection, consolidate and increase spending on existing safety net programs and improve their coverage; prioritize interventions that strengthen human capital (such as conditional cash transfers); invest in social safety net infrastructure, such as unified registries for beneficiaries; increase the use of modern targeting techniques; strengthen governance and accountability; and increase communication to potential beneficiaries about the programs available to them.

Complex political processes, the increasing polarization of society, and a difficult security environment make policymaking challenging. To set in motion a virtuous circle in which political transition and economic transformation reinforce one another, policymakers need to adopt a participatory approach, engage with different segments of society, and build coalitions for reform.

SET POLICY PRIORITIES TO ENHANCE THE CHANCES OF ACHIEVING A BEST-CASE OUTCOME BY 2030

The following actions in each country in the region would enhance the chances of the best-case scenario materializing:

➤ Invest in citizens. Equip them with the tools to seize opportunities through high-quality training and education, and protect the most vulnerable.

➤ Prepare for a new, sustainable, and inclusive growth paradigm, by investing in early childhood health and education and improving living conditions of ethnic groups and minorities.

➤ Enable the private sector to invest, reap economic opportunities, compete globally, and create productive jobs, particularly for youth.

➤ Encourage the education of girls and increase the participation of women in the labor force.

➤ Focus on the well-being of citizens by strengthening health, social services, and the social safety net.

➤ Undertake labor market and education reforms.

➤ Reinvent government. Recalibrate the public sector to accommodate the realities of the 21st century.

➤ Protect the environment. Remove energy subsidies, invest in clean energy, protect water supplies, and use energy and water efficiently.

➤ Undertake major regional infrastructure projects in energy, water, and transport (ground and air transport) to substantially improve links among the major countries in the region.[35]

➤ Deepen trade integration within the region and with the rest of the world. Doing so could yield large direct gains from higher exports and productivity-enhancing F.D.I., and catalyze reforms in other areas that help countries compete.

LAUNCH A MINI–MARSHALL PLAN

Such a plan should include a commitment to coordinate a high-level economic commission involving the World Bank, the International Monetary Fund, the United Nations and its specialized agencies, and other relevant international and regional development agencies. These bodies would work with MENA governments in a coordinated way to craft a multi-year, regional development agenda that would involve funds not only for reconstruction and the resettlement of millions of refugees, but also for regional projects. The European Recovery Program—the original Marshall Plan—involved about $150 billion in today's prices, spent over a four-year period (about 1.5 percent of America's G.D.P. a year between 1948 and 1951). A MENA recovery program must be on a similar scale if it is to achieve the desired outcomes.

In order to raise the region's growth and make a real dent in its extremely high youth unemployment rates (approaching 30 percent), the private sector needs to be revitalized, particularly in Egypt and Iran. Instruments like the Catalytic Finance Initiative and related funds by the International Finance Corporation, with participation of the private sector, governments of advanced and emerging economies, as well as strategic investments by the sovereign wealth funds of the G.C.C. countries, should therefore be integrated into this mini–Marshall Plan.

The regional economic powers, together with the international community, should also consider creating an infrastructure and development bank for MENA, which would provide long-term financing for regional projects as well as major country-level projects with positive regional spillover effects. Such projects, which could be co-financed by the private sector and follow the public-private participation model, should be conceived and undertaken only in countries that implement major domestic reforms along the lines outlined above. The reforms are the sine qua non for achieving the desired growth and job creation in each country and reaping the complementary growth effects from increased economic integration, both within the region and internationally.

ENDNOTES

1. As a result of the substantial drop (about 60 percent) in the price of oil in 2014-2015, the major oil exporters in the region, particularly the G.C.C. members, are facing large budget and current account deficits for the first time in many years. The region's fuel exporters' budget balances shifted sharply from an average surplus of more than 5 percent of G.D.P. in 2008-13 to projected deficits in excess of 12 percent of G.D.P. in 2015-16. The shift was even more pronounced for the G.C.C., whose combined budget shifted from a surplus of about 11 percent of G.D.P. in 2008-13 into projected deficits of about 13 percent of G.D.P. in 2015-16. Similarly, the combined current account balance of payments of the region's oil and gas exporters shifted from an average surplus of about 14 percent of G.D.P. (or about $390 billion a year) in 2008-13 into projected deficits of about 4 percent of G.D.P. (or about $90 billion a year) in 2015-16. Official reserves have already declined in a number of major fuel exporting countries, e.g. Saudi Arabia alone reduced its official reserves by an estimated $100 billion by end-2015, and is expected to resort to further borrowing from international capital markets in 2016 to protect its reserves. Moreover, total assets of Sovereign Wealth Funds (S.W.F.) funded by oil and gas have declined by nearly 10 percent (about $400 billion) since 2014. The decline in S.W.F. assets has been particularly pronounced in Saudi Arabia while some of the other G.C.C. members have continued to accumulate assets, but even these countries, such as the U.A.E., Kuwait and Qatar, which have small populations and relatively large international reserves and S.W.F. and are better able to weather the sharp declines in the prices of oil and gas, have had to reduce public spending and rollback subsidies to protect their fiscal buffers. A recent estimate by I.M.F. staff indicates that based on rough calculations, prior to the oil price decline, the G.C.C. countries were projected to have a combined fiscal surplus of about $200 billion in 2015-2020, but are now are expected to have a combined fiscal deficit of about $450 billion during the same period, a turn-around of about $650 billion in the projected change in net assets with important economic and financial implications for the region and the global economy. See Rabah Arezki, Adnan Mazarei, Ananthakrishnan Prasad, "Sovereign Wealth Funds in the new era of oil," Vox (2015),

accessed May 19, 2016, http://www.voxeu.org/article/sovereign-wealth-funds-new-era-oil.

2. Measured by G.D.P. in 2014 in US dollars in purchasing parity prices (PPP), Saudi Arabia was the 14th largest economy in the world, followed by Turkey (17th), Iran (18th), and Egypt (22nd). In terms of 2015 population size, Egypt ranked 15th in the world, Iran 17th, Turkey 18th, and Saudi Arabia 46th.

3. Ross Harrison, "Defying Gravity: Working toward a Regional Strategy for a Stable Middle East," Middle East Institute (2015), accessed May 19, 2016, http://www.mei.edu/content/article/defying-gravity-working-toward-regional-strategy-stable-middle-east; and Ross Harrison and Shahrokh Fardoust, "Time for a U.S. Regional Strategy for the Middle East," National Interest, May 25, 2014, accessed May 19, 2016, http://nationalinterest.org/feature/time-us-regional-strategy-the-middle-east-10528.

4. The literature on international cooperation analyzes situations and strategic settings where all out war among states is considered to be too costly as an option. However, the quality of "peace" (i.e. no "all out war") can differ substantially depending on the strategies the concerned states pursue and the level of cooperation they are willing to work toward and ultimately attain. It turns out that the more states care about future payoffs (benefits that might accrue to each state in the absence of conflict), the easier cooperation is to achieve. This is because the more states value future, the less willing they are to pursue policies or actions that may result in short-term gains at the cost of long-term benefits that may accrue to them through improved relationships and cooperation. See Andrew H. Kydd, International Relations Theory: The Game-Theoretic Approach (Cambridge: Cambridge University Press, 2014).

5. Hedi Larbi, "Connecting Countries to Stabilize the Middle East," The Middle East Institute 4 (2016), accessed June 8, 2016, http://www.mei.edu/sites/default/files/publications/PP4_Larbi_RCS_Infrastructure_web.pdf.

6. "World Economic Outlook Update," IMF (2016), accessed May 19, 2016, http://www.imf.org/external/pubs/ft/weo/2016/update/01/pdf/0116.pdf; and Ayhan Kose, Franziska Ohnsorg, and Kaushik Basu, Global Economic Prospects: Spillovers amid Weak Growth (Washington D.C.: International Bank for Reconstruction and Development / The

World Bank, 2016) accessed May 19, 2016, http://pubdocs.worldbank.org/pubdocs/publicdoc/2016/1/697191452035053704/Global-Economic-Prospects-January-2016-Spillovers-amid-weak-growth.pdf.

7. Several recent studies provide in-depth analysis of labor market/employment issues in MENA. In most countries in the region, the main job problem is insufficient economic growth and, particularly in oil-importing countries, lack of job creation. Recent estimates indicate that the current pace of annual economic growth (about 2–3 percent) will have to increase to at least 6 percent during the next two decades to address the region's unemployment problem, given the region's rapidly growing labor force and the high desirability of raising female labor force participation rate, which are currently among the lowest in the world. Faster growth is necessary but not sufficient for well- paying jobs in the formal sector, however. Doing so will require improving the quality of education; increasing access to skills building/upgrading programs; and substantially improving the business environment to enable firms to compete and innovate. Countries will need to reduce regulatory barriers, particularly against female workers, in labor markets and remove distortions that discourage labor-intensive activities in all sectors of the economy. For more detailed discussion of these issues, including major structural differences between oil exporters and importers in the region, as well as sectoral differences in the size of employment creation elasticity with respect to the overall economic growth and sectoral activities, particularly infrastructure, see Antonio Estache, Elena Ianchovichina, Robert Bacon, and Ilhem Salamonm, Infrastructure and Employment Creation in the Middle East and North Africa (Washington D.C.: World Bank, 2013), accessed May 19, 2016, https://openknowledge.worldbank.org/bitstream/handle/10986/12237/NonAsciiFileName0.pdf?sequence; and for detailed policy discussion of the implications of changes since the Arab Spring for the labor markets in MENA see Roberta Gatti et al., Jobs for Shared Prosperity: Time for Action in the Middle East and North Africa (Washington D.C.: World Bank, 2013), accessed May 19, 2016, https://openknowledge.worldbank.org/handle/10986/13284, and Marc Schiffbauer, Abdoulaye Sy, Sahar Hussain, Hania Sahnoun, and Philip Keefer, Jobs or Privileges: Unleashing the Employment Potential of the Middle East and North Africa (Washington D.C.: World Bank, 2015), accessed May 19, 2016, https://openknowledge.worldbank.org/handle/10986/20591.

8. For a detailed analysis of major global economic, social, and environmental issues over the long term and their policy implications at the national and international levels, see Franklin Allen, Jere R. Behrman, Nancy Birdsall, Shahrokh Fardoust, Dani Rodrik, Andrew Steer, and Arvind Subramanian, eds., Towards a Better Global Economy: Policy Implications for Citizens Worldwide in the 21st Century (Oxford: Oxford University Press, 2014), accessed May 19, 2016, https://global.oup.com/academic/product/towards-a-better-global-economy-9780198723455?cc=us&lang=en&.

9. For a summary of research on long-term economic growth in advanced and developing countries, see Jere Behrman and Shahrokh Fardoust, "Towards a Better Global Economy Project: Overview and Policy Options," in Franklin Allen, et al., eds, Towards a Better Global Economy. Long-term projections of economic growth generally assume no major macroeconomic and financial crisis over the projection time horizon. They also assume away major climate change, war, or regional conflict–induced disasters with global consequences. While these assumptions may result in optimistic projections, such projections do not incorporate substantial changes that could occur as a result of possible policy changes that may result in deeper structural reforms which may in turn result in significant acceleration of growth in future. In general, however, the pace of growth is expected to gradually slowdown in all global regions over the next two to three decades, largely as a result of the convergence effect (technology catch-up) and aging of populations in a number of large economies. Based on this approach, the projected slowdown of average growth of trend G.D.P. in the period to 2030 (in comparison to average trend growth rate of trend output in the previous two decades) is about 0.5 percent per annum in advanced economies and 0.8 to 1 percent per annum in developing countries.

10. Trade by the region's oil exporters accounts for more than three-quarters of the trade to output ratio in MENA. With the sharp declines in oil prices in the past year, this ratio is likely to fall significantly, particularly if lower oil prices persist and the governments in these countries are forced to cut back on their imports and public spending.

11. For a recent report by the World Resources Institute, see Andrew Maddocks, Robert Samuel Young, and Paul Reig, "Ranking the World's Most Water-Stressed Countries in 2040," World Resources Institute, August 26, 2015, accessed May 19, 2016, http://www.wri.org/blog/2015/08/ranking-world%E2%80%99s-most-water-stressed-countries-2040.

12. See Nancy Birdsall with Christian Meyer and Alexis Sowa, "Global Markets, Global Citizens, and Global Governance in the 21st Century" (Working Paper 329, Center for Global Development and the Global Citizen Foundation: Washington D.C., 2013), accessed May 19, 2016, http://www.cgdev.org/sites/default/files/Birsdall_Meyer_Sowa_global-citizens-for-layout_wcvr_1.pdf.

13. Monika Aring, "Report on Skill Gaps" (UNESCO and EFAGMRL: Paris, 2012), accessed May 19, 2016, http://unesdoc.unesco.org/images/0021/002178/217874e.pdf.

14. A recent assessment by the World Bank indicates that while most countries in the MENA region have had impressive achievements in terms of school enrollment rates and increased literacy, for a significant portion of students across the region "schooling has not been synonymous with learning." See "Education in the Middle East and North Africa," The World Bank, January 27, 2014, accessed May 19, 2016, http://www.worldbank.org/en/region/mena/brief/education-in-mena; and Jere Behrman and Nancy Birdsall, "Information, Assessment and the Quality of Education around the World in a Changing Global Labor Market: Making More People Winners," Global Citizen Foundation (2015), accessed May 19, 2016, http://www.gcf.ch/wp-content/uploads/2016/01/Behrman_Birsdall-Information-Assessment-and-the-Quality-of-Education.pdf.

15. David Cuberes and Marc Teignier, "Gender Gaps in the Labor Market and Aggregate Productivity," University of Sheffield (2012), accessed May 19, 2016, http://www.sheffield.ac.uk/polopoly_fs/1.186609!/file/serps_2012017.pdf.

16. For a discussion of arguments put forward by Thomas Piketty on inequality in the Middle East see: Jim Tankersley, "This Might be the Most Controversial Theory for What's Behind the Rise of ISIS," Washington Post, November 30, 2015, accessed May 19, 2016, https://www.washingtonpost.com/news/wonk/wp/2015/11/30/why-inequality-is-to-blame-for-the-rise-of-the-islamic-state/; on the other hand, a World Bank report on this topic concludes that growing and broadly shared dissatisfaction with the quality of life (based in perception surveys) were the main reasons for the uprisings during the so called Arab Spring. According to this report, the middle classes "were frustrated by their deteriorating standards of living due to a lack of job opportunities in the formal sector, poor quality public services, and the lack of government accountability." See Lili Mottaghi, Elena Ianchovichina, and Farrukh Iqbal, Inequality, Uprisings, and Conflict in the Arab World (Washington D.C.: International Bank for Reconstruction and Development / The World Bank, 2015), accessed May 19, 2016, http://www-wds.worldbank.org/external/default/WDSContentServer/WDSP/IB/2015/10/13/090224b0831415a3/3_0/Rendered/PDF/Inequality00up0ct0in0the0Arab0World.pdf.

17. Aasim Husain, Natalia Tamirisa, and Martin Sommer, Regional Economic Outlook: The Middle East (Washington, DC: International Monetary Fund, 2015), accessed May 19, 2016, https://www.imf.org/external/pubs/ft/reo/2015/mcd/eng/pdf/menap1015.pdf. According to the report, countries in MENA that were in conflict during 2011–15 suffered an average output decline of 2.25 percentage points a year as a result. Countries that did not experience conflict but had neighbors that did also tended to have lower G.D.P. growth. Conflicts also increased inflation and reduced foreign direct investment inflows.

18. For a discussion of spillovers effects in the region, see Regional Integration and Spillovers: Middle East and North Africa (Washington D.C.: World Bank, 2016), pp 132-176, accessed May 19, 2016, https://www.worldbank.org/content/dam/Worldbank/GEP/GEP2016a/Global-Economic-Prospects-January-2016-Spillovers-MENA.pdf.

19. The size of the peace dividend will depend on a multitude of factors. Ending a conflict is highly beneficial, because peace ends further destruction. But significant and sustained benefits require a reduction in military expenditures and their reallocation on reconstruction and humanitarian needs of the affected population and in projects with high economic and social returns (resulting in growth and job creation). To ensure sustained and sizeable peace dividend, the concerned

countries need to reform their economies and institutions and also invest in the region's stability through greater cooperation and economic cooperation (as done in Europe and East Asia after World War II). For a thoughtful, albeit somewhat dated, analysis of the potential peace dividend in the Middle East, see Stanley Fischer, Dani Rodrik, and Elias Tuma, The Economics of Middle East Peace (Cambridge: MIT Press, 1993); see also I.M.F. report cited in a footnote above on the estimated effects of conflicts of the last five years on economic growth of the MENA region. A recent World Bank report on the economic effects of war and peace in MENA argues that an end to the civil wars "will improve macroeconomic indicators through restoring security, increase in investment, and reconstruction activity. Social indicators will also improve as public resources that were used for military expenses could be shifted to education and health. But the pace and pattern of economic recovery in the short term is typically not smooth, as post-conflict countries inherit a weak economy, damaged physical, human and social capital, widespread poverty and high unemployment particularly among youth." MENA Quarterly Economic Brief, January 2016: The Economic Effects of War and Peace, (Washington D.C.: World Bank, 2016), accessed May 19, 2016, http://www.worldbank.org/en/region/mena/publication/mena-quarterly-economic-brief-january-2016.

20. Zubair Iqbal, "Iran's Post-Sanctions Economic Options," The Middle East Institute 11 (2016), accessed May 19, 2016, http://www.mei.edu/sites/default/files/publications/PF11_Iqbal_IranPostSanctions_1.pdf.

21. Bernard Hoekman, "Intra-Regional Trade: Potential Catalyst for Growth in the Middle East," The Middle East Institute (2016), accessed May 19, 2016, http://www.mei.edu/sites/default/files/publications/Hoekman_PDF%20%282%29.pdf

22. Ibid.

23. For a brief explanation of regional trade agreements and lessons of experience, see Box 2 in the main text.

24. In addition to Iran, Pakistan, and Turkey, the ECO includes Afghanistan, Azerbaijan, Kazakhstan, the Kyrgyz Republic, Tajikistan, Turkmenistan, and Uzbekistan. The aggregate G.D.P. of ECO members was $4.7 trillion in 2014, and its population was 420 million.

25. The assessment included the following agreements: E.U.-MENA FTA (Algeria, Egypt, Jordan, Lebanon, Morocco, Palestinian Authority, Syria and Tunisia); US-MENA P.T.A. and US-Israel FTA (Jordan, Morocco, Bahrain, Oman, Israel, and Lebanon); Turkey-MENA FTA (Egypt, Morocco, Palestinian Authority, Syria, Turkey, and Tunisia); PAFTA; and Agadir Agreement (Egypt, Jordan, Morocco, and Tunisia)

26. For an assessment based on gravity- modeling see Caroline Freund and Alberto Portugal-Perez, "Assessing MENA's Trade Agreements," in The Arab Spring: Implications for Economic Integration, Michael Gasiorek, ed. (London: Centre for Economic Research, 2013).

27. Agadir Agreement for the establishment of a free trade zone between Arabic Mediterranean countries (Egypt, Jordan, Morocco, and Tunisia) came into force in 2007.

28. For an informative analysis of the history of cooperation in the MENA region see Paul Salem, "Building Cooperation in the Eastern Middle East," Carnegie Endowment for International Peace 24 (2010).

29. In the W.T.O.'s publicly available assessment, regional agreements have allowed groups of countries to negotiate rules and commitments that go beyond what was possible at the time multilaterally. Some of these rules paved the way for agreement in the W.T.O. Services, intellectual property, environmental standards, and investment and competition policies are all issues that were raised in regional negotiations and later developed into agreements or topics of discussion by the W.T.O. The groupings that are important for the W.T.O. are those that abolish or reduce barriers on trade within the group. However, the W.T.O. recognizes that under certain circumstances, RTAs can hurt the trade interests of other countries. According to the W.T.O., under normal circumstances, setting up a customs union or free trade area would violate the W.T.O.'s principle of equal treatment for all trading partners (most-favored nation). But GATT's Article 24 allows regional trading arrangements to be set up as a special exception, provided certain strict criteria are met. W.T.O. members are bound to the RTAs in which they participate. As of 2015, nearly all W.T.O. members had notified the W.T.O. of their participation in one or more RTAs (some countries are party to many RTAs, leading to a "spaghetti bowl," which could cause distortions). Since the creation of the W.T.O., in

1995, more than 400 arrangements covering trade in goods or services have been notified (124 were created between 1948 and 1994).

30. "Facts and Figures on Regional Trade Agreement," World Trade Organization, accessed May 19, 2016, https://www.wto.org/english/tratop_e/region_e/regfac_e.htm; and Joannes Linn, "Central Asian Regional Integration and Cooperation: Reality or Mirage?" in The Economics of the Post-Soviet Eurasian Economic Integration (Washington D.C.: Brookings, 2012), accessed May 19, 2016, http://www.brookings.edu/~/media/research/files/papers/2012/10/regional-integration-and-cooperation-linn/10-regional-integration-and-cooperation-linn.pdf.

31. See Hoekman, "Regional Integration".

32. Ibid. According to recent data, the LPI for Tunisia and the United Arab Emirates has deteriorated somewhat.

33. P.T.A. are in effect in all regions. Bilateral P.T.A. are becoming the norm, often between countries in different regions. South-South P.T.A. represent about two-thirds of all P.T.A., and North-South P.T.A. about one-quarter.

34. Rules of origin exist in P.T.A. to preserve the value of preferences accorded to PTA members when they maintain different external tariffs. The ways in which they are calculated in different P.T.A. can inadvertently impede trade. Typically, PTA members define a percentage of the value added that must originate in another PTA member for the product to be deemed eligible for preferential tariff treatment. Rules of origin prevent products from entering the member country with lower external tariffs for transshipment to another PTA member that maintains higher tariffs against the third country's goods. As a result, the rules of origin penalize regional producers by forcing them to source from less efficient suppliers located within the region.

35. In a new strategy for MENA, the World Bank has proposed regional projects in energy, water, and education. It estimates the costs of meeting Libya's infrastructure needs at about $200 billion, rebuilding war-torn Syria at about $170 billion, and meeting Yemen's humanitarian needs at $274 million over the next 10 years. According to its estimates, the conflict with ISIS in the Levant will have cost the region about $35 billion in lost output over this period. The region's massive refugee problem, the biggest since World War II, will have additional financial implications that will be massive; see "Our New Strategy," The World Bank, November 5, 2015, accessed May 19, 2016, http://www.worldbank.org/en/region/mena/brief/our-new-strategy.

CHAPTER FOUR

INTRA-REGIONAL ENERGY COOPERATION:

UNLOCKING THE MIDDLE EAST'S POTENTIAL

JEAN FRANCOIS SEZNEC

INTRODUCTION

For the past few generations, it has been hard to blame those pessimistic about the future of the Middle East. Certainly, in early 2016, the region appears to have fallen into a state of permanent decay. On the other hand, it would be unfair to forget some of the achievements of the past 40 years, many of which have been based on the region's natural comparative advantage of plentiful and low-cost energy. Energy in the Middle East does not consist merely of the extraction of crude oil or natural gas (N.G.), but also includes the development of large energy-based industries such as chemicals, fertilizers, cement, and metals.

However, when it comes to mutually beneficial energy relations, there has been very little regional cooperation, even in the richest areas of the Middle East. Of course, the mere production of crude oil and N.G. does not necessitate much local exchange, but it should have at least encouraged substantial trade between, for example, Algeria and Morocco, Qatar and Saudi Arabia, Iraq and Kuwait, or Oman and the United Arab Emirates. Until now, however, the majority of relations between energy consumers and producers has been inter-regional in character as opposed to intra-regional, meaning it has occurred predominantly between the Middle East's energy producers and the industrial world's consumers, including those in Europe, North America, and the Far East. This lack of energy and industrial commerce between Middle Eastern countries is mostly due to political reasons. Countries across the Middle East and North Africa (MENA) have not developed relations based on trust, let alone resolved age-old conflicts and rivalries. Essentially, the lack of energy cooperation has been due to a lack of good governance.

Naturally, if this trend of little cooperation and subpar governance continues, we will see more of the same. MENA countries, and in particular those of the Gulf, will compete not only among themselves, but also with other world producers such as Russia and now the United States, for their share in global crude oil and N.G. markets. Better-endowed countries with a vision to develop industrial downstream ventures, in particular the U.A.E., Qatar, and Saudi Arabia, will move away from their dependence on energy sales and start investing their resources into downstream, value-added products, most notably petrochemicals and fertilizers.[1] However, without intra-MENA cooperation, these industries will find themselves in a familiar predicament, competing with each other for limited markets. Indeed, this is already occurring. Large Saudi chemical, fertilizer, and aluminum production is competing with similar products from Kuwait, Morocco, Algeria, and Qatar, in markets across China, the United States, Europe, and even India.

This condition of counterproductive competition does not have to continue. With some global vision by the region's leaders, we could see cooperative arrangements between neighbors that would minimize their respective production costs, maximize their production levels, and allow all to compete with the world's major producers of advanced goods.

HISTORICAL INTRA-REGIONAL COOPERATION

Admittedly, there have been myriad attempts by regional powers to cooperate on energy issues. Yet, as history shows, many of these have been wrecked by political differences and regional conflict. Decades ago, Iraq and Syria started cooperating on a mutually beneficial pipeline connecting the Kirkuk oil fields in northern Iraq to the Syrian port terminal of Banias on the Mediterranean. Brought online in 1952, the Kirkuk-Banias pipeline marked a significant point of evolution for Iraq's oil industry. It also provided Syria with preferentially priced oil for domestic use, thus allowing Syria's own oil production to be exported at advantageous market prices. The arrangement, however, would prove to be short-lived. In 1956, when the pipeline was still under Anglo-French ownership, Syrian forces attacked and badly damaged it in response to the British and French invasion of the Sinai Peninsula, as well as Iraq's acceptance into the Baghdad Pact. While it would come back online shortly thereafter, operations were halted once again in 1972 over tariff disputes, effectively putting the pipeline out of use until 2001. It was then that Saddam Hussein used the pipeline to bypass export-crippling U.N. sanctions, a practice that ended when the pipeline became a target of U.S. airstrikes during the 2003 invasion.[2]

It was in response to the 1970s and 1980s Iraq-Syria tariff disputes, as well as concerns over export security arising from the Iran-Iraq war, that Iraq's Hussein initiated a concerted effort to diversify his country's export routes. One such initiative was the construction of a pipeline through Saudi Arabia to the Red Sea port of al-Muajjiz near Yanbu, known as the I.P.S.A. Ironically, the Saudis shut down this attempt at export security in retaliation for Iraq's 1990 invasion of Kuwait, once again demonstrating how geopolitical rivalries supersede economic cooperation. The I.P.S.A. has been upgraded and operated by Saudi Arabia for domestic use ever since.[3] Similarly, the Trans-Arabian Pipeline (known as the Tapline), which had transported oil from Saudi Arabia through Lebanon and Jordan to the Mediterranean Sea and provided revenue for Jordan, Syria, Lebanon, and Saudi since 1950, was also closed by Saudi Arabia in response to Jordan's support for Iraq after the latter's invasion of Kuwait.[4] Admittedly, the Tapline had increasingly grown out of favor starting in 1975 partially due to the growth of supertanker trade, but also due to transit fee disputes emanating from Syria and Lebanon.

PRESENT INTRA-REGIONAL COOPERATION

Presently, upon this checkered background of cooperation exist a number of intra-regional energy projects in various stages of success and failure. The prime example of success among these is the Dolphin Gas Project. Conceived in 1999 and becoming operational in 2007, the project involves the transportation of natural gas from Qatar's North Field in Ras Laffan to the U.A.E. and Oman. Costing over $7 billion and holding an export capacity of 3.2 billion standard cubic feet per day, the Dolphin Pipeline is the Gulf's first cross-border gas project. However, the project was delayed for several years by Saudi Arabia's steadfast opposition. The Saudi objections were based on the fact that the pipeline would traverse Saudi territorial waters, a claim that the U.A.E. never accepted. The border dispute at the junction of Qatar, Saudi Arabia, and the U.A.E. has never been settled and although Saudi Arabia finally allowed the project to proceed, it did so begrudgingly and could always revive the problems. Even between the U.A.E. and Qatar, the price negotiated by the parties many years ago is subject to much bickering. The contract specifies that Qatar will be paid $1.4/mmbtu,[5] which is much lower than the usual netback of $6/mmbtu that Qatar was getting for its exports of L.N.G. to the Far East. After the energy price crash of mid-2014, the netback to Qatar on its Far East sales is much lower today, probably below $4/mmbtu. The Dolphin Project's capacity could have been expanded greatly had both parties agreed to a fair price. The Qataris know that the U.A.E. exports its own L.N.G. at world prices, which went as high as $18/mmbtu to Japan in the 2010s, while importing gas by pipeline from Qatar at the $1.4/mmbtu rate mentioned above. When both parties can sit down with realistic views on prices, perhaps a compromise can be reached. In the meantime, the U.A.E. is spending vast sums developing tight gas formations, which may cost up to $6/mmbtu through a joint venture with Occidental Petroleum, and may even one day be open to importing gas from Iran.

The Maghreb-Europe Pipeline further demonstrates the difficulty for intra-regional cooperation. While the pipeline is predominantly used to transport Algerian N.G. to Spain and Portugal, a portion of the pipeline goes through Morocco, hence bringing in an intra-regional aspect. Though the pipeline had been discussed for decades, its development was impeded by the political deadlock between Algeria and Morocco due to the conflict in the Sahara, and the pipeline did not become feasible until the 1988 U.N. agreement eased tensions.[6] Admittedly, the conflict is not fully resolved, but the pipeline provided a starting point for cooperation between Algeria and Morocco, and has even resulted in the limited sale of Algerian gas to Moroccan power plants via the pipeline.[7] It is this nascent energy relationship that acts as an example of future opportunities for mutually beneficial cooperation, an example that this chapter will discuss at length. Unfortunately, the relationship between the two neighbors has taken a turn for the worse and the burgeoning relationship has come to a complete dead-end. Since the N.G. sent from Algeria to Spain is transferred under extensive international agreements and loans, the disagreements have not stopped the flow. However, Algeria now uses other pipelines to Europe: one directly to Spain and the other through Tunisia.

The troubled relationship between the Iraqi Kurds and Baghdad, and the subpar performance of the A.G.P., provide further examples of the region's troubled attempts at cooperation. With the Kurds striving for greater autonomy, Baghdad insisting on stronger centralization, and energy revenues fueling both sides' budgets, an amicable long-run profit-sharing agreement for Iraqi energy resources seems largely improbable. Oppositely, in the case of the A.G.P., which brings Egyptian N.G. to Jordan, Syria, Israel, and Lebanon, and even procured cooperation from Turkey and Iraq, the issue is not geopolitical relations, but Egypt's own domestic affairs. Egypt's logic-defying energy subsidies and serious domestic N.G. shortages, coupled with constant targeting of the pipeline by militants, have collectively shut down the pipeline's operations. Moreover, despite Egypt's recent massive gas discovery at the Zohr field, it is still doubtful that the North African country will resume N.G. exports anytime soon. In addition to these examples, numerous other ongoing projects have been proposed, including the Iran-Iraq-Syria Friendship Pipeline, and the competing Qatar-Turkey pipeline, which would run through numerous states in the Gulf and the Levant. Both remain held up due to financial and geopolitical roadblocks.

INTER-REGIONAL COMMERCE AND ITS DOMESTIC RAMIFICATIONS

Considering the size of the international energy trade, the amount of energy cooperation between Middle Eastern states is minuscule. A natural evolution of trade took place between the markets that needed energy, mainly in the industrial world, and those able to produce it in the Middle East. This developed into well-tread routes that have not evolved. In particular, the Gulf states and North Africa have traded oil for goods with Europe, the United States, and the Far East since the 1950s. There were no efforts to develop markets within the Middle East, in great part because there was little to exchange.

Saudi Arabia was looking to modernize in order to start providing its citizens with living standards similar to those enjoyed in Europe and the United States. To do so it needed cars, air conditioners, TVs, and implements and machinery of all sorts, none of which could be found in the countries of the Middle East. Certainly in the 1970s, Iraq and Syria, under the impetus of the Ba'ath party, sought to develop consumer goods industries.[8] Iraq in the 1970s was producing televisions, washing machines, and other household goods for its own market and closed its borders to imports to encourage domestic production. It was also during this period that Iraq's Ba'athist leadership built heavy industrial complexes such as the petrochemical complex at Basra and the iron and steel mill at Khor al-Zubair.[9] It tried to sell many of its consumer products to neighbors through fairs held from time to time in Bahrain or Dubai. However, the quality of these products was extremely poor and could in no way compete with more advanced and better-designed Western, Japanese, or Chinese goods. Hence, exchanges between Middle East countries remained mostly nonexistent. Furthermore, Iraqi and Syrian products, which had been developed according to Soviet models of distribution and manufacturing, were rejected even by the Iraqis and Syrians themselves. Eventually, the local plants shut down and borders were slowly opened to Eastern and Western products, albeit with significant tariffs to maintain some income for the state. In Iraq, this transition away from domestic production was also catalyzed by the descent into war with Iran.

On the other hand, the Gulf countries did not close their borders to overseas products. While there were efforts to develop manufacturing within the Gulf, mainly in the U.A.E. and Saudi Arabia, the model of development was quite different from the Soviet style seen in Iraq. The Gulf countries, especially Saudi Arabia, provided substantial incentives to state-owned and private companies to develop manufacturing using Western and Japanese technologies. Joint ventures were greatly encouraged. For example, in the early 1980s, SABIC started establishing manufacturing bases through 11 joint ventures with the likes of Sumitomo and Mitsubishi. Their products were made at the highest standards and initially sold by the foreign partners overseas. In development economics terms, the Gulf states followed an 'export-led growth' model that capitalized on their natural comparative advantages, primarily in downstream products, instead of the 'import substitution' employed in Syria and Iraq.

Today, SABIC ranks among the world's top petrochemical companies. It has learned or bought technologies from its foreign partners, established its own research centers, and is filing for its own patents, all while still working with Western and Japanese firms on technologies it has yet to master. This approach has led them to become the second largest chemical company in the world. SABIC's growth has admittedly had nothing to do with the other countries of the Middle East. Instead the company has followed a purely North-South, or East-West, model of trade, opposed to a South-South, regionally cooperative one, which could have potentially beamed beneficial results for Saudi Arabia and its neighbors.

By the same token, the development of the U.A.E.'s economy, and Dubai's in particular, is primarily oriented toward the Far East, Europe, and Africa. The Jebel Ali Port, a key part of Dubai's economy that has grown into the third-largest container port in the world, receives myriad goods that are transformed, stored for redistribution, or re-exported. To a certain extent, however, there is a Middle East component to this exchange. Many international companies, like Chrysler, General Motors, and Sony, bring containers through the Jebel Ali Port and unload the containers in huge warehouses in the Jebel Ali Free Trade Zone. They then re-export the spare parts and products in smaller batches by road or air to other countries of the region. In some cases, firms will actually manufacture goods in Jebel Ali for export to countries like Pakistan or Iran. This allows the firms to take advantage of Dubai's low-cost foreign labor, much of which comes from India or Pakistan, instead of manufacturing directly in the subcontinent. These exports then give the firms the right to legally take foreign exchange out of Pakistan or Iran, a practice that would otherwise be limited by often strict capital controls. These arrangements do not seem to qualify as Middle East cooperation though. The goods are manufactured using imported raw materials or semi-manufactured products, assembled with imported labor, and finally exported; however, the local content is minimal. Moreover, in the Pakistani case, the practice is more of a systematic effort by merchants to bypass Pakistan's stifling commercial and financial regulations. Where this pattern of commerce has little benefit for Pakistan or Iran, Dubai benefits substantially. Its financial sector receives funds from companies who rent offices, warehouses, and homes. Similarly, its merchants sell cars, furniture, and all manner of advanced services to the foreign industries and their employees. Accordingly, it is not a win-win exchange. Instead, there is ultimately a transfer of funds out of Pakistan and Iran to Dubai, resulting in a net loss to those two countries and a net gain for the emirate.

One of the win-win cooperative efforts that had the potential to develop between the Gulf countries and the rest of the Arab Middle East was the effort to capitalize on MENA's large labor pool to develop the Gulf's services and industries. Indeed, at one point there were over two million Egyptian workers in Saddam Hussein's Iraq, mainly in agriculture and construction. When Egypt aligned itself against Iraq in the First Gulf War, these Egyptian laborers, who had contributed greatly to Iraq's agricultural development and supplied critical services and skills when Iraq was entrenched in war, were treated ruthlessly and often deported without access to their savings or belongings.[10] While there are to this day a good number of Egyptians and Moroccans in various Iraqi service industries, the inability to fully capitalize on this capable and willing Arab labor pool shows how easily regional political factors derail potential economic endeavors. In fact, while Arab workers initially dominated the expatriate population, presently most of the expatriate labor in the Gulf comes from South or Southeast Asia. This transformation was quick and dramatic. Where Arabs represented 72 percent of the Gulf's expatriate population in 1975, by 1985 63 percent of the Gulf's expatriate workforce was Asian.[11]

Research by the Kuwait Financial Center in 2015 estimated that there are 25 million expatriate workers in the Gulf, with the majority coming from India, the Philippines, Bangladesh, Pakistan, Indonesia, and Sri Lanka, and a minority portion coming from Egypt and Yemen. These laborers, engineers, and accountants, who constitute upwards of 75 percent of the private labor force, produce substantial remittance outflows, which were estimated to reach $100 billion in 2015,[12] up from $70 billion in 2012.[13] While admittedly Egypt and Yemen do receive a minority share of these remittances, the vast majority goes to benefit non-Arab communities. A larger share of these jobs and remittances could have been a major example of the Middle East as a whole benefiting from oil revenues. Unfortunately, there has been a systematic effort by the Gulf states to limit the flow of Arab expatriates. This effort has arisen due to political, economic, and social factors.[14] In 1990, Saudi Arabia deported 700,000 Yemenis after the Sanaa government supported Saddam Hussein's invasion of Kuwait.[15] Similarly, as previously mentioned, Iraq sent back the majority of its Egyptian workers in 1990. Relatedly, the U.A.E. has been wary of Egyptian expatriates ever since the days of Gamal Abdel Nasser, initially due to fears of Arab nationalism, and more recently due to a weariness toward the Muslim Brotherhood.[16]

Opposed to this aversion to cooperation, a mutually beneficial and natural exchange could have found the Gulf welcoming Arab workers in order to further spread the benefits of the Gulf's energy wealth, while simultaneously fulfilling its domestic labor needs. Instead, the Gulf countries have worried about the potential 'Egyptianization' of their own societies.[17]

With all these factors in mind, it seems that the international economics concept of developing one's natural and comparative advantage for the betterment of all is foreign to the Middle East. Indeed, the World Trade Organization's concept of trade as a win-win situation is subordinated in the Middle East to a concept of trade and commerce as means of establishing control over another state or society. This may be a holdover from the colonial era, or it may be a byproduct of suspicious attitudes rife among diverse groups, or both. Either way, it seems that factors quite ingrained in the soul of leadership and people alike are limiting efforts at regional cooperation.

Should Middle Eastern states continue with business as usual, the wealth of the few will increase and continue to grow based on the East-West or North-South exchanges mentioned above. Intra-regional links will remain low and the common benefits of international trade at the regional level will not happen. Countries like Egypt or Syria, when at peace, will continue to flail about development, but remain hopelessly stuck to their third world status, while the Gulf states reach levels at par with or above Western standards.

POTENTIAL FOR FUTURE COOPERATION

One cannot expect people's attitudes to change overnight. Yet, they can be expected to see the benefits of modern economic development. If exchanges can be promoted without political, ethnic, or sectarian baggage, the benefits of win-win exchanges could develop.

The low-hanging fruit of cooperation, which could be established in the immediate future and provide political-free benefits to all the parties involved, seem to be few and far between. Nonetheless, there appear to be three areas of energy-related cooperation that could maximize benefits to all parties:

1. The creation of trade and manufacturing exchanges between Morocco and Algeria for N.G., phosphates, advanced fertilizers, and various finished products
2. Industrial investments and trade within the Gulf Cooperation Council, namely Qatari N.G. exchanged for Saudi or U.A.E. products
3. Trade and investments between Iran and the Gulf countries

1. MOROCCO-ALGERIA

The Moroccan-Algerian case is perhaps the most egregious example of power politics destroying the great potential of a region. Morocco has the largest phosphate reserves in the world and has developed infrastructure to maximize the return on this resource. It has established some of the world's most modern and advanced techniques for the extraction and processing of phosphate. For example, it has developed the Port of Jorf Lasfar, which receives and processes phosphate from the mines in Khouribga some 95 miles away. In the past, the phosphate had to be cleaned, loaded on trains, and transported to either Jorf Lasfar or Casablanca. Once there, it could only be exported as rock phosphate of little value to be refined into usable fertilizer in other countries. Today, at the Port of Jorf Lasfar, cleaned rock phosphate can be made into phosphoric acid through the addition of water and sulphuric acid, then dried and exported as phosphoric acid or processed further by the addition of ammonia into diammonium phosphate (DAP), a much more valuable product. However, the cost of transport and the amount of water necessary for production diminishes the Moroccans' profit margins significantly. To mitigate this, Office Chérifien des Phosphates (O.C.P.), the phosphate company of Morocco, designed and built a pipeline from Khouribga to Jorf Lasfar, which now transports a slurry of phosphate for almost one-tenth the cost and saves huge amounts of water, in a very dry climate. Further, it built an industrial zone in Jorf Lasfar to attract foreign investors to make the DAP for export to their own country. O.C.P. also makes its own DAP for export mainly to South America and Europe. However, O.C.P. is not as competitive as it should be. The production of phosphoric acid and DAP requires large volumes of sulphur and ammonia. Most sulphur produced today is a by-product of crude oil extraction, and ammonia is made with the methane from natural gas. O.C.P. currently purchases these two products from countries far and wide, including from Saudi Arabia, at international prices and at significant transportation costs, in turn burning potential revenue.

The lost opportunity for intra-regional cooperation arises when one realizes that Algeria, Morocco's neighbor, is one of the world's largest producers of sulphur and ammonia. Yet, neither Morocco nor Algeria wish to trade or invest in each other's industries. Should Algeria and Morocco accept to work together, it could produce fertilizers at the most advantageous price in the world. A simple joint venture in Jorf Lasfar could receive gas directly from Hassi R'mel in the Sahara and convert it into ammonia. In the same manner, sulphur could be delivered from Algeria. In return, Algeria could be an investor in a value-adding downstream industry from its oil and gas, hence allowing for both increased revenue and diversification. Both countries would undeniably benefit greatly. One could even imagine that the problem of the Sahrawi people, most of whom have lived in refugee camps since the late 1970s as a result of the Western Sahara War, could be resolved in the same manner. The Moroccan Sahara has phosphate mines, the product of which is sent to Laayoune, the capital of the territory and home to the territory's only harbor. Morocco has invested very little in developing these resources, and the harbor is old and inefficient. The phosphate is transported over 60 miles by conveyor belt, cleaned using sea water, and not made into the more profitable products of phosphoric acid and DAP. Here again, Algeria's resources offer a possible economic solution. The gas reservoirs of Algeria are even closer to Laayoune than they are to Jorf Lasfar. This presents the possibility of another Algerian-Moroccan joint venture to develop a modern phosphate infrastructure for the benefit of both countries as well as for the great benefit of the Sahrawi people. This may not happen until the status of the territory is fully settled to the satisfaction of all the parties. However, it is not inconceivable that cooperation on purely economic and mining issues could lay the foundation for a settlement that benefits all involved.

2. QATAR-SAUDI ARABIA

Another example of cooperation that could take place at relatively low cost is the potential for Qatar to sell natural gas to Saudi Arabia. The kingdom is short of natural gas, mainly because its amazing economic growth of the past 40 years has taxed its resources. Saudi Arabia requires huge amounts of natural gas to desalinate water for its 32 million people, generate electricity for its increasingly sophisticated cities, and act as feedstock for its chemical, fertilizer, and metals industries. Admittedly, Saudi Arabia does have a large resource of N.G., which it extracts from the crude oil it produces, and which, unlike other states in the region, it has decided not to export in order to encourage domestic industrialization. This industrial policy has been a huge success, but the population has grown exponentially, so much so that the demand for N.G. has grown to surpass Saudi's large supply.

To try and alleviate this N.G. deficit, Saudi Aramco, the national oil company of the kingdom, has spent a great deal of effort and capital to develop new sources of N.G. not dependent on crude oil extraction (also called 'dry gas'). It has had success finding large deposits of "dry" N.G., but this new N.G. is sour and rich in hydrogen sulfide, making it very dangerous and costly to produce. Other dry N.G. is available as shale gas, especially in the northern part of the country near the newly opened phosphate mines of al-Jalamid and Wa'ad al-Shamal. However, shale gas is also expensive to bring online and requires large amounts of water, which is already in short supply in the kingdom and is only available from fossilized non-renewable phreatic wells. It is difficult to know what the cost of extracting and producing this sour N.G. is, but could be as high as $6/mmbtu. Accordingly, even with the domestic price of gas in the kingdom rising from $0.75/mmbtu to $1.25/mmbtu in late December 2015, the extraction of sour N.G. is not only difficult, but also fiscally counterproductive.[18]

Once again, a quick look at Saudi's neighbors highlights a significant missed opportunity for cooperation. Near the industrial areas in Saudi Arabia's Eastern Province lies Qatar's Northern Dome N.G. reservoir, the largest in the world. It would be eminently efficient for Qatar and Saudi Arabia to build a short pipeline from the Northern Dome to Jubail and Ras al-Khair, where the phosphate rock is being processed. The potential fruits of this option are further highlighted by the severe financial strain Qatar is feeling presently. While Qatar holds a massive capacity to produce and export Liquid Natural Gas worldwide, it does so at a price that is linked to that of crude oil, a price that has been in free-fall for over a year. Consequently, at this time, Qatar profits very little for the L.N.G. it exports, including for the previously profitable L.N.G. sent to Japan and Korea. As of early 2016, prices for L.N.G. to Japan are about $9/mmbtu, which, after accounting for all of Qatar's costs—mainly transportation, manufacturing, and dues to J.V. partners—results in a netback profit of only $4/mmbtu. This is a steep fall from prices that hovered around $16/mmbtu for the last five years, which had in turn provided double digit netback profits. Tellingly, the I.M.F. estimates that Qatar's gross revenues from L.N.G. exports have fallen over 25 percent since 2011,[19] and with hydrocarbon exports acting as Qatar's main source of revenue, it is not surprising that Qatar was forced to post a fiscal deficit for the first time in 15 years.[20]

It seems that a deal could and should be reached between Qatar and Saudi Arabia. Riyadh could purchase ample amounts of N.G. from Doha at $3/mmbtu, thus cutting the need to develop very expensive sour gas reserves. For Qatar, this would do away with the need to turn its N.G. into L.N.G., in turn producing savings of $2/mmbtu or more, reducing L.N.G. plants' huge maintenance requirements, and providing a stable source of demand for its product. In return, it could invest in the numerous Saudi chemical companies. This would create more N.G. demand while simultaneously assisting Saudi develop its burgeoning industrial companies. Truly open borders for products and investments in the G.C.C. could catalyze major growth for both countries, while also making them less dependent on the vagaries of global commodity markets.

Just like cooperation between Morocco and Algeria could make the two countries economic powerhouses through the capitalization of their respective natural advantages, Qatari-Saudi cooperation could make both countries competitive with chemical juggernauts like Germany's B.A.S.F. or the United States' Dow Chemical Company. Yet, such course can only happen if basic issues of sovereignty are resolved. On the other hand, the benefit of cooperation could rapidly build trust between parties, thereby achieving what thousands of meetings and promises at the G.C.C. have not.

3. G.C.C.-IRAN

Perhaps the most difficult challenge is developing cooperation between the Arab Gulf states and Iran. The burden of bad blood between Saudi Arabia and the Islamic Republic is difficult to overcome. Both states fear isolation, and until the Joint Comprehensive Plan of Action, the Iranians felt isolated and surrounded by enemies seeking to overthrow their regime. As of January 2016, though, it seems that the shoe has found itself on the other foot. Saudi Arabia talks and acts as if it were isolated and left alone to face wolves from across the Gulf in Tehran.

Saudi Arabia's present perception of an Iranian threat, and Iran's past, yet similar, feeling, could perhaps be alleviated through economic cooperation. Had all the Gulf powers worked together to develop their economies, they could by now be world-scale industrial powers. A parallel can be drawn with the extremely bloody confrontations between France and Germany in the 19th and 20th centuries which ended with a seemingly pedestrian agreement on coal and steel exchanges. This agreement evolved into the European Union and vastly enriched France, Germany, and the countries around them. No doubt after the bloodletting of World War II, the French and German political leadership made the decision to use economic cooperation to bring the people together. It could be similar in the Gulf. Iran and the Gulf states have much they could cooperate on. For example, just as Qatar can sell gas to Saudi Arabia, Iran could sell gas to the U.A.E., Oman, Kuwait, Iraq, and even Saudi Arabia. In turn, the Gulf states could invest in manufacturing facilities in Iran, import Persian agricultural products instead of importing them at a steep cost from afar, and join efforts in building more advanced chemical, fertilizer, and metal processing facilities. As has been shown, the economic slate is large and could be successful, especially considering that the Gulf neighbors enjoy a combined market of over 120 million consumers and are close to the huge markets of South Asia and the Far East.

Oman has already seen this potential for cooperation. It stands ready to sign an agreement with Iran to import Iranian N.G. for its industrial development in Sohar and other areas of the country. This would require some major investments in an underwater pipeline from the Iranian coast to Oman, which, while technically difficult, is by no means impossible. By the same token, the U.A.E. could also relatively easily start importing N.G. from Iran. In fact, pipelines from Iran to Sharjah's sea border, and from the sea border to the coast of Sharjah, already exist. All it would technically require is to verify and hook up the lines to start the flow. Nevertheless, these few meters of hook-up require political will on both ends of the pipeline, which may or may not be present and could potentially be complicated by the nature of the U.A.E.'s domestic politics, where one emirate does not always agree with another on how to benefit from foreign cooperation.

CONCLUSION

Cooperation in energy implies cooperation in modernization of economies, including joint ventures in chemicals, fertilizers, aluminum, and other metals. All these downstream productions will allow the Gulf to decrease its primary function as a mere fuel reservoir for Europe or China. It would also create jobs and stable wealth based on value-added production rather than mere extraction. Nevertheless, it may be the sad conclusion that such cooperation can only happen after disasters similar to those of 1914-1918 or 1939-1945 in Europe and Asia: disasters which, while ultimately fostering the roots of cooperation, cost tens of millions of lives, destroyed entire countries and societies, and continue to leave an imprint.

This kind of catastrophe is not necessary. If leaders, possessing traits similar to those of the late Saudi King Abdullah or the present Iranian President Hassan Rouhani, have a will to bring people together, separate from extreme ideologies, the sphere of economics and commerce provides a relatively fast and beneficial opportunity to do so. Both sides of the Gulf have vast energy resources that are disparate enough to lead to cooperation. The Saudis have crude oil, the Iranians natural gas. The Saudis have capital and know-how in chemicals, fertilizers, and metals, the Iranians have knowledge of other chemicals and fertilizers and a large educated work force. Clearly, some of the basics for cooperation are already present. Now all that is needed are leaders of vision and good will from across the Gulf to recognize these resources for the opportunity they truly are. Similar conclusions can be drawn in the rest of the Middle East. A potential Moroccan-Algerian economic cooperation could boost the economy of both countries, employ masses of their unemployed, and bring hope to the Sahrawi conundrum. Better use of available skills and labor from Egypt in the Gulf market would bring sorely needed remittances from the oil-rich Gulf to the Egyptian economy. Altogether, it appears that economic cooperation between Middle Eastern countries would bring about major benefits to all their citizens. However, such cooperation requires leaders with a vision that goes beyond ideological and historical barriers to focus on the future of their countries and the youth, who are the true wealth of the region.

ENDNOTES

1. "Downstream in the Persian Gulf-2," Oil and Gas Journal, September 22, 1997, accessed April 28, 2016, http://www.ogj.com/articles/print/volume-95/issue-38/in-this-issue/petrochemicals/downstream-in-the-persian-gulf-2.html.

2. Neela Banargee and Felicity Barringer, "A Nation at War: Oil; Iraq Pipeline To Syria No Big Secret, Experts Say," The New York Times, April 17, 2003, accessed April 28, 2016, http://www.nytimes.com/2003/04/17/world/a-nation-at-war-oil-iraq-pipeline-to-syria-no-big-secret-experts-say.html.

3. Anthony H. Cordesman and Nawaf Obaid, National security in Saudi Arabia: Threats, Responses, and Challenges (Westport, CT: Praeger Security International, 2005), 55.

4. Asher Kaufman, "Between Permeable and Sealed Borders: The Trans-Arabian Pipeline and the Arab-Israeli Conflict," International Journal of Middle East Studies 46, no. 01 (2014): 95-116, http://dx.doi.org/10.1017/S002074381300130X.

5. MMBTU, or MBTU, stands for one million British Thermal Units (BTU). A BTU is a measure of the heat energy in fuel and is equal to the amount of heat required to raise the temperature of one pound of water by one degree Fahrenheit. It is a widely used measure in the power, steam generation, heating and air conditioning industries. Natural gas is usually measured in BTUs and priced in millions of BTUs. A common rule of thumb to easily estimate income from any gas production is that 1,000 cubic feet of natural gas will produce about 1 million BTUs.

6. Jonathan Stern, "Gas pipeline co-operation between political adversaries: examples from Europe," Report Submission to Korea Foundation (London: Chatham House, 2005), 9.

7. Abdelghani Henni, "Algeria to supply gas to Morocco from September," Arabian Oil and Gas, August 2, 2011, accessed April 28, 2016, http://www.arabianoilandgas.com/article-9275-algeria-to-supply-gas-to-morocco-from-september/.

8. Onur Ozlu, "Iraqi Economic Reconstruction and Development," (Washington, DC: Center for Strategic and International Studies, 2006), 9-10, http://www.mafhoum.com/press8/249E16.pdf.

9. Jonathan E. Sanford, "Iraq's Economy: Past, Present, Future," Report for Congress (Washington, DC: Congressional Research Service, June 3, 2003), http://www.au.af.mil/au/awc/awcgate/crs/rl31944.pdf.

10. See Panayiotis J. Vatikiotis, The Middle East: From the End of Empire to the End of the Cold War (New York: Routledge, 1997), 174; Lindsay Carroll and Muthanna Edan, "There and back again: Egyptian workers remember their time in Iraq," Egypt Independent, March 21, 2013, accessed April 28, 2016, http://www.egyptindependent.com/news/there-and-back-again-egyptian-workers-remember-their-time-iraq.

11. Andrzej Kapiszewski, "Arab Versus Asian Migrant Workers in the G.C.C. Countries," United Nations Expert Group Meeting on International Migration and Development in the Arab Region (Beirut: United Nations, May 15-17, 2006), 7, accessed April 28, 2016, http://www.un.org/esa/population/meetings/EGM_Ittmig_Arab/P02_Kapiszewski.pdf.

12. "Gulf expat workers 'send home $100 billion,'" AFP, June 9, 2015, accessed April 28, 2016, http://news.yahoo.com/gulf-expat-workers-send-home-100-billion-112029035.html.

13. Alberto Behar, "Labor Market Reforms to Boost Employment and Productivity in the G.C.C.," Annual Meeting of Ministers of Finance and Central Bank Governors (Kuwait: International Monetary Fund, October 25, 2014), 6, https://www.imf.org/external/np/pp/eng/2014/102514a.pdf.

14. Kapiszewski, "Arab versus Asian migrant workers in the G.C.C. countries."

15. Youssef M. Ibrahim, "Saudi Curbs on Yemeni Workers Sets Off a Migration," The New York Times, October 22, 1990, accessed April 28, 2016, http://www.nytimes.com/1990/10/22/world/mideast-tensions-saudi-curbs-on-yemeni-workers-sets-off-a-migration.html.

16. See Andrzej Kapiszewski, Nationals and Expatriates: Population and Labour Dilemmas of the Gulf Cooperation Council States (Reading: Ithaca Press, 2001), 133-144; Lori Plotkin Boghardt, "The Muslim Brotherhood on Trial in the UAE," The Washington Institute for Near East Policy, April 12, 2013, accessed April 28, 2016, http://www.washingtoninstitute.org/policy-analysis/view/the-muslim-brotherhood-on-trial-in-the-uae.

17. Liesl Graz, The Turbulent Gulf: People, Politics and Power (London: I. B. Tauris, 1992), 220-221.

18. Simeon Kerr, "Saudis face fuel price jump under new austerity plan," Financial Times, December 30, 2015, accessed April 28, 2016, http://www.ft.com/cms/s/0/fbbc4b56-af00-11e5-993b-c425a3d2b65a.html#axzz47F9bh7t1.

19. "Qatar: 2015 Article IV Consultation – Staff Report; and Press Release," Country Report No. 15/86 (Washington, DC: International Monetary Fund, March 2015), http://www.imf.org/external/pubs/ft/scr/2015/cr1586.pdf.

20. "Qatar publishes 2016 budget, projects 46.5 bln riyal deficit," Reuters, December 16, 2015, accessed April 28, 2016, http://www.reuters.com/article/qatar-budget-idUSL8N14532X20151216.

CHAPTER FIVE

INTRA-REGIONAL TRADE:

POTENTIAL CATALYST FOR GROWTH IN THE MIDDLE EAST

BERNARD HOEKMAN

INTRODUCTION

It has often been argued that countries in the Middle East and North Africa (MENA) can do much more to leverage international market opportunities to accelerate economic growth and job creation. Excluding petroleum exports, the MENA region,[1] with over 400 million people, exports roughly the same amount as Switzerland.[2] With a population of over 500 million inhabitants and an average per capita income of some $36,000 in 2014,[3] the European Union is a major market in close geographic proximity to many MENA states. India, China, other parts of Asia, as well as sub-Saharan Africa, offer dynamic markets and great potential as sources of demand for goods and services. Major economies in the region offer good trade growth prospects as well, most notably Iraq and Iran, both countries that in the past have played an important role in the regional economy.

Harnessing this potential is a necessary condition for the MENA region to generate the broad-based economic growth and job creation it so urgently needs. The pursuit of policies by many governments in the region, designed to benefit specific politically connected groups in society, and an unwillingness to establish an environment supportive of private sector dynamism have proven very costly.[4] They helped to generate the dynamics that resulted in the conflicts convulsing many parts of the region and the resulting destruction of property, refugee flows, and internally displaced people. The asymmetrically distributed benefits of the policies implemented before the Arab Spring also created a significant opportunity cost in the form of reputational harm done to the policy recommendations long advocated by international organizations such as the European Union, International Monetary Fund, and World Bank. Avoidance of an overvalued exchange rate, an open trade and investment regime, pro-competitive regulation, contestable markets, transparency, accountability, and rule of law remain fundamental elements of any incentive framework conducive to sustained high rates of investment in tradables, employment growth, and rising household real incomes. Overcoming public distrust, generating the political support needed for implementing policy reforms supportive of investment and trade, and establishing the institutions shown to be necessary for sustained high growth in other parts of the world are key challenges confronting MENA policymakers.

MENA countries vary widely in the degree to which they are integrated into the global economy. As discussed below, some countries are at the top of globalization rankings for specific dimensions of international integration. Most countries do not participate in the forms of value chain production and trade that have driven growth in East Asia and in Central and Eastern European countries. A prominent feature of the region is that there is only limited trade between neighboring countries, despite regional integration long having been a purported goal of the Arab states. A variety of initiatives have been pursued in the past 50 or so years to promote Arab cooperation, including gradual market integration under auspices of the Arab League, such as the Pan-Arab Free Trade Agreement (PAFTA),[5] and the creation of a common market involving Saudi Arabia, Kuwait, the United Arab Emirates, Qatar, Bahrain, and Oman within the Gulf Cooperation Council (G.C.C.). In some dimensions, such as intra-regional capital and labor flows, Arab states are relatively highly integrated, but intra-regional trade in manufactured products within MENA and with neighboring economies such as Turkey is far below levels observed in many other regions.[6]

There has been extensive analysis of the reasons why MENA countries 'punch below their weight' in economic terms on global markets and why there has been only limited success on the part of energy exporters to diversify. Such factors include state dominance of the economy and mismanagement of the real exchange rate and associated 'Dutch disease.' The role of the state has been reflected in high shares of government employment; extensive subsidies with associated fiscal burdens; 'crony capitalism;' high barriers to trade to protect (connected) incumbents; weak economic governance and 'red tape' resulting in high transaction costs; and an absence of effective pro-competitive regulatory frameworks. Addressing the reasons for the region's longstanding underperformance is important from a political stability and social perspective. Other parts of the world have shown that more effective exploitation of world markets, reflected in increasing exports of higher value-added goods and services, will generate both employment opportunities and higher wages and household incomes.

This chapter briefly reviews the extent to which MENA countries are integrated into the global economy and with each other, and some of the relevant policy areas that impact trade performance and investment incentives. The specific focus is on the question of whether re-energizing efforts to integrate markets regionally can help address the various factors thought to impede the implementation of policies needed for a broader economic growth strategy. Clearly a precondition for any such initiatives for the countries currently mired in conflicts is a re-establishment of peace, political stability, and economic security. The discussion that follows does not engage with the here-and-now challenges of ending conflicts, nor does it address directly the short-term fiscal consolidation and macroeconomic challenges that are currently confronting many governments as a result of low energy prices and weak global demand, except to note that this may potentially change the incentives to pursue regional cooperation more seriously. The focus is on the medium term. A case is made that regional integration can and should play a role in addressing the constraints that, to date, have held countries back in benefiting from international market opportunities, but to do so it must contribute to overcoming the political economy forces that have precluded beneficial trade and investment policy reforms. A business-as-usual approach to intra-regional cooperation is unlikely to do so, given the dismal track record to date.[7] The region needs new approaches that are more pragmatic and directly involve constituencies and interest groups with a clear stake in successful cooperation.

The plan of this chapter is as follows. Section 1 briefly reviews indicators of the extent of international integration of the MENA region, both with respect to the world and intra-regionally. Section 2 summarizes the state of play on trade policy and trade costs, important factors affecting the ability of firms to exploit trade opportunities and support economic growth. Section 3 discusses whether and how regional cooperation could help promote policy reforms that are needed to attract greater investment in the region and increase the participation of firms in the international value chains that are driving global trade. Section 4 concludes.

INTERNATIONAL INTEGRATION: STATE OF PLAY

The MENA region accounted for 6.6 percent of global merchandise trade in 2014.[8] Fuels and other natural resources account for some 77 percent of total export value, manufactures for 20 percent, and agriculture for 3 percent. MENA's share in world exports of manufactures was only 2 percent, similar to its share in global agricultural trade. Regional export growth in the pre-Arab Spring/global financial crisis period was driven mostly by expansion of existing products to new markets and new products to existing markets—that is, along the extensive margin.[9] This can be explained partly by declining sales to a number of traditional export markets in Europe,[10] but is also an illustration of a gradual increase in participation in international production sharing arrangements in sectors such as motor vehicles and aeronautics (Morocco) and chemicals (G.C.C. oil exporters).[11] These were positive developments, but limited to only a subset of countries and did not generate enough new opportunities for workers through the growth of enough productive firms that together could 'move the needle' in contributing to export growth and diversification. The MENA region lacks "teams of world class exporters to surround and emulate the number ones," the firms that are the market leaders in their sectors.[12]

The share of global services exports in 2013, as measured by the balance of payments, is somewhat higher at 2.5 percent. Transportation and travel (tourism) account for the bulk of services exports, with the region as a whole having a 5.2 and 6.5 percent share of the global total, respectively. Egypt, Morocco, and Tunisia rank among the world's 30 largest net exporters of services (in value), helping to partially offset merchandise trade deficits. However, services exports have been mainly concentrated in transport and travel. MENA accounts for only 1.7 percent of global trade in other commercial services, the largest and most dynamic category of global services trade. For all of the three major service categories, no MENA country has a global share that exceeds 1 percent. Egypt comes closest with a 1 percent share of global transportation services (reflecting Suez Canal revenues). At less than 0.3 percent,[13] the region barely figures in global exports of services related to goods—manufacturing services using physical inputs owned by others, a measure of participation in global value chains.

Global flows of F.D.I. tripled in the decade preceding the 2008 financial crisis, but inflows into MENA economies increased at an even higher rate—rising from 0.2 percent in 1990 to 4.6 percent of G.D.P. in 2008. Since 2008, F.D.I. inflows dropped by half, to the equivalent of some 2 percent of G.D.P.[14] In 2013, total F.D.I. inflows were some $45 billion, down from $93 billion in 2008.[15] In addition to the drop in overall inflows of F.D.I., there have been shifts in the allocation since 2008. The U.A.E., Iraq, Kuwait, and Morocco have seen their shares of the total increase substantially, while that of Saudi Arabia has fallen from 42 to 20 percent.[16] With a 22 percent share, the U.A.E. was the largest recipient of F.D.I. in 2013.[17] What has not changed is that in most countries F.D.I. tends to go primarily to the energy and natural resource sector and to nontradables, such as real estate and construction, with little going to export-oriented manufacturing or high-tech services.[18]

The trade and investment data makes clear that there is significant heterogeneity across countries in the region in terms of production structure and trade specialization. For the 'region' in the aggregate, fuels and natural resource exports dominate, with only limited change in recent decades in the share of manufactures. Services are somewhat more competitive, as reflected in higher global trade shares, but the two categories of services where the MENA share is highest are not activities with high value added. On some measures, MENA countries are among the most globalized countries in the world. In a recent compilation of globalization indices that considers labor remittance and F.D.I. flows, as well as trade in goods and services, Lebanon ranks second, after Singapore. Oman ranks fifth, Bahrain 14th, Kuwait 16th, Jordan 17th, and the U.A.E. 22nd.[19] Algeria, Syria, and Iran are the least connected internationally in this exercise, ranked as 115th, 120th, and 143rd respectively.[20] Of course, any such ranking is heavily influenced by what is included in the indicators and the weights given to constituent components. In the case of Iran, the very low ranking reflects the impact of economic sanctions, while the ongoing conflict is a major factor in the case of Syria. Nonetheless, this data serves to illustrate that many MENA economies are closely linked to the international economy. This is partly due to the small size of many of the economies and the structure of specialization—oil exporters often have high trade/G.D.P. ratios, employ ('import') substantial numbers of foreign workers, and generate major inward and outward flows of F.D.I. that, in turn, give rise to remittances and repatriation of investment earnings. Thus, the G.C.C. as a group ranks 31st in the ESCWA exercise, compared to 73rd and 71st, respectively, for the Maghreb and the Mashreq countries.[21]

Such globalization indicators measure 'connectivity' with the world as a whole. Since the global financial crisis, the Arab Spring uprisings, and the violent conflicts that have erupted in several countries, connectivity indices have fallen for many economies, augmented by a drop in the price of oil resulting from weak global demand. However, notwithstanding these disruptive events, compared to 2000 there is still a positive trend for many countries: with the exception of Saudi Arabia, the G.C.C. has become more connected (globalized), as have Egypt, Morocco, and Tunisia. Several major economies, however, registered declines in globalization rankings since 2000, including

Iraq (-71 percent), Saudi Arabia (-22 percent), and Iran (-15 percent).[22] One implication is that Iraq and Iran offer the prospect of substantial trade and investment expansion, including greater intra-regional exchanges.

There is less integration, or interdependence, if the focus is limited to intra-regional trade flows. This has insulated countries, to some extent, from the effects of the conflicts in parts of the region: the direct trade spillovers have been less than they would have been if the region had been more integrated.[23] Intra-regional exports of goods are particularly important for Syria, Lebanon, and Jordan (over 40 percent of total exports) and have doubled for Bahrain and Egypt since 2000, exceeding 20 percent of total trade in 2013. Intra-regional trade in intermediates has also grown, from some 15 percent of the total to the low 20 percent range.

Linkages through movement of people are often stronger than linkages through trade in MENA, even though a large share of foreign workers in G.C.C. countries are not from the region, but instead come from South and East Asian countries. As a share of total migration, intra-Arab flows have stayed essentially constant since 1990, at around 37 percent of the total stock.[24] Many of the workers that send back remittances to their families work outside the region. Only 29 percent of outward remittance flows from Arab countries goes to other Arab countries,[25] although the figure is much higher for some countries—50 percent of remittance flows to Egypt are from workers in the G.C.C.; 60 percent for Jordan. One dimension where intra-regional flows are high is for banking—in 2009 some 60 percent of all foreign banks in Arab countries are of Arab origin, up from 43 percent in 2000.[26]

Goods and services increasingly are produced in regional or global value chains (VCs), with value being added to a product by firms located in different countries. Much of this foreign value comprises services inputs such as research and development (R&D), design, finance, marketing, and distribution. The geographic fragmentation of production is reflected in rising vertical specialization, with firms in countries producing outputs that are exported and further processed in the importing country, which in turn may be exported to a third country, and so forth. Some 30-40 percent of world trade today is vertical in nature.[27] A large share of this VC trade is intra-firm—involving exchanges between plants that are part of the same company—which implies that such trade is closely linked to F.D.I., and that barriers to F.D.I. will constrain the ability of a country to participate in global supply chains.

A striking feature of the MENA region as a whole is that it participates to only a very limited extent in international VCs. In the case of oil and mining product exporters, VC participation is at the upstream stage, providing inputs that are used in other countries—so-called forward linkages in the literature. For oil-importing countries, exports of manufactured and agricultural goods and services account for some 35 percent of G.D.P., which is quite high compared to other developing regions. These exports are largely for final consumption, however, meaning they do not comprise goods that are processed further in the destination market. The same applies for so-called backward linkages, which is the use of imported inputs that are embodied in a processed product that is exported.

An often used crude measure of vertical specialization is intra-industry trade (I.I.T.): a measure of the relative importance of imports and exports of similar products. Analysts have pointed out for decades that levels of I.I.T. for MENA countries are very low. I.I.T. rose somewhat in the 2000s, but remains far below what is observed in other regions. Tunisia has the highest share of I.I.T. in the MENA region, attaining some 40 percent in the late 2000s, followed by Morocco and the U.A.E. The only country in the region with a significant share of components in its total exports—a key feature of vertical specialization—is Tunisia, which saw the share of parts and components in total exports expand from less than 4 percent in 1985 to 10 percent in recent years.[28] Tunisia is also one of the few countries in the MENA region where F.D.I. in manufacturing

FIGURE 1. SHARE OF IMPORTED VALUE ADDED IN EXPORTS, 2005

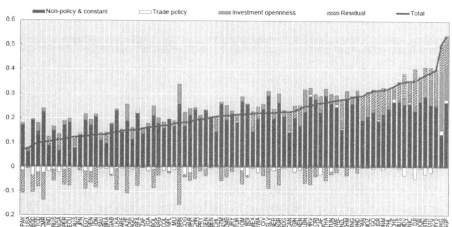

NOTE: SHARE IS GIVEN BY SOLID LINE; BARS INDICATE ESTIMATED CONTRIBUTION OF DIFFERENT DETERMINANTS.

SOURCE: KOWALSKI ET AL. (2015).

sectors is substantial as a share of total F.D.I. inflows—around 15 percent of greenfield investment. As mentioned, export-oriented F.D.I. in several manufacturing sectors is also substantial in Morocco. This has been associated with increasing demand for locally produced inputs: for example, the Renault plant sources 40 percent of its inputs locally, including from suppliers that have also invested in the country.[29]

More detailed analysis of VC participation has become possible as a result of major research projects to measure the value-added content of trade. Figure 1 shows that backward participation in VCs varies across countries in the MENA region; Egypt, Saudi Arabia, and the U.A.E. are at the low end with a share of around 15 percent, followed by Morocco and Turkey with a ratio of some 20 percent. The most integrated MENA countries on this measure of VC participation are Lebanon, Tunisia and Jordan. Over 35 percent of the value of Jordan's gross exports reflects imported intermediate inputs. Relative to what is predicted based on fundamental factors such as G.D.P., the share of manufacturing in G.D.P., and proximity to a global industrial hub, VC participation in many MENA countries is below what is predicted by fundamentals. In a number of cases policy is found to be relatively supportive, but as discussed further below, the O.E.C.D. analysis concludes that trade policies in Morocco, Tunisia, and Egypt constrain VC participation, whereas in all MENA economies included in the sample, F.D.I.-related policies (investment openness) are a positive factor, especially in the countries with the highest VC participation performance—Tunisia, Jordan, and Lebanon.[30]

TABLE 1. BILATERAL TRADE COSTS FOR INDUSTRIAL PRODUCTS (PERCENT)

	Maghreb	Egypt	Mashreq	Fr/It/Sp	Greece
Maghreb	95	126	152	75	151
Egypt	126		112	119	163
Mashreq	152	112	77	149	185
France/Italy/Spain	75	119	149	50	96
Greece	151	163	185	96	
G.C.C.	167	111	96	132	169

SOURCE: SHEPHERD (2011).

Trade costs are often argued to be one reason for the limited participation in VCs. Computations of bilateral trade costs for MENA countries indicate that trade costs are typically twice as high in the region as they are in E.U. countries, especially for trade between Arab countries. Maghreb countries have lower trade costs with Europe than between themselves (Table 1).[31] The cost differentials relate mainly to distance, trade logistics, and the existence of non-tariff measures (N.T.M.s). Trade costs are consistently higher for agricultural products. This reflects the higher transportation costs (per unit value) and time sensitivity of perishables, but also potentially the impact of more controls at the borders and non-tariff measures. In short, MENA's geographic advantages in terms of connectivity to major markets such as the European Union are more than offset by trade costs. Container dwell times are often substantially above the O.E.C.D. average and what prevails in emerging economies in Asia.[32]

Markets for logistics services, including trucking, are fragmented by country, with many small providers and few incentives for consolidation and efficiency gains. There are relatively few active transport corridors between countries in the region.[33]

TRADE-RELATED POLICIES AND COSTS

In the 1990s, many countries made significant progress in lowering import tariffs and other explicit trade restrictions. Tariffs in Egypt, for example, were reduced to less than 10 percent on average, (down from over 40 percent in the late 1980s), most quantitative restrictions were removed, and the trade regime was greatly simplified. Similar reforms were implemented in other Mediterranean MENA countries. A mix of unilateral, autonomous reductions in import tariffs and regional liberalization through trade agreements with each other and with major trading partners, such as the European Union, reduced tariff barriers significantly. Based on the results of a 2008 survey of trading firms, Hoekman and Zarrouk conclude that tariffs were mostly removed on intra-Arab trade and customs procedures were perceived to be much less of a problem than in the late 1990s.[34] In 2001, tariffs were ranked as one of the most important barriers to intra-regional trade; in 2008, they were ranked last. Instead, transport-related infrastructure and real trade costs, such as trade facilitation, were ranked as the most important constraints. More recent assessments come to the same conclusion.[35]

Factors limiting a positive supply response to trade policy reforms include the continued dominant role of the state in many economies[36] and barriers to entry and high costs of investment in new activities resulting from a plethora of regulatory impediments.[37] Even on the trade policy front, less was achieved than was needed to encourage investment in tradable activities. The average uniform tariff equivalent of all applied tariffs (ad valorem and specific) for a number of MENA countries remains substantially above that in other parts of the world.[38] Moreover, the prevalence of N.T.M.s is extensive. Research suggests that the gap introduced between domestic and world prices for a given product as the result of N.T.M.s is typically large in countries for which data is available (Morocco, Tunisia), especially for agricultural goods.[39] While progress has been made in streamlining N.T.M.s over the last two decades, this has been offset by an increase in the use and incidence of technical regulations, product standards, procedural requirements, and administrative processes that result in delays and high costs of compliance. Firm-level surveys by the International Trade Centre reveal that N.T.M.s are considered a major factor impeding trade and reducing profitability, especially for intra-regional flows.[40] Noteworthy is that firms regard procedures and requirements implemented by their own governments as much of a burden on exports as those imposed by foreign countries.

Jaud and Freund argue that in many MENA countries, high trade and transaction costs, partly resulting from overvalued exchange rates[41] and partly a reflection of trade barriers that remain relatively high, are a major factor reducing competition and competitiveness. Trade-related policy reforms, while significant relative to the status quo ante, did not go far enough, especially as countries elsewhere in the world did more to remove barriers to trade and lower operating costs for firms. The continued prevalence of high 'red tape' costs—especially in comparison to 'competing' countries such as Turkey and Central and Eastern Europe—and dominance of the state in the economy limited the positive effects of trade reforms. Behar and Freund conclude that a typical MENA country exports less than half, and as little as one quarter, of its potential, controlling for standard determinants of trade such as country size, income, and distance to partner markets.[42] Similarly, Bhattacharya and Wolde also find that a typical MENA country exports much less than what it should, given fundamental trade determinants,[43] although imports are much closer to what would be expected.[44] Bourdet and Persson estimate that improving export and import procedures to the best practice level prevailing in the region could increase the value of South Mediterranean exports by 34 percent and the number of products exported by these countries by 21 percent.[45] If exporting Mediterranean countries attained best trade practices prevailing in the European Union, predictions estimate that total exports from the countries analyzed would increase by some 40 percent on average. Countries have much to gain from improving sub-regional trade corridors, regional trade facilitation frameworks, and transit systems.

There is robust evidence that a country is unlikely to become a major exporter if its firms do not have access to a wide variety of competitively priced inputs.[46] This includes access to services inputs, such as professional services and logistical support. The competitiveness of firms and their ability to use and participate in VCs is a function of the cost and quality of the inputs they have access to.

Sector-level measures of trade and F.D.I. policies are positively associated with manufacturing productivity: lower levels of trade policy restrictiveness and trade costs help improve the productivity of firms. This applies to services inputs as much as to goods.[47]

Barriers to trade and investment in services sectors often are significant in the region.[48] Expanding production and exports of services will often require F.D.I. However, as noted previously, F.D.I. goes primarily to the energy/natural resource sector and to nontradables (real estate and construction), with little going to export-oriented manufacturing or high-tech services.[49] Averaging across countries, services trade restrictiveness indices (S.T.R.I.)—a measure of barriers to trade and investment in services—in MENA is twice as high as in Europe and Central Asia (Figure 2).

FIGURE 2. OVERALL SERVICES TRADE RESTRICTIVENESS INDEX BY REGION, 2010

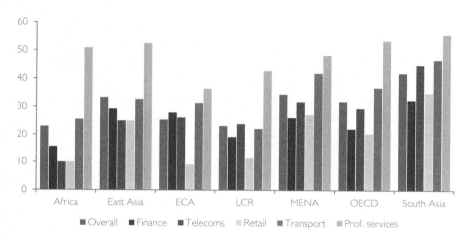

NOTE: INDICES RANGE FROM 0 TO 100, WITH 100 BEING COMPLETELY CLOSED TO FOREIGN COMPETITION. DATA IS ONLY AVAILABLE FOR 2010.

SOURCE: COMPILED FROM WORLD BANK, HTTP://IRESEARCH.WORLDBANK.ORG/ SERVICESTRADE/DEFAULT.HTM.

Morocco has the least restrictive services trade and investment policies among MENA economies, consistent with some of the sectoral performance measures discussed below. Professional and transport services tend to be the most restricted sectors in the MENA regions (Figure 3); the latter will have negative consequences for the efficiency of logistics-related services; the former for the productivity performance of firms in general given that professional services are one channel for the diffusion of knowledge regarding good practices (management consulting, accounting, legal services, etc.).

Jafari and Tarr have estimated the ad valorem tariff equivalents (A.V.E.s) implied by the S.T.R.I.s reported by the World Bank, using the methodology developed by the staff of the Australian Productivity Commission.[50] These suggest that there is significant variance in A.V.E.s across sectors and countries, with Morocco standing out as the country with the lowest levels of discrimination against foreign providers of air and road transport among the North African countries, but with significant levels of protection in the maritime transport sector (Table 2). Such high levels of trade restrictions reduce the ability of firms to participate in value chain-based production.

FIGURE 3. SERVICES TRADE RESTRICTIVENESS INDICES BY SECTOR, 2010

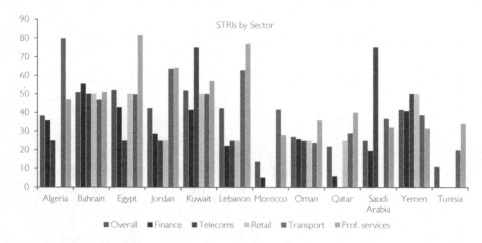

NOTE: INDICES RANGE FROM 0 TO 100, WITH 100 BEING COMPLETELY CLOSED TO FOREIGN COMPETITION.

SOURCE: COMPILED FROM WORLD BANK, HTTP://IRESEARCH.WORLDBANK.ORG/ SERVICESTRADE/DEFAULT.HTM.BLE 2. ESTIMATED AD VALOREM TARIFF EQUIVALENT OF S.T.R.I.s (PERCENT)

SECTOR	ALGERIA	EGYPT	MOROCCO	TUNISIA	TURKEY	BULGARIA	ROMANIA
ACCOUNTING	56	56	27	79	75	20	37
LEGAL SERVICES	52	73	47	69	73	47	47
AIR TRANSPORT	55	40	0	39	44	0	37
RAIL TRANSPORT	93	93	59	90	93	84	84
ROAD	30	12	8	21	15	15	15
BANKING	14	44	2	10	2	1	5
INSURANCE	28	35	26	29	14	17	18
FIXED LINE	10	18	13	12	6	5	5
MOBILE LINE	10	13	9	9	5	4	5
RETAIL	5	7	1	6	1	1	1
MARITIME	22	58	51	54	26	11	0

SOURCE: JAFARI AND TARR (2015), BASED ON WORLD BANK S.T.R.I. DATA.

All this matters for economic performance. Hoekman and Shepherd show that local services productivity is an important determinant of manufacturing productivity at the firm level, with services productivity mattering more for those firms that use s ervices relatively intensively in their overall input mix, and that this in turn impacts on merchandise trade performance.[51] They also find that S.T.R.I.s are one determinant of the value of bilateral merchandise trade flows. Policies affecting investment in retail distribution and transport are particularly important—a result that is intuitive, given that these services directly affect the ability of goods producers to get their production to market.

A country that maintains high barriers to trade in services, and that does not have a supportive business environment for investment, effectively taxes its firms and impedes their ability to be or become competitive on world markets. If there are both high tariffs on imports of intermediate products and barriers to trade and investment in services, this will negatively affect the prospects for firms to connect to international production networks and global supply chains.

ADDITIONAL MEASURES TO BOOST INTEGRATION

Of course, more than an open trade regime is needed to develop competitive services sector offerings domestically. Infrastructure, education, and the quality of institutions and governance matter greatly. Beverelli, Fiorini, and Hoekman find that the positive economic effects of more open services trade regimes on downstream sectors are strongly conditional on the quality of economic governance and related institutions.[52] The implication is that countries with better institutional and business environments will benefit from a more open services trade regime. Beverelli et al. argue that their finding may be due to the characteristics of services and services trade. The non-storability of many services often will require a foreign firm to invest or otherwise establish a physical presence in an importing market to provide a service. This in turn subjects the firm to local regulation and the prevailing business environment.

A large part of the competitiveness reform agenda revolves around improving the operation of services sectors. Trucking services are an example. Informality and relatively short distances prevent the emergence of a network of high-quality medium-size transport operators, which has implications not only for logistics, but also for road safety and urban management. Intermediary professions (e.g., brokers, agents) also tend to be fragmented, with insufficient quality control and nationality requirements for brokers in some countries, reducing competition. These are areas where some countries have been pursing action. Morocco has implemented measures to abolish nationality requirements for brokers, promoted the development of new logistics services for the manufacturing industry (e.g., logistics zones in Tangier and Casablanca), opened up the sector to F.D.I., and adopted new customs procedures that are more suitable for logistics activities.[53]

The World Bank's Logistics Performance Indicators (L.P.I.s) provide a comprehensive measure of the overall quality of logistics services across 160 countries.[54] LPI level has been found to be an important determinant of the trade costs that prevail between any given pair of countries: improving LPI performance would reduce average bilateral trade costs ten times more than an equivalent percentage reduction in average tariffs.[55] Many countries have registered improvements in LPI scores since this data began to be collected in 2007, although Tunisia and the U.A.E. are perceived by transporters and traders

FIGURE 4: LOGISTICS PERFORMANCE INDEX, 2014

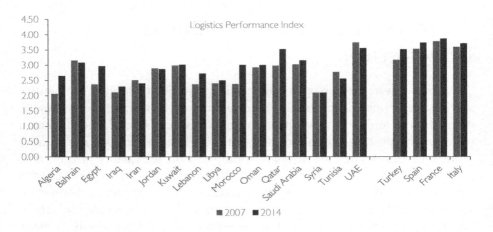

SOURCE: WORLD BANK, HTTP://LPI.WORLDBANK.ORG/.

as having seen a deterioration in trade logistics performance during the 2007-14 period. There is substantial heterogeneity in country performance, with the G.C.C. countries perceived to have the best logistics performance, approaching that observed in the European Union. (Figure 4).

Road transport is the dominant mode of regional transport. The region has extremely limited railway connectivity. However, air transport linkages have expanded substantially in the last 15 years, and there have been major improvements in liner shipping connectivity. Between 2004 and 2014 the U.A.E., Morocco, Egypt, Saudi Arabia, Oman, Lebanon, Bahrain, and Jordan all registered an increase in liner shipping connectivity, in some cases more than tripling (Morocco, Lebanon). Four MENA countries are in the global top 20 for liner shipping connectivity: the U.A.E. (ranked 14th in 2014), Morocco (15), Egypt (17) and Saudi Arabia (18).[56] That said, transport and logistics related costs remain a major burden.[57]

ADDRESSING SOURCES OF UNDERPERFORMANCE: (HOW) CAN REGIONAL COOPERATION HELP?

While there is still much to be done to improve the incentive structure confronting firms in tradable activities, some MENA countries have increased rates of participation in international VCs—e.g., Tunisia and Jordan—and some have been successful in attracting F.D.I. in advanced manufacturing sectors—e.g., Morocco. On some dimensions, policy regimes in a number of MENA economies are comparable to those in countries that have been much more successful in leveraging trade opportunities into sustained economic growth.[58] What is missing is sufficient volume, or a sustained step increase in export production and performance, driven by productive firms that are leaders in their sector.[59] Research has identified a number of policy factors that underlie the weak trade performance, and there have been decades of piecemeal and partial efforts to put in place a more supportive incentive framework. The challenge is to recognize and deal with the political economy factors that result in policies—and the absence of policies—that create high transaction costs and uncertainty.

There is a vast literature that generally finds that better performance on the types of indicators discussed above is associated with better economic outcomes. While this literature is useful at a general level, it is not always helpful in assisting governments and stakeholders to identify priority areas for reform or to mobilize and sustain action to improve matters. In the case of MENA countries, there is a long-standing line of research that points to the dominant role of the state as an employer, including in industrial activities and rent-seeking and rent-protection efforts by politically connected agents, as well as through trade policy-related lobbying.[60] Post-Arab Spring, the importance of such 'crony capitalism' has become more transparent and clearly documented in several of the countries concerned (Egypt, Tunisia), based on new data that became available on the ownership and control of industries, and the behavior of companies that were politically connected to the regime.[61]

In practice, there will often be several policy areas that jointly need to be the focus of reform efforts. Dealing with one without dealing with others that reduce the contestability of a market or create high costs may make little difference. A consequence is that top-down efforts to improve a country's performance on one or more specific trade policy metrics may not have the desired impacts as they do not change the underlying political economy dynamics. An example is a program to reduce import tariffs for goods that are subject to exclusive distribution arrangements: lower tariffs may then not do anything to lower prices for consumers; instead what used to be collected as tariff revenue by the government will now simply be transferred to exclusive license holders. Major efforts to automate customs so as to improve clearance times may do little to reduce the cost it takes to get goods from the port to the retailer or the factory gate because of a lack of competition in the road transport sector. The same is true for international cooperation. Fixing a customs post on a land border with a neighboring country may do little if the neighbor has an inefficient regime that creates blockages or generates high transactions costs. In many areas of policy, bilateral or regional cooperation is a necessary condition for reducing trade transactions costs or permitting any trade to occur at all. Examples include access to and interconnection of telecom and financial services, the treatment of e-commerce transactions, digital trade and data security, the ability of providers of services that are based in one country to use infrastructure in another, and so forth. More specifically, there may be a need for investment in regional connectivity and associated infrastructure.

There is undoubtedly scope for regional integration to boost trade and related economic activity in MENA countries. This is most obviously the case for countries that have been or are in conflict—Iraq, Iran, Syria—and that historically have traded with each other or are simply neighbors. In other parts of the region, it is less obvious that intra-regional trade has great potential relative to trade with the rest of the world. Part of the question here is whether regional initiatives can help capture gains in areas outside narrowly defined trade in goods or services and more generally be used to deal with the political economy underlying the policies—and absence or ineffectiveness of policies— that have led to low-level equilibrium traps and reduced the economic returns to past reform efforts.

Economic integration with neighboring markets has been an effective component of the growth strategies of many countries. Free trade agreements (F.T.A.s) offer one path toward greater regional integration; customs unions and common markets another. An F.T.A. allows members to retain full independence or sovereignty regarding external tariffs on third countries, while the parties provide tariff-free access to imports originating in their countries. A customs union requires members to adopt the same trade policy, i.e., the same external tariffs, as well as mechanisms to distribute tariff revenues to member countries and to determine what external trade policy should be. Members of customs unions are precluded from negotiating F.T.A.s with other countries. Research has shown that the greatest benefits from trade agreements come from the deep aspects of the agreements involving removal of N.T.M.-related costs, not from the preferential tariff liberalization.[62]

PAFTA and the G.C.C. are the two primary trade integration agreements among MENA countries.[63] The G.C.C. is the deepest integration arrangement in the region, with the aim being to create a common market and monetary union among the six member states. The transition period to the G.C.C. customs union—the common external tariff—was fully completed in 2015, and substantial progress has been made in permitting cross-border movement of citizens and capital. PAFTA is a looser arrangement that operates under the auspices of the Arab League. It includes the G.C.C. members as well as the Maghreb and Mashreq states.[64] The focus of PAFTA has been on removal of tariffs on intra-PAFTA trade. This was mostly achieved by the late 2000s with the exception of excluded lists of products, which in some cases cover a large number of products—as in the case of Algeria. Moreover, restrictive rules of origin mean that traders may still have to pay tariffs.[65] Surveys suggest that various N.T.M.s are more important as a source of intra-regional trade barriers, including product standards and regulatory requirements.[66]

In principle, the aim of PAFTA is to extend services trade and investment policies as well as non-tariff barriers to intra-PAFTA exchange, but little progress has been achieved in these areas. Arab League countries have indicated that the long-term goal is to establish an Arab customs union/common market.[67] Achieving this will prove to be difficult given the need to agree on common policies in a variety of areas, including a common external tariff. The strong resistance by states in the region to cede sovereignty suggests that the customs union/common market path is not a credible prospect.[68] PAFTA permits members states to conclude bilateral or regional trade agreements with other countries. Most MENA countries have F.T.A.s with the European Union; many have a F.T.A. with the United States; and some have concluded F.T.A.s with Turkey. PAFTA members have also signed F.T.A.s amongst subsets of Arab countries—as in the example of the 2003 Agadir Agreement between Egypt, Morocco, Tunisia, and Jordan. This goes further than PAFTA in the area of rules of origin, government procurement, and other non-tariff policies. The G.C.C. is, of course, the premier instance of a deeper integration arrangement among a subset of PAFTA members.

Research has consistently found that MENA trade agreements have done little to promote trade.[69] One reason is that with the exception of the G.C.C., Arab countries have generally failed to seriously implement most of the preferential trade agreements that have been agreed upon since the 1960s. Fawzy argues that concerns over the distribution of gains from integration across and within countries, a desire to retain national sovereignty, and the potential adjustment costs resulting from increased competition explain the weak implementation.[70] This suggests a need to put in place institutional mechanisms that can address the political economy factors impeding closer integration. It also suggests focusing on policy areas where sovereignty concerns are less prevalent and the economic payoffs to joint action are significant. The potential payoffs of targeting cooperation to further integrate the markets for services and factors of production—key 'inputs' that determine productivity and competitiveness of firms—appear to be large, suggesting that this could be a focus of regional cooperation.

It is doubtful that an ambitious 'top-down' regional initiative of the type that has long been a central feature of MENA international relations will do more than has been possible in the past to remove N.T.M.s. This observation may not apply to the deep and comprehensive free trade agreements (D.C.F.T.A.s) that the European Union is seeking to negotiate with Tunisia and Morocco. However, even in that context, much depends on the design of the associated implementation mechanisms, the degree to which convergence with E.U. norms in the various policy areas will occur, and how much this will result in greater efficiency (lower trade costs). Experience with D.C.F.T.A.s with countries in Eastern Europe suggests that to be effective in generating improved trade conditions for firms, there is a need to tailor them to the specific institutional circumstances of a partner country and for flexibility in both the substance and sequencing of implementation of reforms.[71]

POTENTIAL AREAS OF COOPERATION

Hoekman and Messerlin conclude that focusing (limiting) cooperation efforts to specific policy issues where there are clearly defined benefits for specific groups or stakeholders may offer greater prospects to reduce trade costs and integrate markets.[72] Focusing on areas of cooperation where issues of sovereignty are less problematic and the economic payoffs to joint action (cooperation) are significant should help increase support for regional integration initiatives. Trade facilitation and better regional connectivity to lower trade transaction costs are possible focal points. Given that any border crossing by definition involves two countries, effective trade facilitation will require cooperation. The same is true for enhancing the contestability of transport services markets—such as air and road transport—through agreement on the equivalence of standards, or through agreement to permit transporters supply services without confronting additional costs or entry barriers, are actions that benefit all sectors of economic activity. Another potential area for deeper cooperation could involve the establishment of regional regulatory bodies to oversee network services (telecommunications, electricity, railways, air transport).[73] Many of the countries in the region have adopted competition laws, but there are large differences in the substance of competition regimes. Cooperation in this field, building on international experience, could generate significant benefits, including as a means to combat 'crony capitalism'-type anti-competitive arrangements. While substantive convergence in such sensitive areas of economic policy will be difficult, regional cooperation could help increase transparency, awareness, and accountability through objective analysis and advocacy.

What is needed are approaches that identify the policy areas that matter most in terms of negative impacts on (potential) exporting firms and that require action by two or more governments. This must start with generating information on how complementary 'bundles' of policies impact incentives to invest. The way policies and public expenditure (investments) are designed and implemented by governments differs significantly from how businesses go about assessing investment decisions and organize their production. Businesses think 'supply chains,' whereas governments focus on specific policy instruments that are under the control of a particular authority or entity. Progress in addressing barriers to trade may be facilitated if the value chain methodology used by businesses is applied to identify desirable policy reforms and priorities for cross-border or regional cooperation.[74] This need not occur in the framework of a formal trade agreement or extant Arab integration initiatives such as PAFTA.

Trade agreements are potential instruments to reduce the effects of protectionist policies and N.T.M.s. The problem is that if political will is missing, and political economy forces are too strong, implementation of an agreement will be partial at best. Past Arab integration initiatives have been ambitious on paper, aiming for the creation of common markets and an economic union. This continues to be the case: in 2009 the Arab League agreed to pursue an Arab Customs Union, to be operational by January 2015. This deadline, as have many before it, came and went. In practice, the political will and commitment to implement such initiatives have been missing and this continues to be the case.[75] A necessary condition for reducing N.T.M.-related trade costs is that negatively affected interest groups have sufficient incentives to sustain the focus and effort needed to ensure implementation of reforms. The challenge is to identify areas where there are clear 'win-wins' in the sense that groups in the different countries involved have strong incentives to push for cooperation by their governments to implement desirable reforms, and to put in place mechanisms through which such groups can hold their governments accountable for results.

The traditional approach to negotiating trade agreements fits poorly with the reality of how international production is organized. Trade agreements are not designed with a view to assist governments to put in place a policy environment that will support vertical specialization and integration of firms into international value chains. They generally do not engage much with private sector interests or communities that have a strong stake in reducing cross-border trade frictions. Hoekman suggests that one way of determining priorities and defining an action agenda is through the creation of public-private partnerships that involve the active engagement of the business community, economic policy officials, and civil society groups, organized around the supply chain as a whole in a sector.[76] In practice, there often will be several factors that generate impediments to trade. If only one policy area is addressed, another may turn out to be equally constraining. To most effectively lower trade costs, information is needed on the specific sources of trade frictions. To generate such information, mechanisms need to be designed that support cooperation between the groups in society that are negatively affected.

Rather than seeking to address trade problems through traditional government-to-government negotiations and trade agreements, bottom-up, specific initiatives may be more effective in mobilizing the engagement and support of business on both sides of a border. Business representatives and industry organizations have hands-on knowledge of the impacts of prevailing policies and the potential returns to investment in specific areas. Business interests and affected communities on both sides of a border are likely to have many common interests in lowering trade costs. Such bottom-up efforts will by their nature involve subsets of countries and may well be limited to bilateral cooperation. In other instances a number of countries will be implicated, for instance in infrastructure-related investments and related policy reforms to enhance connectivity within a region. What the focal points for cooperation might be are endogenous and need to be determined through public-private partnerships and processes along the lines just discussed. This can build on the extensive research and analysis of sources of trade costs and market segmentation in the region, some of which was discussed in Section 2. The main point is that top-down textbook types of regional integration are unlikely to be effective. This does not mean they are not relevant or should be abandoned, but that businesses and communities need to be mobilized in ways that trade agreements have not done and are unlikely to do. Indeed, there may be scope to use existing institutional mechanisms to provide an 'authorizing framework' for the proposed integration à la carte approach.

Conclusion

Addressing the constraints that, to date, have prevented many MENA countries from benefiting more fully from the opportunities offered by both regional and global markets can potentially do much to help generate the employment and income growth that is so urgently needed. For regional integration to be a useful instrument for governments to do what is needed, it must contribute to overcoming the political economy forces that have held Arab countries back for decades. It is not at all obvious that intra-Arab cooperation based on traditional trade and investment agreements will be able to play such a positive role. Outside of the G.C.C., the track record to date has been dismal. Those countries that have done best essentially have gone their own way and focused on either the large market to the north (Morocco/Tunisia—European Union) or pursued a global strategy anchored on diversification into services (U.A.E.).

There are two complementary ways of regarding opportunities to pursue regional cooperation with a view to promoting cross-border trade and investment. One is to view it through the lens of supporting or cementing peaceful relations—as was the case for the establishment of the European Coal and Steel Community in 1951. Another is to take a more narrow economic perspective and to focus on projects and programs that generate direct gains to communities in participating countries by addressing coordination failures and capturing economies of scale. Whatever point of view is taken, it is important that efforts to re-energize regional integration efforts be part of a strategy to make Arab countries more competitive in general. What is needed are measures that will stimulate investment (F.D.I. and domestic) and employment in export activities broadly defined, including direct and indirect exports of services. The latter are a key driver of overall productivity and may be one area where on a sectoral basis there are incentives for regional cooperation to play a positive role, such as connectivity, network infrastructure and related services.[77]

Regional cooperation may be best pursued on an à la carte, bottom-up, pragmatic basis—as opposed to relying on the type of trade agreements that have been the focal point to date in the region and largely failed to deliver. Formally, the top-down, traditional approach toward regional integration continues to be the purported goal in the context of the Arab League—as exemplified by the stated goal of moving from the Pan-Arab Free Trade Area to a customs union. The difficulties that were experienced by G.C.C. countries in agreeing to a common external tariff, despite being a group of countries that mostly had low tariffs to start with, illustrate how difficult it will be to achieve this objective. It would seem more feasible, both politically and in terms of generating win-win outcomes, to use the PAFTA structure that is already in place as an umbrella to pursue measures that are more piecemeal. These could be limited to subsets of countries that have direct interests in joining forces on specific investment/infrastructure programs or collaborating to reform specific policies (non-tariff measures) that preclude investment by the private sector in projects that involve value chain activities spanning a number of MENA countries.

The historical experience of Europe points to the large potential payoffs of creative use of regional cooperation to generate economic incentives to sustain peace and security. If countries in the region are able to pursue a similar strategy, building pragmatically on multiple fronts on a decentralized basis, this can help establish conditions for greater shared prosperity. If, instead, they continue to pursue a business-as-usual approach of prioritizing regional competition over cooperation, this will increase the pressure on individual countries and polities to accept and implement urgently needed economic policy reforms on their own.

ENDNOTES

1. The MENA region in this chapter comprises the countries in the Middle East (the G.C.C., Iraq, Iran, Jordan, Lebanon, Syria, and Yemen) plus the following North African countries: Algeria, Egypt, Libya, Morocco and Tunisia. For more on the brittleness of Iranian power, see Thomas Juneau, "Iran: Rising but Unsustainable Power, Unfulfilled Potential," in Iranian Foreign Policy since 2001: Alone in the World, ed. Thomas Juneau and Sam Razavi (London: Routledge, 2013), 18-39.

2. Jean-Pierre Chauffour and Bernard Hoekman, "Harnessing existing trade and investment opportunities," in The Arab Spring: Implications for Economic Integration, ed. Michael Gasiorek (London: Centre for Economic Policy Research, 2013), 95-112, accessed April 5, 2016, http://www.voxeu.org/sites/default/files/Arab_Spring.pdf.

3. "European Union," The World Bank Data Website, accessed April 6, 2016, http://data.worldbank.org/region/EUU.

4. Hafez Ghanem, The Arab Spring Five Years Later: Toward Greater Inclusiveness (Washington, DC: Brookings Institution Press, 2015).

5. Also called the Greater Arab F.T.A. or GAFTA.

6. "Regional economic outlook: Middle East and Central Asia," (Washington, DC: International Monetary Fund, 2015).

7. See Samiha Fawzy, "The Economics and Politics of Arab Economic Integration," in Arab Economic Integration: Between Hope and Reality, ed. Ahmed Galal and Bernard M. Hoekman (Washington, DC: Brookings Institution, 2003), 13-37; and Bernard M. Hoekman and Khalid Sekkat, "Arab Economic Integration: Missing Links," Journal of World Trade 44, no. 6 (2010): 1273–1308.

8. The data in this paragraph are based on country-level statistics reported in the W.T.O. statistics database. The W.T.O. includes North African states in Africa; as a result W.T.O. aggregates are not used. Data quality for some of the MENA is often very poor; this will affect the calculation of overall shares which are best regarded as indicative of broad patterns. Nicholas Blanford, "Deconstructing Hezbollah's Surprise Military Prowess," Jane's Intelligence Review, October 24, 2006.

9. Elena Ianchovichina, "Sustaining the Recovery and Looking Beyond, MENA Regional Economic Developments and Prospects Report," (Washington, DC: World Bank, 2011), accessed April 5, 2016, http://documents.worldbank.org/curated/en/2010/10/15023563/sustaining-recovery-times-uncertainty-regional-economic-outlook.

10. Paul Brenton, Lulu Shui, and Peter Walkenhorst, "Globalization and Competition from China and India: Policy Responses in the Middle East and North Africa," in Trade Competitiveness of the Middle East and North Africa: Policies for Export Diversification, ed. José R. López-Cálix, Peter Walkenhorst, and Ndiamé Diop (Washington, DC: World Bank, 2010), 227-266.

11. In the case of Morocco, this reflects F.D.I. by automobile producers such as Renault and a number of its suppliers such as Leoni, and investment by EADS (Airbus) and some of its suppliers, e.g., Safran. "The Report: Morocco, 2014," (London: Oxford Business Group, 2014).

12. Mélise Jaud and Caroline Freund, Champions Wanted: Promoting Exports in the Middle East and North Africa (Washington, DC: World Bank, 2015), 2.

13. "International Trade Statistics 2015," (Geneva: World Trade Organization, 2015), 126, accessed April 5, 2016, https://www.wto.org/english/res_e/statis_e/its2015_e/its2015_e.pdf.

14. "Global Economic Prospects: Middle East and North Africa," (Washington, DC: World Bank, 2016), 123-176, accessed April 5, 2016, http://elibrary.worldbank.org/doi/abs/10.1596/978-0-8213-9889-0.

15. "Draft Background Note: Recent FDI Trends in the MENA Region," (Cairo: Organization for Economic Co-operation and Development, 2014), 4.

16. Ibid.

17. Ibid.

18. "Sustaining the Recovery and Looking Beyond, MENA Regional Economic Developments and Prospects Report," (Washington, DC: World Bank, 2011), accessed April 5, 2016, http://documents.worldbank.org/curated/en/2010/10/15023563/sustaining-recovery-times-uncertainty-regional-economic-outlook; and Organization for Economic Co-operation and Development, "Draft Background Note: Recent FDI Trends in the MENA Region," (Cairo: Organization for Economic Co-

operation and Development, 2014).

19. United Nations Economic and Social Commission for Western Asia, Assessing Arab Economic Integration: Towards the Arab Customs Union (Beirut: United Nations, 2015), accessed April 5, 2016, https://www.unescwa.org/publications/assessing-arab-economic-integration-towards-arab-customs-union.

20. Ibid.

21. Khalid Sekkat, "Is there anything special with intra-Arab foreign direct investment?," Journal of Economic Integration 29, no. 1 (2014): 139-64.

22. Ibid.

23. "Global Economic Prospects: Middle East and North Africa," (Washington, DC: World Bank, 2016), 123-176, accessed April 5, 2016, https://www.worldbank.org/content/dam/Worldbank/GEP/GEP2016a/Global-Economic-Prospects-January-2016-Middle-East-and-North-Africa-analysis.pdf.

24. This does not take into account the large international refugee flows as a result of the conflicts in Iraq and Syria.

25. "Assessing Arab Economic Integration: Towards the Arab Customs Union," (Beirut: United Nations Economic and Social Commission for Western Asia, 2015), 116-119, accessed April 5, 2016, https://www.unescwa.org/publications/assessing-arab-economic-integration-towards-arab-customs-union.

26. Ibid.

27. Przemyslaw Kowalski, Javier Lopez Gonzalez, Alexandros Ragoussis, and Cristian Ugarte, "Participation of Developing Countries in Global Value Chains: Implications for Trade and Trade-Related Policies," OECD Trade Policy Papers, no. 179 (Paris: OECD Publishing, 2015), accessed April 5, 2016, http://www.oecd-ilibrary.org/trade/participation-of-developing-countries-in-global-value-chains_5js33lfw0xxn-en.

28. Alberto Behar and Caroline Freund, "The Trade Performance of the Middle East and North Africa," Middle East and North Africa Working Paper Series, no. 53 (Washington, DC: World Bank, 2011), accessed April 5, 2016, http://siteresources.worldbank.org/INTMENA/Resources/WP53.pdf.

29. Indraneel Bardhan, "Is North Africa the next frontier for vehicle manufacturing?," Automotive World, July 23, 2015, accessed April 5, 2016, http://www.automotiveworld.com/analysis/north-africa-next-frontier-vehicle-manufacturing/.

30. "Participation of Developing Countries in Global Value Chains: Implications for Trade and Trade-Related Policies."

31. Ben Shepherd, "Trade Costs in the Maghreb 2000-2009," Developing Trade Consultants Working Paper DTC-2011-9, 2011.

32. What follows draws on From Political to Economic Awakening in the Arab World: The Path of Economic Integration, ed. Jean-Pierre Chauffour (Washington DC: World Bank, 2012), accessed April 5, 2016, http://dx.doi.org/10.1596/978-0-8213-9669-8.

33. Ibid.

34. Bernard Hoekman and Jamel Zarrouk, "Changes in Cross-Border Trade Costs in the Pan-Arab Free Trade Area, 2001–2008," World Bank Policy Research Paper no. 5031 (Washington, DC: World Bank, 2009), accessed April 5, 2016, http://documents.worldbank.org/curated/en/2009/08/11017288/changes-cross-border-trade-costs-pan-arab-free-trade-area-2001-2008.

35. Chahir Zaki, "How Does Trade Facilitation Affect International Trade?," European Journal of Development Research 27, no. 1 (2015): 156-85, http://dx.doi.org/10.1057/ejdr.2014.36.

36. "From Privilege to Competition: Unlocking Private-Led Growth in the Middle East and North Africa, MENA Development Report," (Washington, DC: World Bank, 2009), accessed April 5, 2016, http://documents.worldbank.org/curated/en/2009/01/11409150/privilege-competition-unlocking-private-led-growth-middle-east-north-africa.

37. Marc Schiffbauer, Abdoulaye Sy, Sahar Hussain, Hania Sahnoun, Philip Keefer, "Jobs or Privileges: Unleashing the Employment Potential of the Middle East and North Africa," (Washington, DC: World Bank, 2015).

38. Jean-Pierre Chauffour and Bernard Hoekman, "Harnessing Existing Trade and Investment Opportunities," in The Arab Spring: Implications for Economic Integration, ed. Michael Gasiorek (London: Centre for Economic Policy Research and FEMISE, 2013).

39. Patricia Augier, Olivier Cadot, Julien Gourdon and Mariem Malouche, "Non-tariff measures: Regional cooperation and competitiveness through regulatory governance," in The Arab Spring: Implications for Economic Integration,

ed. Michael Gasiorek (London: Centre for Economic Policy Research and FEMISE, 2013).

40. "Making regional integration work: Company perspectives on non-tariff measures in Arab States," (Geneva: International Trade Centre, 2015).

41. Freud and Jaud, Champions Wanted; and Natural Resource Abundance, Growth and Diversification in MENA, ed. Ndiame' Diop, Daniela Marotta and Jaime de Melo (Washington, DC: World Bank, 2012).

42. Behar and Freund, "The Trade Performance of the Middle East and North Africa."

43. Hirut Wolde and Rina Bhattacharya, "Constraints on Trade in the MENA Region," Working Paper 10/31 (International Monetary Fund, 2010).

44. This is a well-established result in the literature, see e.g., Nicolas Péridy, "Toward a Pan-Arab free Trade Area: Assessing Trade Potential Effects of the Agadir Agreement," The Developing Economies 18, no. 3 (2005): 329-45.

45. Yves Bourdet and Maria Persson, "Expanding and Diversifying South Mediterranean Exports through Trade Facilitation," Development Policy Review 32, no. 6 (2014): 675-99.

46. Freud and Jaud, Champions Wanted.

47. Joseph Francois and Bernard Hoekman, "Services Trade and Policy," Journal of Economic Literature 48, no. 3 (2010): 642-92.

48. Novella Bottini, Mohamed Ali Marouani, and Laura Munro, "Service Sector Restrictiveness and Economic Performance: An Estimation for the MENA Region," The World Economy 34, no. 9 (2011): 1652-78; Ingo Borchert, Batshur Gootiiz and Aaditya Mattoo, "Policy Barriers to International Trade in Services: Evidence from a New Database," World Bank Economic Review 28, no. 1 (2014): 162-88.

49. "Sustaining the Recovery and Looking Beyond, MENA Regional Economic Developments and Prospects Report" (Washington, DC: World Bank, 2011), accessed April 6, 2016, http://documents.worldbank.org/curated/en/2010/10/15023563/sustaining-recovery-times-uncertainty-regional-economic-outlook; "Draft Background Note: Recent FDI Trends in the MENA Region," (Cairo: Organization for Economic Co-operation and Development, 2014), accessed March 26, 2015, http://www.oecd.org/mena/investment/Draft%20Note_FDI%20trends%20in%20MENA_Dec.%202014.pdf.

50. Yaghoob Jafari and David G. Tarr, "Estimates of Ad Valorem Equivalents of Barriers Against Foreign Suppliers of Services in Eleven Services Sectors and 103 Countries," Policy Research Working Paper 7096 (The World Economy, 2014), DOI: 10.1111/twec.12329; see Christopher Charles Findley and Tony Warren, Impediments to Trade in Services: Measurement and Policy Implications (London and New York: Routledge, 2010).

51. Bernard Hoekman and Ben Shepherd, "Services Productivity, Trade Policy and Manufacturing Exports," The World Economy (2015), accessed April 6, 2016, DOI: 10.1111/twec.12333.

52. Cosimo Beverelli, Matteo Fiorini, and Bernard Hoekman, "Services Trade Restrictiveness and Manufacturing Productivity: The Role of Institutions," working paper RSCAS 2015/63 (European University Institute, 2015).

53. Jean-Pierre Chauffour, ed., From Political to Economic Awakening in the Arab World: The Path of Economic Integration (Washington, DC: World Bank, 2012), accessed April 5, 2016, http://dx.doi.org/10.1596/978-0-8213-9669-8.

54. See "Logistics Performance Index," The World Bank, accessed April 8, 2016, http://lpi.worldbank.org/.

55. Jean-François Arvis, Yann Duval, Ben Shepherd, and Chorthip Utoktham, "Trade Costs in the Developing World: 1995–2010," Policy Research Working Paper 6309, (Washington, DC: World Bank, 2013).

56. This index is compiled by UNCTAD. See: "UNCTADSTAT," United Nations, accessed April 8, 2016, http://unctadstat.unctad.org/wds/TableViewer/tableView.aspx?ReportId=92.

57. Mustapha Rouis and Steven R. Tabor, Regional Economic Integration in the Middle East and North Africa: Beyond Trade Reform (Washington, DC: World Bank, 2012).

58. Przemyslaw Kowalski, Javier Lopez Gonzalez, Alexandros Ragoussis, and Cristian Ugarte, "Participation of Developing Countries in Global Value Chains: Implications for Trade and Trade-Related Policies, Trade Policy Paper 179 (Paris: O.E.C.D., 2015).

59. Freund and Jaud, Champions Wanted.

60. Adeel Malik and Bassem Awadallah, "The

Economics of the Arab Spring," Working Paper WPS/201123 (World Development, 2011).

61. See Ishac Diwan, Philip Keefer, Marc Schiffbauer, "On top of the Pyramids: Cronyism and Private Sector Growth in Egypt," The World Bank (2014), accessed April 6, 2016, http://siteresources.worldbank.org/EXTABCDE/.

62. Bernard Hoekman and Eby Denise Konan, "Deep Integration, Nondiscrimination and Euro-Mediterranean Free Trade," in Regionalism in Europe: Geometries and Strategies After 2000, eds. Jurgen von Hagen and Mika Widgren (Amsterdam: Kluwer Academic Press, 2001), 171-194.

63. There is also the Arab-Maghreb Union but this is effectively defunct as a result of long-standing political tensions and closure of the border between Morocco and Algeria.

64. Algeria became the most recent member, joining in 2009.

65. Bernard Hoekman and Jamel Zarrouk, "Changes in Cross-Border Trade Costs in the Pan-Arab Free Trade Area, 2001–2008," World Bank Policy Research Paper No. 5031 (Washington, DC: World Bank, 2009), accessed April 5, 2016, http://documents.worldbank.org/curated/en/2009/08/11017288/changes-cross-border-trade-costs-pan-arab-free-trade-area-2001-2008.

66. Making regional integration work.

67. "Arab Integration: A 21st Century Development Imperative," (New York: United Nations Economic and Social Commission for Western Asia, 2013).

68. Research suggests that the economic benefits of establishing a customs union are limited, unless this generates very substantial improvements in connectivity and reductions in trade costs. See "Assessing Arab Economic Integration: Towards the Arab Customs Union," (New York: United Nations Economic and Social Commission for Western Asia, 2015).

69. Caroline Freund and Alberto Portugal-Perez, 2013, "Assessing MENA's Trade Agreements," in The Arab Spring: Implications for Economic Integration, ed. Michael Gasiorek (London: Centre for Economic Policy Research, 2013).

70. Fawzy, "The economics and politics of Arab economic integration."

71. DCFTA negotiations were launched in 2013 but halted in July 2014 after four rounds of talks by Morocco, which indicated it wanted to assess the results of impact assessments it had commissioned, reflecting concerns expressed by Moroccan industry and NGO groups that a DCFTA would not benefit the country. See Guillaume Van der Loo, "Enhancing the Prospects of the E.U.s Deep and Comprehensive Free Trade Areas in the Mediterranean: Lessons from the Eastern Partnership," CEPS Commentary (Brussels: Centre for European Policy Studies, 2015).

72. Bernard Hoekman and Patrick Messerlin, "Initial Conditions and Incentives for Arab Economic Integration: A Comparison with the European Community," in Arab Economic Integration: Between Hope and Reality, eds. Ahmed Galal Bernard Hoekman (Washington DC: Brookings Institution, 2013).

73. Hoekman and Sekkat, "Arab Economic Integration."

74. Bernard Hoekman, Supply Chains, Mega-Regionals and Multilateralism: A Road Map for the WTO (London: Centre for Economic Policy Research Press, 2014).

75. Fawzy, "The economics and politics of Arab economic integration."

76. Hoekman, Supply Chains.

77. Examples of areas where bilateral or regional cooperation could have significant economic payoffs are discussed in Chauffor, From Political to Economic Awakening in the Arab World; and Malik and Awadallah, "The Economics of the Arab Spring."

Chapter Six

Regional Infrastructure Cooperation:

Connecting Countries to Stabilize the Middle East

Hedi Larbi

Introduction

Building on a well-known wisdom that commercial ties reduce the risk of conflicts among countries,[1] we believe that economic cooperation can help break the cycle of conflicts in the Greater Middle East (G.M.E.) and lay the foundations for stability and inclusive development. This chapter is devoted to cooperation in regional infrastructure by identifying several policy reforms and physical projects that would require little political capital, but impact significantly on the economy and society.

Multi-country cooperation can start modestly through bilateral arrangements and extend gradually to cover the rest of the region. Development of regional infrastructure, especially in transport and energy sectors, can play a critical role in promoting economic cooperation and achieving the huge unrealized economic welfare imparted by increased trade in the region.

The G.M.E. region should seize this opportunity to meet the urgent demands of their people for jobs, dignity, stability and prosperity. The countries in the region are encouraged to implement whatever actions and measures possible at their level or bilaterally to improve the national and cross-country infrastructure and business environment. Countries can take unilateral measures to remove the barriers and upgrade their physical infrastructure.

It is in the interest of all states to align their policies, regulations and technical standards with good practices to facilitate further regional cooperation and market integration in the long-term. The ultimate goal of such a pragmatic approach is to go beyond the current politically-imposed paralysis, reap the huge welfare potential of economic cooperation to improve the living standards of the people and lay the foundation for a more prosperous and peaceful Middle East.

Status Quo of Competition-over-Cooperation and Lost Opportunities

Major constraints are holding back economic cooperation among G.M.E. countries. There are enormous opportunity costs resulting from not tapping the economic potential offered by regional cooperation. The very low intra-regional trade in goods and services, and highly restricted labor mobility, are among the missed business opportunities. This is due not only to the lack of political vision, but also other constraints such as regulatory barriers, highly restrictive service trade policies, non-tariff trade barriers, and supply-chain inefficiencies. For example, despite recent improvements, the efficiency of customs procedures in many Middle Eastern countries is still quite low compared to their trading partners outside the region. The majority of facilities at border crossings are in poor condition; a stringent enforcement of the rule of origin is still in practice by many countries for manufacturing goods; the transit regime is still burdensome, requiring costly escorts; and efficient logistics services are still missing as reflected by the latest logistics performance index—Egypt ranks 62 out of 155 countries, Jordan 68, Lebanon 85, and Iraq much lower at 141. [2]

The G.M.E. region suffers from high trade costs mostly due to weak trade facilitation frameworks, including infrastructure services and customs procedures. For many years now, failure to create open policies, adequate infrastructure and streamlined facilitation at border crossings have hindered transit traffic between countries, resulting in long delays at borders. The cost of trade between neighbors is typically twice as high among MENA countries as compared with those in Western Europe. For example, Turkey's trade costs with Arab countries, even adjusting for distance, are around 80 percent higher than those with the European Union. [3] Furthermore, non-tariff measures and technical barriers, such as licensing requirements or standards regulations are costly. The lack of infrastructure for promoting a reliable regional energy market, despite its potential, and little regional cooperation in the I.C.T. sector constitute more impeding factors for regional cooperation. It should be noted that these factors affect the competitiveness of regional countries in general and thus reduce their share of global markets. However, many of these constraints can be removed without much political capital due to their technical aspects.

THE BENEFITS OF COOPERATION

Many reasons militate in favor of more regional cooperation in the Middle East. The region has a favorable geography in terms of territorial contiguity, shared history and numerous free trade agreements and economic complementarities. Indeed, trade complementarities among G.M.E. states are high and comparable to index levels among countries elsewhere in the world that have achieved successful regional economic cooperation. The six founding members of the European Economic Community (E.E.C.), the NAFTA countries, and more recently the Eastern European Enlargement within the E.U. all had an average trade complementarity index of a little less than 60 when they signed their trade agreements. As a comparison, a rough estimate of this index for G.M.E. states range between 45 and 55 (a measure of the extent to which one of two countries exports what the other country imports). This is high by international standards.

The potential for wider economic cooperation is tremendous and perhaps key to addressing the massive challenges facing the region. With a combined population of more than 400 million, and a nominal G.D.P. of around $3.0 trillion,[4] complemented with their proximity to major European and Asian markets, and access to transportation corridors, trade among G.M.E. countries is still extremely low at less than 8 percent of their total trade. The potential for intra-regional trade is high, and tapping into this is essential for high growth and employment creation in a region lacking economic diversification, competitiveness, and modern governance institutions.

Two World Bank reports—Regional Economic Integration in MENA in 2013,[5] and Over the Horizon: A New Levant in 2014[6]—quantified the economic impact of deeper regional cooperation, which showed it was a positive-sum game for all countries involved. Under a scenario of reducing some non-tariff measures, lowering transport costs and liberalizing services trade, all countries can significantly increase their national income by 1 to 2 percent per year. Therefore, the cost of not promoting economic cooperation is extremely high for the entire region.

Connecting people through integrated regional infrastructure is definitely one of the areas where G.M.E. states can foster a reasonable level of economic cooperation. In return, this will also help create a more enabling political environment for further regional integration. This chapter proposes a few quick wins by investing in infrastructure, and more specifically in the gas, electricity, transport and facilitation sectors. These sectors are selected owing to their ability to foster huge unrealized trade potential of goods in the region.

Development and interconnection of a regional power grid and transportation/distribution of natural gas can help create a regional energy market with tremendous social and economic benefits to the energy-rich countries—G.C.C., Iran, Iraq, Algeria and Libya—and consumer countries as well—the rest of the region. Improved regional transport infrastructure, such as roads and railways, along with streamlined customs services and facilitation at border crossings are important measures to reduce transportation costs and stimulate regional trade of goods.

In both sectors there are a few actions countries can take at the regional, sub-regional or country level to dramatically improve economic integration. This chapter will focus on possible steps to be taken at country level that require minimum or no political capital, but can help promote regional cooperation. I.C.T. and other infrastructure sectors have been researched by regional (ESCWA) and international (World Bank) institutions and found to require important policy and regulatory reforms, which cannot happen without substantial political engagement and cooperation from regional states.

FEASIBLE OPTIONS FOR COOPERATION

FACILITATION AND POLICY REFORMS

Pragmatism and gradual development can go a long way in developing economic cooperation. Broadly, the recommendations to be presented here are a selection of similar measures to those made consistently by other studies over the last decades. However, very few of these recommendations have been implemented at country or, at best, at sub-regional levels. Lack of political will, complexity of the reforms and poor institutional capacity explain the lack of progress in regional projects and economic cooperation.

Drawing on lessons from past experiences, we propose only a selection of measures and actions to be taken at the country level or in the context of bilateral arrangements between countries willing to foster their economic cooperation. Bilateral arrangements have been more effective since they are usually easier to achieve: pass legislation and harmonize physical standards, procedures and regulations. Over time, successful bilateral arrangements—including coordination and harmonization—can inspire other neighboring countries--particularly their private sectors, when they realize the economic gains they can reap from effective economic cooperation. The cooperation space would gradually grow until integrating all or at least a large number of countries in the region.

Streamlining customs and facilitation services: With the exception of Turkey and to some extent the G.C.C., trade facilitation and logistical performance are poor. Consequently, nominal and effective cost of trade handling and processing is high. Transport corridors are primarily road corridors and to a much less extent sea lines.

Facilitation—customs and other administrative clearances at borders crossings, including ports and airports—are cumbersome, lengthy and costly. Attempts to address this important issue at sub-regional levels met with bureaucratic procrastination and little success. However, many countries of the G.M.E.—Jordan, Turkey, West Bank and Gaza, Lebanon, Syria—have benefited from adopting Asycuda World, a computerized system designed to handle trade data and accelerate the clearance process at borders crossings. It is highly recommended that all G.M.E. countries adopt this system along with streamlined clearance processes. This will not need much coordination between countries, and will enable states to exchange similar trade information online well ahead of time of the actual arrival of goods to the borders and dispose of enough time to prepare for effective clearance.

Jordan-Iraq, Jordan-Saudi Arabia, Iran-Turkey, Iran-Iraq, Israel/Palestinian Authority-Jordan are pairs of countries that could rapidly benefit from joining Asycuda. The United Nations Conference on Trade and Development can assist countries in adopting and training people on the use of Asycuda World. This would be a major step toward simplification and cost reduction of trade in the region.

In the same vein, several other measures can be undertaken by each country or in a coordinated way with immediate neighbors, such as adopting favored trader regimes with light inspections and technical controls for a Golden List of traders according to nature of goods. Overtime, this list would expand and provide complementarity from country to country.

Common standards for transport and logistics service-providers is another area where countries can make progress if deployed in a smart manner. In transit traffic movement in the European Union, states require traders to rely on standard quality of service from freight forwarders, customs brokers, logistics providers, and trucking companies. By adopting similar best practice standards in this area, as Jordan and Turkey have done, countries will eventually harmonize their standards without resorting to lengthy bureaucratic mechanisms.

Likewise, by adhering to the current transport international regime principles, countries will greatly facilitate the treatment of transit road traffic across countries. All the above measures require little political capital since they are done at country level. If adopted, they can tremendously improve trade regimes and efficiency of each country with its neighbors and by extension within the region. The pairs of countries mentioned above are good candidates to start harmonizing their transport and logistics standards.

TRANSPORT INFRASTRUCTURE

Transport infrastructure is currently not a serious impediment to economic cooperation either within the region or between the region and the rest of the world. The main corridor highways have adequate capacity, though they will require upgrading in the medium-to-long term to accommodate future traffic. Port capacity in the region is adequate and states have plans to expand their ports when necessary. Railway transport is the weakest link in the transport chain in the region, except in Turkey, Iran and soon in the G.C.C. countries—a major network is being developed linking all G.C.C. countries. Railway transportation is underdeveloped in the region and is not a first order priority. Until the region stabilizes and economic cooperation and trade reaches a critical mass, it is difficult to justify large capital investments into thousands of miles of railway infrastructure.

Upgrading, modernization and expansion of the physical facilities of border crossings is an urgent priority. With few exceptions, most border stations were not designed to accommodate high trade volumes, offer quality service and accommodate public administration, and transport providers and users. Ideally, it is highly advised to coordinate between countries on both sides of a border to maximize the benefits, and that each country proceed within its own space and modernize its border terminals. This will give first implementers serious comparative advantages and may encourage neighboring countries to follow suit.

Upgrading road corridors. Most G.M.E. states invested heavily in road infrastructure and have master plans for future roads development. While countries agree to upgrade and further develop regional roads leading to main border crossings, they rarely if ever coordinate to ensure that regional roads are upgraded simultaneously on both sides of the border. Past attempts to coordinate road investment were largely unsuccessful.[7] However, in a few instances, emulation and competition among countries have proved to be more effective in accelerating decision-making on both sides of the border.[8]

The construction of East-West and North-South corridors in the Maghreb is underway. To reap the full benefits of this major investment, particularly the ongoing Maghreb motorway, Egypt and Morocco should proceed with improving their connections with Libya and Algeria respectively.

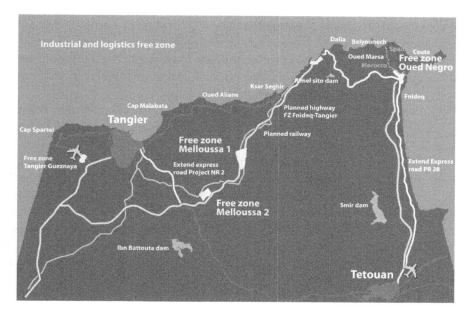

Source: UN-Habitat , 2012.[9]

These are decisions that each country can make on its own to improve the road conditions and capacity and thus reduce the transport cost of goods exchanged cross countries. Once stabilized, Libya will then join the efforts.

Maritime transportation between some states can offer an effective alternative to or complement road transport. The North Africa, the Persian Gulf, as well as eastern Turkey, Iraq and eastern Syria can be easily and effectively served by internal maritime services. Most of the maritime services should be operated by the private sector to create market opportunities beyond political consideration. In the context of shipping, the efficiency of the ports in the region will need to be highly improved (see above facilitation, custom services). Finally, a sea corridor between the G.C.C. and Iran is the shortest, cheapest and most efficient transportation mode.

ELECTRICITY AND GAS

The potential for cooperation in the energy sector, especially in power and gas, is theoretically huge and practically achievable despite the many difficulties further regional integration of this sector has been facing. Indeed, many regional countries have large reserves of oil and gas and produce large quantities of hydrocarbon products and electricity. By contrast, other countries—Iraq, Lebanon, Egypt, Yemen, Syria—have been facing frequent power disruptions, which impose a heavy burden on their economic performance. The energy demand in the G.M.E. is forecast to grow by an average annual rate of about 4.5 percent by 2030.[10] This will require the region to increase its current generation capacity by more than 50 percent requiring an investment of more than $500 billion. However, one of the most significant bottlenecks in developing new power generating capacity is the supply of the required fuel, especially gas owing to its economic and environmental attributes.

In recent years, gas availability in the region has turned into a serious issue as a result of increased demand and limited production of gas-rich countries such as Saudi Arabia, Iraq, Iran and even Egypt. Moreover, unlike oil that is normally traded in free market, gas and electricity trade requires construction of cross-border infrastructure facilities and well-structured market regulations that are not yet entirely in place. In addition, cross-border projects are complex, take time to prepare and face many technical, institutional and implementation challenges. This is why even the few bilateral power interconnections and gas supply contracts—Jordan-Egypt, Lebanon-Egypt, Iraq-Jordan, among others—have never developed over time and have suffered major implementation deficiencies.

A pragmatic approach is to tap the economic benefits imparted by regional energy cooperation. The possibility to overcome these bottlenecks is real and the potential to increase gas production in the region is huge. With the lifting of sanctions on Iran, the largely untapped gas reserves of Iraq, the existing production capacity of Algeria, the G.C.C. and Egypt, and the recent gas discoveries in the eastern Mediterranean, the regional demand for gas and electricity can be easily met at a competitive cost for regional economies. In the medium and long-term, once oil and gas prices have recovered to meet the production cost, the realization of such a potential along with the development of a well-structured power and gas market in the region will generate significant benefits to the region's economies. Abundant cost-effective energy supply will enable the region to create a more diversified and competitive economy.

Notwithstanding the number of institutional, regulatory and technical constraints to the expansion of electricity and gas trade in the G.M.E., countries may want to adopt an opportunistic strategy whereby each country, at its own pace and depending on its authorizing environment, pursues sector policies that meet the requirements of well-structured regional gas and electricity markets. To the extent possible, bilateral harmonization of sector policies could help tremendously to achieve seamless sub-regional and then regional cooperation. A practical way is for each country to gradually develop and implement a sector strategy consisting of:

1. Aligning their policies and regulatory frameworks in the electricity and gas sectors with the good practice example offered by Turkey. Ankara has pursued a vision of becoming an energy hub in the region and has

successfully restructured its gas and electricity sectors in line with E.U. practices and according to the standards that facilitate cross-border energy trade. In parallel, countries should expand their bilateral gas and/or electricity contracts (Jordan-Egypt, Syria-Lebanon, Turkey-Iran, Jordan-Iraq, and so forth). Implementation of this strategy will enable most G.M.E. countries to achieve an important institutional convergence in the energy sector while, at the same time, improving the efficiency of their own energy sector in a tremendous way. This is an important step toward harmonization of the energy market institutions that is necessary for an effective energy trade and cooperation in the region;

2. Proceed with priority projects of expansion and strengthening of the cross-border gas and electricity regional networks. These projects consist of physical investments countries can implement with some coordination with neighbors or existing sub-regional structures provided they are consistent with international standards (see (1) above).

The recent return of Iran to the energy market opens new opportunities for gas and electricity cooperation in the region. Many countries of the region suffer large energy deficit while Iran has large reserves of gas and has built power generation capacity. Turkey, Iran and Iraq can lead the region in developing major gas pipelines to feed the entire region and beyond at a competitive cost.

INFORMATION, COMMUNICATION AND TECHNOLOGY

The potential contribution of the I.C.T. sector to regional cooperation is enormous. I.C.T. is a powerful enabler of complex supply chain integration. In addition to transport infrastructure and services, I.C.T. services can greatly improve connectivity and enhance trade cooperation among G.M.E. states and between these countries and the rest of the world. A close examination of the I.C.T. sector in the region reveals tremendous complementarities and opportunities. In many G.M.E. countries, foreign direct investment (F.D.I.) in telecommunications has represented up to 40 to 50 percent of all F.D.I. in the past few decades. Opportunities for economies of scale and investments in technology upgrading (G4, broadband infrastructure, and high speed internet) and human capital development are prodigious if sector development is planned for the regional market and not only national demand.

There is also a strong opportunity for the mobile applications and software markets to grow beyond national borders and create greater value added at a regional level, benefiting from economies of scale derived from a large size of the market offered by the Middle East. Business process outsourcing, IT outsourcing, or crowdsourcing are other areas where the region is lagging behind and could otherwise offer potential for job creation through I.C.T.-enabled trade of professional services in and outside the region. These and other opportunities would have a significantly positive economic and social impact on the people of the region. For example, empirical evidence shows that a 10 percent increase in broadband penetration is associated with an increase in exports by over 4 percent.[11] International communication prices drop by more than two to three times when appropriate regional reforms and infrastructure are implemented.[12] Enhanced business process outsourcing that applies specifically to high value services and manufacturing industries can benefit the region if appropriate reforms are introduced and regionally coordinated in the sector.

Numerous impediments, mainly of regulatory nature, must be removed if regional opportunities are to be realized. Most trade regimes in the region have no specific regulations for trade in I.C.T. goods and services, unless they are related to services falling within already regulated markets (such as financial sector). In most G.M.E. states, including Turkey and Saudi Arabia, there are no regulations specifically applicable to business process outsourcing, IT outsourcing, or telecommunications services. Services such as software development, mobile apps, gaming, micro-work, and e-contracting are subject to conventional trade regulations that impede their development. Regulatory barriers to market entry, licensing, and business conduct remain significant compared to other regions.

This situation is further complicated due to countries taking very different approaches—except the G.C.C.—to services liberalization, as illustrated by the diverse extent of GATS liberalization commitments among the region's W.T.O. members. In many instances, the extent of commitments reflects the status quo or even less than the prevailing situation, especially for members of the W.T.O.'s precursor, the General Agreement on Tariffs and Trade. These commitments have been assessed to be relatively modest and include several restrictions on the participation of non-national investors or operators. While regional I.C.T. service liberalization has begun in some countries, especially Jordan, Turkey and the G.C.C. countries, the process lags behind in the rest of the region. The situation is less worrisome than infrastructure and technology upgrading, though major efforts are called upon in the next years, particularly in countries where broadband infrastructure and high speed internet services are yet to be further developed.

Enhanced regulatory frameworks and harmonization in I.C.T. could help the region benefit from the many opportunities offered by the sector, including job creation and greater levels of regional economic cooperation. Many of the necessary regulatory and policy reforms for a better integrated regional I.C.T. sector will require a great deal of political support and engagement of major stakeholders to create a conducive political economy environment for these reforms to take root, both at the national and regional levels.

Further regional cooperation in the I.C.T. sector is a winning strategy for all Middle Eastern countries. Contrasted to other infrastructure and utility sectors, the I.C.T. sector enjoys unique features that could facilitate regional cooperation. The sector is largely liberalized compared to other infrastructure sectors; its services are delivered mostly by large and influential private operators; its customers include a large cohort of youth eager to be continuously connected to state-of-the-art technology, regardless of where these are produced; this youth constituency can play a major role in bringing about the policy changes needed in the sector; and technology innovations are rapid and have powerful appeal. It is, thus, politically wiser, economically more productive and socially desirable to unleash the economic potential of a more integrated regional I.C.T. sector in the G.M.E.

A strategy of gradual integration through bilateral harmonization can be adopted to enable countries to build internal consensus and catch up with the frontrunner. In this regard, Turkey, Jordan and the G.C.C. can be considered as models of well-developed policy and regulatory frameworks for the I.C.T. sector. Gradual, but rapid, alignment of other countries' policies and legislation with those of the G.C.C., Jordan, and Turkey can promote harmonization of regional I.C.T. policies. Such harmonization will promote regional cooperation and further integration while minimizing political resistance to policy reforms.

In addition to improving and synchronizing the regulatory framework, G.M.E. states may want to consider the following investment opportunities in the sector: support existing large constituencies across borders, implementation of bilateral or sub-regional cooperation and policy alignment on existing good practices by frontrunners in the region. The priority actions and measures are as follows. Private sector operators in the I.C.T. sector can team up with regional civil society and youth associations and setup a Regional Regulatory Advisory Council (R.R.A.C.) to provide I.C.T. policy advice, help build public sector regulatory capacity and provide support to young start-ups in the sector. This can help encourage the development of sector regulations and policy frameworks that can lead to better competition, lower prices and higher quality of key telecom sector services crucial for the development of the I.C.T sector.

In the same vein, regional professional associations (PRAs) can be established by the private sector in the various countries. PRAs can take the lead in creating regional virtual hubs for software development, mobile apps, and gaming to facilitate exchanges of experiences and pooling knowledge, promote joint ventures and merging deals in the region. Such hubs can benefit from the nature of I.C.T. services that can break geographic barriers and enable cooperation beyond borders for IT developers and service providers. PRAs can also facilitate exchange of skilled labor in the area of I.C.T. through virtual experience sharing and distance technical assistance provision, thus bypassing the key barrier to free flow of skilled human capital in the region.

In this respect, promoting free movement of skilled human capital is a prerequisite to the enhancement of trade in I.C.T. services as it allows the industry to exchange know-how, technical skills, and experience in various cutting-edge and rapidly developing I.C.T. areas. R.R.A.C. and PRAs can set up regional entrepreneurship and technology centers to offer first class training for I.C.T. professionals to remain up to international standards, and promote regional start-ups in the sector. Likewise, they can also organize regional conferences and annual country-level meetings to debate the sector issues and agree on relevant actions to further regional cooperation and sector development.

All of these actions are highly needed. They address failures or gaps that neither the market nor governments are addressing. With regard to physical investments, each country has its own investment plans to strengthen their networks and upgrade to higher telecommunication technologies. While expediting these plans, countries should ensure that regional broadband or fiber networks are rapidly developed and that cross borders connections are completed. In this regard, countries of the region can leverage on the largely under-used fiber infrastructure held by non-telecom utilities, such as electricity and railway companies, to enhance cross-border internet connectivity at a minimum cost.

OPPORTUNITIES FROM CONFLICT

The ongoing wars and animosity among regional states would dampen the will of the most determined proponents of economic cooperation. However, the current situation could also present unprecedented opportunities for those states that want to play an important role in the future development and stability of the G.M.E. Few countries in the region can position themselves in this role and lead the proposed gradual and pragmatic economic cooperation process. Through developing commercial ties and facilitating free trade of goods and services with their neighbors, they can demonstrate the high value of economic cooperation in the region. The reconstruction of Iraq is an excellent opportunity for both immediate neighbors, Turkey and Iran, to increase their engagement in the institutional and physical reconstruction effort of the war-torn country. Creating joint ventures with Iraqi investors and the business community will help build a vibrant Iraqi private sector to create jobs and improve the living conditions of ordinary Iraqis, which in turn increases the demand for Turkish and Iranian goods and services. Reconstruction of Syria, once stabilized, is another opportunity for Jordan, Lebanon, Turkey and Iran. In view of the size and complementarities of their economies, Turkey and

Iran can play a major role in initiating this strategic approach of regional cooperation and demonstrate to their neighbors the political and economic benefits of engaging in regional economic cooperation to prevent conflicts and spread prosperity.

If the reconstruction process is strategically planned with the objective to build an integrated regional infrastructure and a competitive regional industry to support such a process and meet the increasing demands of the people, the G.M.E could emerge from the current destructive juncture as one of the largest, most prosperous, and most stable markets.

RECOMMENDATIONS

The economic opportunities offered by the reconstruction of various states— Iraq, Syria, Libya, Yemen to name a few—and the infrastructure backlog of other G.M.E. states are tremendous. Below are some examples where regional states can explore cooperation to their mutual benefit.

Roads: We recommend that countries upgrade and improve the quality and capacity of their road corridors with a priority to those main roads leading to the main borders crossings with their immediate neighbors. Among the roads infrastructure priorities, countries could gradually build the following major regional corridors: Turkey-Syria-Jordan-G.C.C. (through Saudi Arabia); Turkey-Iraq, Turkey-Iran; Iran-Iraq-Syria-Lebanon, including a regional link between Iraq-Jordan-West Bank and Gaza.

Energy: Numerous important regional energy projects have already been identified. Most countries of the region have plans for these and other energy sector development policies. The priority projects countries can proceed with include:

➢ Upgrading of the transmission links interconnecting Iraq's Qa'im substation and Syria's Tayem. This is a single circuit 400 kV of about 102 miles. Each country can upgrade its own section. This is an important interconnection for future trade of electricity, not only between the two countries, but in the region as part of the main regional transmission line—Syria, Iraq, Iran and Turkey.

➢ Expanding and strengthening the transmission corridor from Egypt to Syria. This is a critical transmission project to facilitate regional electricity trade and cooperation and help transport large volumes of electricity. Each country can proceed with the construction of its own segment, including reinforcement of interconnections with neighboring countries. This major line is necessary to strengthen the national grid of each country. When one or more countries of the region has electricity surplus, it can be used to supply countries which suffer power deficit, for example Syria to Lebanon.

➢ Construction of a new interconnection between Jordan and the Occupied Palestinian Territories and a 30 mile double circuit 220 kV line from El Arish in Egypt to Gaza are highly recommended to alleviate the energy deficit the Palestinian territories have been suffering from.

➢ Building a second 400 kV transmission line between Egypt and Jordan and another between Iraq and Jordan would increase the capacity of electricity trade within the entire Middle East.

➢ Given the huge power deficit Iraq and other countries in the region are incurring and the destruction of the national grids of conflict countries, it is recommended to build several large generation plants (a total of 1.0 GW) in stable countries (G.C.C. and Jordan) in the region to feed countries in need and help them jumpstart their economies as soon as peace and stability are restored. Immediate candidates for an integrated electricity market are Egypt-Jordan-Saudi Arabia, and Turkey-Iraq-Iran. Several of these countries have the capacity to rapidly upgrade their market institutions to facilitate regional cooperation, and enjoy good market size and a high level of energy supply. They have the potential to positively influence the rest of the region.

➢ Egypt, Turkey, Iran and Iraq are encouraged to engage in constructive discussion about developing regional gas hubs and related institutions in partnership with the private sector. The latter would provide financing, technology and management capabilities of regional gas infrastructure and market institutions.

➢ Completion of the Arab Gas Pipeline through construction of two segments within Syria (Furglus-Aleppo and Aleppo–Kilis) and one segment in Turkey (Kilis–Gaziantep). The construction of these parts can be phased over time depending on the availability of gas either from Egypt or Turkey or both to sell to countries in short supply.

➢ Construction of Iraq-Jordan gas pipeline to transport gas from Iraq's northern and/or southern gas fields—once developed—to Jordan and then to Lebanon and Syria through the Arab Gas Pipeline should be considered.

➢ Preparation (feasibility study) of the Iraq-Syria gas pipeline. This pipeline of about 30 miles would transport gas from the Akkas gas field in Iraq's western desert to Syria to fire power generation plants and produce electricity to both countries. This would be highly beneficial to Iraq with a generation gap of about 50 percent of its electricity demand.

➢ Start planning for an important future gas pipeline (800 km) between Iraq and Syria. This pipeline will be an important gas outlet for Iraq and a major feeder into the Arab Gas Pipeline, which aims at encouraging trade between countries of the region, including Turkey and Iran.

➢ Given the massive electricity shortage in Iraq, the construction of a second 400 kV line from Iraq to Turkey through the substation in Dohuk, northern Iraq, would tremendously help Iraq and position Turkey in the region's energy market.

These are physical investments regional states can realize for their own needs, but will also serve energy trade in the region if interconnections are coordinated with neighbors. Many of the economic challenges facing MENA countries are solvable with greater integration within the neighborhood.

ENDNOTES

1. Immanuel Kant, Perpetual Peace: A Philosophical Essay, trans. Mary Campbell Smith (London: Thoemmes Press, 1992).

2. "Global Rankings 2014," Logistics Performance Index, The World Bank, accessed April 11, 2016, http://lpi.worldbank.org/international/global?sort=asc&order=LPI%20Rank#datatable.

3. World Bank. 2011. Regional Cross-Border Trade Facilitation and Infrastructure Study for Mashreq Countries. Washington, DC. © World Bank. https://openknowledge.worldbank.org/handle/10986/12509 License: CC BY 3.0 Unported.

4. Author estimate based on various I.M.F. data.

5. Mustapha Rouis and Steven R. Tabor, Regional Economic Integration in the Middle East and North Africa: Beyond Trade Reform (Washington D.C.: World Bank Publications, 2012), accessed April 11, 2016, http://elibrary.worldbank.org/doi/abs/10.1596/978-0-8213-9726-8.

6. Omer Karasapan and Mark Volk, Over the Horizon: A New Levant (Washington D.C.: World Bank, 2014), accessed April 11, 2016, http://siteresources.worldbank.org/INTMENA/Resources/QN127.pdf.

7. See Reuters, "Bahrain-Qatar causeway on hold – sources," Arabian Business, June 7, 2010, accessed April 11, 2016, http://www.arabianbusiness.com/bahrain-qatar-causeway-on-hold-sources-281536.html. The Bahrain-Qatar Causeway was announced in 2001, construction was to begin in 2008. As of April 2016, construction has not begun. See also, "Can it really be bridged?," The Economist, July 31, 2008, accessed April 11, 2016, http://www.economist.com/node/11849068. The deal for the Bridge of Horns, between Djibouti and Yemen was signed in 2008. Eight years later, construction has not begun.

8. "Building bridges: How the world's terrestrial links stack up," Gulf News, April 11, 2016, accessed April 11, 2016, http://gulfnews.com/news/gulf/saudi-arabia/building-bridges-how-the-world-s-terrestrial-links-stack-up-1.1708571. The King Fahd Causeway links Bahrain and Saudi Arabia, and opened in 1986.

9. Mona Serageldin, Regional Corridors and Cooperation, 2nd ed. (Nairobi: United Nations Human Settlements Programme UN-Habitat, 2012), 118, accessed April 11, 2016, http://www.unhabitat.org.jo/en/inp/Upload/143424_Pages%20from%20StateofArabCities_high-17.pdf.

10. World Bank. 2010. Potential of energy integration in Mashreq and neighboring countries. Washington, DC: World Bank. http://documents.worldbank.org/curated/en/2010/06/12909378/potential-energy-integration-mashreq-neighboring-countries

11. Natalija Gelvanovska, Michel Rogy, and Carlo Maria Rossotto, Broadband Networks in the Middle East and North Africa: Accelerating High-Speed Internet Access (Washington D.C.: International Bank for Reconstruction and Development / The World Bank, 2014).

12. Ibid., 48.

CHAPTER SEVEN

CLIMATE CHALLENGES IN THE MIDDLE EAST:

RETHINKING ENVIRONMENTAL COOPERATION

GERALD STANG

INTRODUCTION

Pathways toward improved regional cooperation in the Middle East are rarely smooth, and the environmental arena is no exception. Rarely benefiting from high-level political attention or a surfeit of resources, environmental issues have been too easily pushed to the sidelines by other priorities. However, a series of demographic and climactic factors may be reversing this trend, with new threats emerging to economic progress and regional stability. The common environmental challenges faced by regional states present opportunities for improved policy-making and closer cooperation at regional and subregional levels.

After 50 years of rapid population growth, industrialization, and irrigated farming expansion, the MENA region is pressing against the limits of available water, air, land, and biodiversity resources. Water scarcity is at the top of the worry list, as an arid climate, overdrawn aquifers, and poor water management threaten water shortages across the region. Continuing increases in demand and the worsening impacts of climate change will sharpen this threat. Air pollution has become the number one health threat in a region with increasingly dense and polluted cities. Land degradation, desertification, urban sprawl, and worries about dependency on food imports have reshaped land use as more marginal lands are brought under irrigation, further exacerbating the water challenge.[1] The biodiversity problem plays out most notably in marine areas where overfishing and pollution from land are ruining fish stocks and threatening ecosystems.

FIGURE 1. ANNUAL PER CAPITA RENEWABLE WATER RESOURCES IN THE ARAB REGION 1960-1999 AND PROJECTIONS FOR 2025

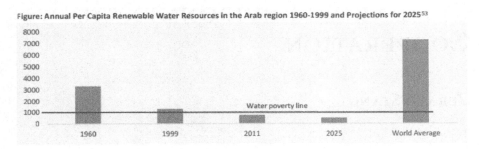

Figure: Annual Per Capita Renewable Water Resources in the Arab region 1960-1999 and Projections for 2025[53]

SOURCE: REEM NEJDAWI, MONIA BRAHAM, JANA EL-BABA, CAMERON ALLEN, AND FADI HAMDAN, ARAB SUSTAINABLE DEVELOPMENT REPORT - TECHNICAL SUMMARY (BEIRUT: UNESCWA, 2015), P.25.

These challenges are not uniformly distributed, of course, and neither are the political and socioeconomic realities in which they play out. The impacts of these environmental challenges on the health of the population, the functioning of the economy, and even social stability vary significantly within countries and across the region. The entire region, however, is predicted to be affected by significant heating and drying trends over the coming decades as climate change takes hold. Taken together with continuing demand increases, these climate impacts are likely to add stress to existing resource challenges, with serious potential consequences for the economy, and for social and political stability, particularly in the most fragile situations where resilience is low.[2] Much has been made of the idea that the spiral into the Syrian conflict may have been facilitated by the 2006-10 drought that forced as many as 1.5 million farmers to migrate to the cities, contributing to social instability. Similarly, the Darfur conflict was often described, including by U.N. Secretary General Ban Ki-Moon, as being greatly influenced by ecological crisis. Of course, both these places have exclusionary governments, a history of political violence, major social divisions, uneven economic progress,

FIGURE 2. NORTH AFRICA POPULATION DENSITY

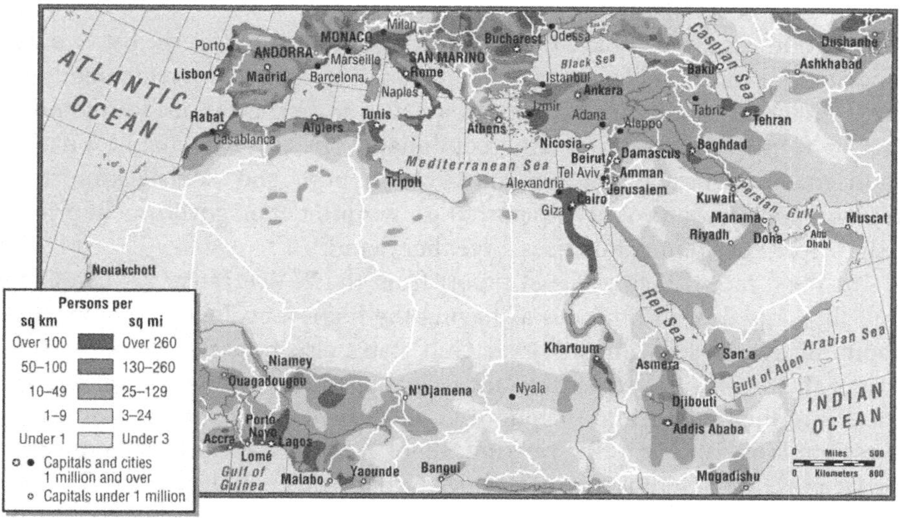

SOURCE: "NORTH AFRICA POPULATION DENSITY," ROEBUCKCLASSES.COM, ACCESSED APRIL 18, 2016, HTTP://WWW.ROEBUCKCLASSES.COM/MAPS/PLACEMAP/NAFRICASWASIA/ NAFRICAPOPDENSITY.JPG.

and a quintupling of the population in 50 years. Given this complexity, climate change cannot be labeled as the cause of conflict, but is often referred to as a threat multiplier that can add stress to already difficult situations.[3]

The most worrisome climate change issue is its unpredictability—with sufficient resources and smart policies, hot and dry conditions can be planned for, but sudden shocks can overcome local resilience and contribute to the likelihood of fragility, conflict, and forced migration. Optimists might argue that as the Middle East is a historically dry region, dealing with limited water resources is not a new challenge, and social, architectural, and agricultural practices reflect this. Thus, recent water usage patterns notwithstanding, societies and governments generally retain awareness of, and a history of adaptation to, water constraints, and so should have significant resilience as they go from dry to very dry in the decades ahead. Pessimists, however, might argue that such optimism is misplaced given the relatively low level of public environmental consciousness, a history of poor governance, and silo approaches that limit communication, cooperation, or the sharing of best practices in the region.

Environmental Protection in the Region

Environmental issues have historically ranked quite low on the list of public priorities for most governments in the region. However, resource demands and environmental conditions are worse than ever, and expectations for the future are far from positive. Thus, some combination of citizen demand, financial inducements, international pressure, or support and socialization from regional cooperation could help push the environment up government priority lists, before environmental crises force their hand.[4]

The most recent Living Planet report from the W.W.F. ranks Kuwait, Qatar, and the United Arab Emirates as having the highest ecological footprint per capita in the world, with the other Gulf states also near the top. Across the rest of the region, and across the globe, developed countries are clustered near the top of the ranking and the poorest countries near the bottom. Comparing these rankings to the E.P.I. ranking, there is a notable lack of connection between wealth and environmental performance, as is found in much of the rest of the world. The E.P.I. has Israel as the highest ranked country in the region (49th), followed by Tunisia, Jordan, and Algeria. The poorest states have little ecological footprint, but lack adequate resources to dedicate to developing clean drinking water, treating wastewater, addressing threats to human health (including household air pollution from solid fuels), or protecting species and habitats. While these rankings have value, there are no universally agreed markers of good environmental management. And there are many factors involved in environmental performance beyond the making and implementing of good environmental policy, including population density, natural resource abundance, and level of economic development.

What are the incentives of the policymakers and what policies do they choose to shape the behavior of citizens? It has been argued that the debt restructuring processes of the 1980s showed that authoritarian Arab governments were more responsive to external pressures than to domestic demands.[5] How true does this remain today in the world of 24-hour transnational cable channels and post-'Arab Spring' populations? An environmentally informed and active public could change their own habits, pressure their governments, and be more receptive of government action in this area.[6] While the transformations of the 'Arab Spring' have brought issues of government accountability to the fore across the region, there remain serious doubts about progress on the issue. There are also doubts about how high environmental concerns are for MENA publics, which may prioritize the same serious economic and security challenges as their governments. The most concerning environmental challenges for the public are the same as anywhere else—those that impact health and quality of life: polluted air, dirty water, and poor waste disposal. Climate change is too nebulous and long term, and even seemingly hypothetical, to be a priority for most people around the world. Doing nothing has proven to be the 'too easy' option.[7]

The eternal challenge of environmental protection is the distribution of costs imposed by the negative externalities that result from our production and consumption activities. Who pays to clean up the air, treat the water, and pick up the garbage? A key goal of effective environmental action is to incentivize the internalization of these costs by the polluter, so that the government or other actors don't have to pay to clean up or, as is too often the case, suffer from what is not cleaned up. Most governments around the world rely on regulatory instruments that involve a command and control approach to monitor and enforce adherence to environmental standards. In some areas, there is increasing use of economic incentives such as taxes, fees, or subsidies to encourage behavioral change, in addition to information-based instruments and voluntary instruments.[8] In the MENA region, many command and control

TABLE 1. ECONOMIC AND ENVIORNMENTAL RANKINGS

	G.D.P. PER CAPITA (CURRENT U.S. $) - WORLD BANK 2014	WWF ECOLOGICAL FOOTPRINT PER CAPITA- GLOBAL RANKINGS 2014	ENVIRONMENTAL PERFORMANCE INDEX- GLOBAL RANKINGS 2016
KUWAIT	43,594	1	113
QATAR	96,732	2	87
U.A.E.	43,963	3	92
BAHRAIN	24,855	9	86
SAUDI ARABIA	24,161	33	96
ISRAEL	37,208	34	49
LEBANON	10,058	46	94
LIBYA	6,573	47	119
IRAN	5,443	57	105
TURKEY	10,515	63	99
MAURITANIA	1,275	71	160
JORDAN	5,423	78	74
TUNISIA	4,421	81	53
EGYPT	3,199	84	104
ALGERIA	5,484	90	83
SYRIA		97	101
IRAQ	6,420	102	116
MOROCCO	3,190	105	64
SUDAN	1,876	107	170

	G.D.P. PER CAPITA (CURRENT U.S. $) - WORLD BANK 2014	WWF ECOLOGICAL FOOTPRINT PER CAPITA- GLOBAL RANKINGS 2014	ENVIRONMENTAL PERFORMANCE INDEX- GLOBAL RANKINGS 2016
SOMALIA	543	124	180
YEMEN	1,408	138	150
PALESTINIAN TERRITORIES	2,966	151	--
COMOROS	810	--	152
DJIBOUTI	1,814	--	164

regulatory instruments have been written into law, and implementing agencies have been developed, notably since the 1990s.[9] However, the continued environmental degradation would seem to indicate the limited effectiveness of these instruments, which require effective governance systems to enforce. MENA countries have been ruled mostly by authoritarian regimes—with limited political accountability—which have too often used the state to distribute economic rents rather than make long-term investments in their economies, societies, and environments.[10]

Though inaction is too common, some progress has been made at national and regional levels. In the Gulf region, there has been a proliferation of initiatives on solar power, green cities (notably Abu Dhabi's Masdar Initiative[11]), and improved building codes, as well as a gradual recognition of the problem of over pumping groundwater for domestic food production. Across the wider region, multiple countries, from Egypt to Somalia to Qatar, have begun to integrate the Sustainable Development Goals into their development plans. Both within and outside of government, there is a large and growing community of experts who recognize the need to address environmental issues. This 'epistemic community' is connected internationally, through U.N. agencies or transnational NGOs considered domestically non-threatening, and have thus been allowed influence over their policy area, if not always sufficient resources.[12]

The international connections of this community have been very important. International bodies such as UNEP, U.N.D.P., and the World Bank play a significant role in supporting institutional capacity building and the pursuit of concrete environmental projects. While MENA countries have historically been more likely to join multilateral environmental agreements only after their entry into force, international engagement is increasing as political leaderships in many MENA countries see value in engaging in these processes.[13] The most recent and most powerful example comes from the United Nations Framework Convention on Climate Change negotiation process, the outcome of which has significant implications for global energy demand, domestic energy use, and the severity of climate impacts. However, despite increased connections with international processes, regional environmental cooperation remains relatively weak.[14]

WHERE ARE WE TODAY IN TERMS OF REGIONAL COOPERATION?

Similarities in water, land use, urban pollution, and climate change pressures have not translated into effective joint responses. Divided by deserts, and with only a limited number of shared challenges as specific focal points for cooperation, the intergovernmental initiatives in which regional states discuss environmental issues—and there are a surprising number of them—have resulted in unimplemented reports, strategies, and protocols. A major reason for this is that meeting participants, whether environment ministers or technical experts, often lack the authority to move beyond consultations or report writing, turning cooperation initiatives into talk fests.[15]

At the broadest level in the region—though still exclusionary of Iran, Israel, and Turkey—is the Arab League, which established CAMRE in 1986. CAMRE has met regularly and has launched multiple intergovernmental initiatives, including the Arab Initiative for Sustainable Development, the Arab Region Environmental Information Network, the Arab Union for Sustainable Development and Environment, and the Joint Committee on Environment and Development in the Arab Region. Each of these have been involved to varying degrees in policy research, information sharing, and bridge building. All roads lead back to CAMRE and, from there, to the national governments which remain the locus of decision-making and policy implementation.

Civil society organizations are also active across the region. In addition to the regional branches of international organizations such as the I.U.C.N. and W.W.F., there are several regional organizations, including AFED, the most well-known regional environmental NGO with academic, business, and media partnerships; the Arab Network for Environment and Development, a network of more than 250 NGOs; the Arab Union for Sustainable Development and Environment; and the Arab Water Council. They operate with varying degrees of government connection. The Arab Water Council has government ministers on its board, while AFED works independently but invites government representatives to its events and sees them as an essential part of the audience for the work.[16] All of them have observer status at CAMRE meetings, remaining connected to the regional cooperation discussions, even if little happens after the ministers disperse to their capitals.

SUBREGIONS

The Arab League and its bodies include a broad and far from cohesive membership, therefore it has not moved toward becoming an institutionalized center of action. Some subregional efforts, however, have met with success, though even at this level, environmental cooperation has proven difficult to construct in the absence of wider political and economic cooperation processes.

The Gulf Cooperation Council (G.C.C.) has been working on environmental issues since 1986. The political, socioeconomic, and geographic similarities of the six G.C.C. states go a long way to explain its relative cohesiveness and increasing institutionalization. Despite intense competition among its members in many areas, it may hold the most promise of any MENA subregion to move toward integrated environmental governance, though progress remains limited.[17] They have together shifted their agricultural policies away from the focus on improving food self-sufficiency, have developed an environmental action plan (mostly on information sharing), and are increasing work on climate issues. They have also looked at wider strategic dialogue with Turkey, Jordan, and Morocco. The G.C.C. states have developed into global leaders in energy, banking, and airlines, and thus don't suffer from the same governance weaknesses as many other MENA states. They also have a burgeoning environmental leader, the United Arab Emirates, which has clearly decided to improve its environmental performance. It is expanding its domestic policy capacities, created the Abu Dhabi Global Environmental Data Initiative, and is actively cooperating with a wide range of partners, from the United States to the World Bank to AFED. However, real integrated G.C.C. action remains in the realm of the hypothetical.

Two other organizations in the Gulf region are worth noting. The first is the Regional Organization for the Conservation of the Environment of the Red Sea and Gulf of Aden, which is an intergovernmental body dedicated to coastal and marine conservation in the Red Sea, Gulf of Aqaba, Gulf of Suez, and Gulf of Aden. Created in 1995, it involves Djibouti, Egypt, Jordan, Saudi Arabia, Somalia, Sudan, and Yemen, and not Israel or Eritrea. The second is the Regional Organization for the Protection of the Marine Environment, which is comprised all Gulf states, including Iran—which joined in 1978.

The other subregions, the Levant (Lebanon, Palestine, Jordan, Syria, and Iraq) and the Maghreb (Algeria, Libya, Mauritania, Morocco, and Tunisia), have had less success at intergovernmental cooperation, environmental or otherwise. The Levant region has more geographic opportunities to pursue environmental cooperation than the other subregions, with the shared waters of the Jordan, Tigris, and Euphrates basins crossing borders. In practice, however, cooperative efforts that have been attempted have required significant involvement of outside actors, and other than the Jordan-Israel partnership, have not had much success. Today's conflicts preclude any substantive attempts to pursue cross-border environmental cooperation in the Levant.

The Maghreb does not suffer the open conflict that is underway in the Levant, but major political differences have prevented effective action—the

Arab Maghreb Union's charter for environmental protection and sustainable development (1992) has had limited follow-up. Work with the World Bank on separate desertification projects has gone well, but efforts to scale up a regional initiative remain at the planning stage. The Maghreb states have also been those most open to cooperating with, and receiving support from, the European Union and the E.U.-led Union for the Mediterranean. The Mediterranean Action Plans (1975 and 1995) have formed the centerpieces of efforts to assist Mediterranean countries in assessing and controlling marine pollution, formulating environmental policies, and addressing natural resource management. Currently, there are six regional activity centers, five of which are in Europe, one in Tunisia. The European Union and some of its member states also support the Egyptian-led CEDARE, an intergovernmental organization dedicated to water management, land management, and sustainability issues, with Saudi Arabia and Egypt as the lead Arab partners.

INTERNATIONAL ORGANIZATIONS

There are doubts about the capacity and political will of many countries to pursue environmental cooperation, which has led to international organizations playing key roles.[18] The U.N.D.P. focuses on environment and sustainable development as one of its four main fields of action in the region. It runs two major environmental programs: the Water Governance Program for Arab States and the Arab Climate Resilience Initiative, with an active focus on regionality, but the bulk of work is still done individually with national partners.[19] The U.N. Economic and Social Commission for Western Asia (ESCWA) is playing a role in sustainable development issues. The World Bank is partnering with the G.C.C. on marine issues, and with individual G.C.C. countries on capacity building. Importantly, however, the pre-existing weakness of environmental cooperation efforts has meant that the bulk of the international support has been necessarily focused at the national level, where capacity and interest in these partnerships exist. As with other themes in the development world, there has been worthwhile focus on developing programs that are nationally owned, but this focus may mean that an integrative regional focus cannot be prioritized. UNEP is the leading international organization for environmental cooperation in the region, supporting CAMRE and CEDARE, partnering with the other U.N. agencies active in the field (notably U.N.D.P. and ESCWA), and supporting capacity building and policy formulation with national governments across the region.

SHARED WATERS

Since transboundary waters constitute a necessary resource in specific locations, they can be a more concrete issue to cooperate or fight over than other seemingly more nebulous issues such as climate change. Transboundary freshwater resources have contributed to regional conflicts—including between Israel and Syria in the 1950s and 1960s—and have caused ongoing tensions between many states in the region. They have also led to a number of intergovernmental initiatives to promote resource cooperation. Unfortunately, the complexity of transboundary water projects, which tend to encompass political, geographical, and economic aspects requiring long-term cooperation, shared infrastructure, and significant financial investment, often hinders the realization of large-scale cooperative projects.

The Israel-Jordan peace agreement of 1994 addressed freshwater via the formation of a Joint Water Committee to regulate water sharing, infrastructure, and joint project development. Cooperation has continued for 20 years despite wide distrust between the governments. While other initiatives involving Israel and its neighbors have survived, such as the Middle East Desalination Research Center in Oman, they are rare birds. More common are the failures, including the attempt to copy the Israel-Jordan success between Israel and the Palestinian Authority following the Oslo Accords. Unfortunately, the shared water committee has been politicized and decisions dictated by Israel.

In the Tigris-Euphrates basin, decades of tension have followed Turkish and Syrian dam building in the 1960s, punctuated by periodic efforts at cooperation. Syria and Iraq agreed on water sharing in 1974, only to have a military standoff the next year in which water was a key factor. Turkey and Iraq formed a Joint Technical Committee in 1980, and were joined by Syria in 1983, but bilateral and trilateral meetings during the 1980s, 1990s, and 2000s (during which time Turkey has built more than a dozen dams in the basin) have not resulted in meaningful agreements.

One significant regional project, the Red Sea-Dead Sea Canal, will desalinate Red Sea water and transfer the remaining brine to the Dead Sea, producing electricity along the way. A version of the project was agreed in 2005 among Israel, Jordan, and the Palestinian Authority, but political distrust and lack of funds prevented it from materializing. World Bank involvement helped facilitate a deal between Israel and Jordan in 2013, without the Palestinians, and construction of the first phase is now underway.

A large number of other bilateral and trilateral water cooperation efforts exist in the region, of varying levels of effectiveness. These include the Nile Basin Initiative involving Egypt and its upstream partners; Lebanon-Syria cooperation over the Orontes and Nahr al-Kabir al Janoubi rivers; an aquifer agreement involving Egypt, Libya, Chad, and the Sudan; and an aquifer coordination mechanism between Algeria, Tunisia, and Libya.

Regional Environmental Cooperation— Models from Elsewhere

Model 1—The Path to Integration

The European Union represents the world's most comprehensively integrated regional body, with member states pooling portions of their sovereignty and ceding policy-making power in many areas. Created in the post-World War II era, it was intended as an economic partnership to reduce the likelihood of future conflict. As economic cooperation deepened, other areas also began to be addressed, including environmental policy starting in the early 1970s. The European Union has become the leading center for environmental policy-making in Europe, and perhaps the world, with environmental cooperation evolving as a component of a larger effort to form an ever-closer union.

No other region of the world has a comparable political arrangement or set of goals, preferring to limit cooperation to information sharing/discussion efforts or, in a few cases, to the creation of sites of shared managerial authority for specific shared problems. Rather than operating at a continental scale like the European Union, environmental cooperation has been most effectively pursued elsewhere within geographic sub-regions that share similar challenges, and often political sensibilities.

Model 2—Intergovernmental Cooperation

In Northeast Asia, cooperation has taken place through fragmented initiatives, rather than shared institutions.[20] The annual Tripartite Environment Ministers Meeting between China, Japan, and South Korea is a limited success, with the density of exchanges at different levels continuing to increase despite the ups and downs of the wider geopolitical situation. While originally focusing on policy information exchange, they have expanded their efforts to create working groups, joint projects, and dedicated policy dialogues for specific challenges such as air pollution, biodiversity, and chemicals management.[21] Japan's role as a major investor and aid provider has allowed it to assume some regional leadership in environmental cooperation, but it has not pursued deeper integration beyond particular projects.[22]

Model 3—Weak Institutionalization

Three decades of intermittent—but genuine—progress in environmental cooperation have occurred in Southeast Asia, centered on ASEAN.[23] Long derided as ineffective, the 'ASEAN way' of working, focused on consensus and noninterference, has often meant that progress on any issue occurs at the speed of the slowest member of the group. Yet economic and political progress has transformed many ASEAN members, and this has affected the club itself. While effective outcomes of environmental cooperation through ASEAN have been limited, notably poor implementation of the ASEAN Agreement on Transboundary Haze Pollution, the role of ASEAN as a robust discussion forum and the locus for collective action is increasingly secure. As in the Middle East, international organizations, notably UNEP, have played a key role in providing financial and technical support for this evolution.

MODEL 4—HOLLOW PRESIDENTIAL SUMMITS

In South America, cooperation efforts have primarily involved decades of periodic summits filled with impressive rhetoric, primarily on economic and security issues, which lead to limited follow-up. Environmental issues, when raised, are generally derivatives of more important economic initiatives and environmental challenges; while common within each region, they are primarily addressed within national discussions. With limited trade and infrastructure links within each region, there are also few transboundary environmental issues affecting major populations. Their major centers, and their biggest environmental challenges, are separated by vast forests and mountain areas.

A MODEL FOR THE MIDDLE EAST?

The model that most closely fits the Middle East and North Africa today is the hollow presidential summit model. Like South America, Middle Eastern countries have shown a preference for periodic summits with limited follow-up. Rather than being divided by forests as in South America, population centers in the Middle East are often separated by sparsely populated dryland and desert regions, though transboundary water issues are more common—notably in the Levant. Both regions also have a surfeit of subregional integration initiatives. Looking forward, the weak institutionalization model may be held up as a positive example worth moving toward, particularly at subregional levels. While continuing to ensure noninterference and respect for the sovereignty of each member, this model involves the increased regularization of meetings and agendas, the institutionalization of working groups, and the gradual buildup of collective trust in an intergovernmental forum as an entity in itself.

Where Will the Region be in 2030 under a Muddling Through Scenario?

Should the current connected trends in the low prioritization of environmental issues and the hollow pursuit of regional cooperation continue toward 2030, the MENA states will each be forced to face, separately, the problems that arise from the continued overuse and maltreatment of limited natural resources. Each country will have forged its own path in handling the increasingly serious impacts of a dirty, dry environment on human health, economic growth, and social and economic stability.

In such a scenario, efforts to sell sustainable development and green growth are dismissed as disconnected from the economic priorities of populations and political priorities of governments. National governments will not integrate environmental and climate issues into their plans for economic growth, infrastructure expansion, or agricultural development, forgoing opportunities to improve their social and economic resilience to climate impacts. Enforced pollution control measures and improved water management systems will be slow to arrive, except in response to crises. The increasing impacts of climate change are expected to precipitate water stress and heat wave crises, and attendant threats to livelihoods and food security, with increasing frequency.

Despite a trend of growing awareness among publics and decision makers about the similar environmental challenges across the region, atomized national responses—or lack thereof—will predominate. Efforts by the international community will help address some governance capacity issues, and those environmental issues most connected with poverty, such as water treatment and indoor air pollution, but the whole is less than the sum of the parts. Instead of being a shared opportunity for green growth, the world of international climate finance will develop into a new area for sharper competition among MENA states. In such a scenario, environmental cooperation efforts will continue to lag rather than lead to any wider political rapprochements or economic integration.

Where Could the Region be in 2030 Under a Scenario Involving Significant Cooperation?

Forging a more optimistic scenario for regional environmental cooperation would not require revolutionary transformations in politics or policy-making. To start with, there is no shortage of draft plans for environmental cooperation in the region. Much of what is lacking today is follow through and implementation of ideas already under development. As long-established limits on the media and public discourse have been disrupted by new technologies, new media models, and the Arab Spring, there has been a genuine increase in awareness across the region of how neighboring states face similar challenges. Gradually, this consciousness can help facilitate openness to regional and international cooperation, particularly where economic impacts and advantages are clear.

In such a context, improved environmental cooperation would likely involve two complementary processes: first, increased ownership and prioritization of environmental problems by different states, buttressed by civil society actors who help strengthen sustainable development voices in separate national discussions; and second, increased openness to regional cooperation as a tool for addressing environmental problems. This cooperation would play out first with learning and applying the best practices learned from each other's national initiatives, before eventually moving toward the development of integrated initiatives. Such a scenario could be facilitated by the choice of external actors (international organizations, bilateral partners) to prioritize support via regional initiatives that are regionally led, rather than through bilateral processes.

The content of this improved cooperation may be most likely to be developed along three thematic lines: sustainable development, climate change, and managing shared waters.

The sustainable development agenda holds great promise because it allows environmental issues to be integrated into economic planning. With the SDGs and Agenda 2030, developed through a remarkably inclusive U.N. process, sustainable development has become more than an environmental catchphrase. The term is becoming central to many discussions on economic growth and job creation for both developed and developing regions. While not without skeptics, the concept includes a green focus, but is targeted at improving human well-being, an approach that fits well with the priorities of much of the broader MENA public. Importantly, the SDGs have been designed with quite clear, measurable targets, ensuring that they remain high on the agendas of aid agencies and international organizations. While the nature of many of the goals makes them well suited for being addressed through regional initiatives, many of the individual targets are defined at national levels, perhaps providing a counter pressure to expanding efforts beyond the national level.

Climate change is the second likely theme for environmental cooperation. It has long been presented primarily as an adaptation challenge for a dry region that may get drier, with adaptation efforts largely managed at national levels. However, the vast majority of climate finance available—a pie that is expected to expand rapidly—has been dedicated to mitigation, which partly explains why mitigation is increasingly moving up agendas in the region. Mitigation discussions have been the focus of climate change talks at a regional level, rather than adaptation, as Arab states have forged joint approaches to international climate negotiations. Further regional cooperation will be facilitated by continued momentum of global processes, in which MENA governments have become increasingly invested; the ongoing dedication of additional government capacity to climate issues; and the fact that energy is central to climate discussions. Energy issues are always on the agenda for decision makers; if the world's biggest economies are prioritizing climate issues, everybody else will have to take notice, due to the repercussions on their energy systems. Even the region's oil exporters supported the Paris climate deal, and are now trying to figure out how to avoid the worst disruption, that of lower future demand for oil due to climate impact. In this scenario, awareness of the world's limited carbon budget, and subsequent constraints on the wealth of oil exporters, can begin to mitigate the historic 'go it alone' mentality of the oil exporters. This may begin to open them up to cooperation on energy and climate issues with less endowed neighbors. High levels of political and financial support from external actors would also play an important role in driving the process.

Shared waters constitute the third likely theme for regional environmental cooperation. As discussed above, a number of transboundary rivers and aquifers remain sites of contention. A trend toward improved cooperation could lead to real benefits in terms of reduced tensions and more predictable water management.

The formats for pursuing regional cooperation on any of these thematic lines could be developed according to three priorities: building on existing frameworks and agreements, targeting action at the subregional level, and strategic thinking in pursuing narrow projects or broad processes.

1. Rather than reinventing the wheel, the opportunity presented by a shift in political will, priorities, or resources, which open the door to improved cooperation, should be seized by building on existing agreements. This would turn rhetoric into signatures, and signatures into action. There is already a proliferation of initiatives at multiple levels, from low-level intergovernmental technical cooperation, to urban partnerships, to issue-specific civil society initiatives.

2. The different MENA subregions provide the most fertile ground for environmental cooperation, particularly in the G.C.C. The ASEAN model of weak but persistent moves toward institutionalization might be considered the most plausible scenario for G.C.C. optimists. Additionally, if governance could be decentralized within the region—a big 'if'—it would create more centers of effective decision-making. Evidence from

other world regions suggests that local and subnational governments can sometimes cooperate quite widely beyond the national arena as they do not have the same political and pride constraints as national governments.

3. Strategic thinking about the balance of cooperation mechanisms, narrow technical projects, or wider global processes will be required. Narrow and targeted environmental initiatives have often made the most progress in being institutionalized and affecting lives on the ground, such as Israeli-Jordanian water cooperation. It is, however, the broader issues—sustainable development or climate change—for which the sharing of policy experiences and the pursuit of deeper cooperation would be less likely to be trapped in technical bubbles. These broader issues could have the most potential knock on impact in affecting the wider political relationship between countries.

In the end, a scenario involving better environmental cooperation can be expected to result in improved environmental performance over time. This could include bending long-term trajectories on climate and energy in the right direction, reducing the likelihood that climate impacts will lead to fragility or instability, and improving water management across the region. This will occur as lessons are learned, new technologies are more widely applied, and joint investments are pursued. Successful implementation of sustainable development principles in the region could also result in progress in the fight against poverty if efforts to reform inefficient water use in the agricultural sector take into account the unique challenge of the millions of rural poor.

WHAT CAN IMPROVED COOPERATION YIELD IN TERMS OF TRACTION ON ECONOMIC AND POLITICAL FRONTS?

Improved environmental cooperation may have value in facilitating wider cooperation, depending on two factors. The first is how important environmental issues become on national agendas. Will local environmental crises be required to instigate change—not unlike the severe local pollution issues that instigated environmental movements in the West? The more that climate change is recognized as a potential security challenge, the more likely it is that efforts to address it will be integrated with other foreign policy priorities. Second, how successfully can environmental issues be integrated into economic development thinking? Significant growth in international climate finance over the next 15 years could create major incentives to move environmental issues to the center of national and regional policy-making.

At the governmental level, the environment can form a solid plank for continued dialogue, notably in the technical sphere, along with related dialogues on trade, agriculture, and energy, to foster a culture and mechanisms for organizing regional cooperation. External support to facilitate such dialogues can be a good investment. For civil society, the environment can be a relatively apolitical issue, unlikely to trigger pressures and crackdowns that local organizations face on other issues. Thus, environmental discussion can be seen as opening space for civil society in general.

Taking advantage of these opportunities will be a challenge without deeper and more widespread understanding of the problems being faced. No region on Earth is expected to be harder hit by climate change. No other region has already displayed quite so clearly the potential threats to stability and peace that rapid environmental change may bring. Responses at the national level will be necessary, but perhaps not sufficient, for mitigating these threats and forging a sustainable path to development. Improved information sharing, technical cooperation, and political negotiation at regional and subregional levels can play an important role. While it is easy to identify obstacles to improved regional cooperation in the Middle East, these obstacles should not be used as excuses for despair and inaction. Times change and challenges that once seemed impossible can suddenly appear resoluble. Step-by-step and theme-by-theme, it will be important to find pathways to get there.

ENDNOTES

1. While agriculture employs an average of 23% of the population across the region (2010) and generates 6% of G.D.P. (2014), it accounts for more than 85% of water use (2013). See "World Development Indicators database," World Bank, most recent years listed, accessed March 24, 2016, http://data.worldbank.org/datacatalog/world-development-indicators.

2. Lukas Rüttinger, Dan Smith, Gerald Stang, Dennis Tänzler, and Janani Vivekananda, "A New Climate for Peace - Taking Action on Climate and Fragility Risks, (Adelphi, International Alert, Woodrow Wilson International Center for Scholars, and European Union Institute for Security Studies, 2015).

3. Oli Brown and Alec Crawford, "Rising Temperatures, Rising Tensions - Climate change and the risk of violent conflict in the Middle East" (Winnipeg: International Institute for Sustainable Development, 2009).

4. John Waterbury, "The Political Economy of Climate Change in the Arab Region," Arab Human Development Report Research Paper Series (New York: United Nations Development Programme Regional Bureau for Arab States, 2013).

5. Ibid., 20.

6. Ibid.

7. Ibid.

8. Hala Abou-Ali, "Environment and regulations in MENA," in Economic Incentives and Environmental Regulation - Evidence from the MENA Region, ed. Hala Abou-Ali (Cheltenham, UK: Edward Elgar Publishing, 2012), 6.

9. Ibid, 10.

10. Waterbury, "The Political Economy," 13.

11. The Masdar Initiative is a planned sustainable city intended as a showcase for green technologies. See "Masdar: a Mubadala Company," Masdar, accessed April 18, 2016, http://www.masdar.ae/en/#city/all.

12. Waterbury, "The Political Economy," 19.

13. Ratification status and dates updated from Arab Environment: Future Challenges: 2008 Report of the Arab Forum for Environment and Development, ed. Mostafa K. Tolba and Najib W. Saab (Beirut: Arab Forum for Environment and Development, 2008). The review covered the Stockholm Convention on Persistent Organic Pollutants, the Cartagena Protocol on Biosafety, the U.N. Convention to Combat Desertification, the Convention on Biological Diversity, the U.N. Framework Convention on Climate Change, the Kyoto Protocol, the Basel Convention on the Control of Transboundary Movements of Hazardous Waste, and the Vienna Convention on the Protection of the Ozone Layer.

14. Unanimous agreement among authors and interviewees.

15. Najib Saab, Secretary General of AFED, Interview by author, February 11, 2016.

16. Ibid.

17. Dora Kulauzov and Alexios Antypas, " The Middle East and North Africa Sub-regional environmental cooperation as a security issue," in Comparative Environmental Regionalism, ed. Lorraine Elliott and Shaun Breslin (London: Routledge, 2011).

18. Ibid.

19. Executive Board of the United Nations Development Programme, the United Nations Population Fund and the United Nations Office for Project Services, "Regional programme document for Arab States, 2014-2017," December 13, 2013, accessed April 18, 2016, http://www.undp.org/content/dam/undp/library/corporate/Executive%20Board/2014/first-regular-session/English/DPRPDRAS3.doc.

20. Lorraine Elliott, "East Asia and sub-regional diversity Initiatives, institutions and identity," in Comparative Environmental Regionalism, ed. Lorraine Elliott and Shaun Breslin (London: Routledge, 2011).

21. The 17th Tripartite Environment Ministers Meeting among China, Japan and Korea, "Joint Communiqué," April 29-30, 2015, Shanghai, China, accessed April 18, 2016, http://www.env.go.jp/earth/coop/temm/archive/pdf/communique_E17.pdf.

22. Nicole Armitage, "From crisis to Kyoto and beyond: The evolution of environmental concerns in Japanese official development assistance," Discussion Paper No.176 (Graduate School of International Development, Nagoya University , November, 2009), accessed April 18, 2016 http://www.gsid.nagoya-u.ac.jp/bpub/research/public/paper/article/176.pdf.

23. Elliott, "East Asia and sub-regional diversity."

CHAPTER EIGHT

NATURAL COOPERATION:

FACING WATER CHALLENGES IN THE MIDDLE EAST

AYSEGÜL KIBAROGLU

INTRODUCTION

The vital importance of water for human security and sustainable development has received worldwide attention. Much emphasis has been placed on the global status of water, namely water scarcity and a lack of access to clean water and sanitation. Certain regions are far weaker than others in terms of shared surface and groundwater resources between two or more countries. The Middle East and North Africa (MENA) is regarded as one of the most challenged regions in this regard. In addition to the constraints of its natural water resources, MENA suffers from an abundance of issues that compound water security, including a rapidly growing population, disparate economic development, limited amounts of irregularly distributed water supply, negative impacts of climate change and variability, and poor water management and allocation practices both within and between states.

The geopolitical importance of the region, and the conflicts that have consequently resulted, aggravate the usual problems of sharing water in a variety of MENA settings, such as in the transboundary river basins of the Jordan, the Euphrates-Tigris, and the Nile.

While MENA covers 4.9 percent of the total area of the world and contains 4.4 percent of its population, its water resources, which total 484 km³, are only about 1.1 percent of the total renewable water resources of the world. Moreover, large differences exist between MENA's countries and its sub-regions. Globally, the average per capita water availability is close to 7,000 m³/person/year, whereas in MENA, only 1,200 m³/person/year is available. Half of the region's population lives under conditions of water stress.[1]

Moreover, with the population expected to grow from 300 million today to 500 million in 2025, per capita water availability is expected to halve by 2050, with serious consequences for the region's already-stressed groundwater and natural hydrological system.[2] Some 60 percent of the region's water flows across international borders, complicating the resource management challenge. Every major river in the region crosses one or more international border, and

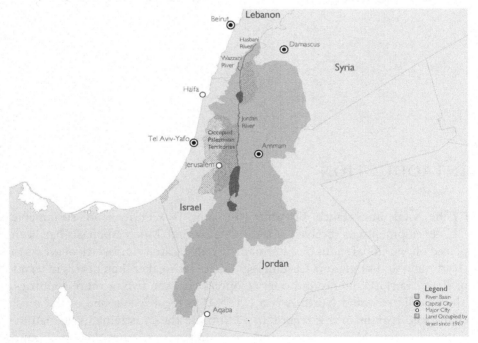

50 percent of MENA's population depends on water flowing from another sovereign state. Political considerations of individual states exert pressure on water policies and often lead to policies that have unforeseen and serious consequences on populations and states downstream.

In addition to being one of the most arid regions in the world, MENA experiences high natural variability in precipitation. With global warming and climate change, variability and aridity are both likely to increase. Researchers have identified an increasing tendency in annual and seasonal drought intensity corresponding with an increasing number of dry days in the rainy season.[3] There is evidence that climate change is already beginning to influence droughts in the area by reducing winter rainfall and increasing evapotranspiration at rates higher than can be explained by natural variability alone. Recent climate simulations all indicate growing water-related risks from higher temperatures, increased evaporative water demands, reductions in future runoff levels, and changes in the timing of runoff.[4]

EXISTING KEY WATER DISPUTES

All the major transboundary river basins in MENA are in sub-regions that have experienced severe political tensions. These political circumstances have aggravated past water disputes, which otherwise might have been solved had the political climate been more favorable. In other words, water disputes were overlaid, or at least influenced, by multifaceted interstate conflicts involving disputes over security, borders, and other issues.[5]

JORDAN RIVER BASIN

The Jordan River system includes Israel, Jordan, Palestinian Authority, Syria and Lebanon. Total water availability in the Jordan basin is very limited. The riparians of the Jordan system place it among the countries with the lowest per capita water availability in the world. To complicate this harsh hydrological setting, the region has been the locus of a protracted political struggle.[6] Since 1967, "resource capture" has been a cause for water disputes in the Jordan basin. Its occupation of the West Bank, Gaza Strip, and Golan Heights gave Israel almost total control over the headwaters of the Jordan River and its tributaries, as well as control over the major recharge region for its groundwater aquifers. Hence, much of the tension over water between the Palestinians and the Israelis relates to discrimination in water allocation, pricing, and delivery systems.[7] Water consumption by Israeli settlers in the West Bank is roughly eight to ten times that of the Palestinians.[8] With rapid population growth (3 percent per year), declining water availability in the West Bank is a tightening constraint on agriculture and human use.[9] To illustrate, water became a bone of contention between Israel and Lebanon in 2002. The Lebanese initiative to divert water from the Wazzani River— the main source of the Hasbani River, which contributes approximately 25 percent of the Jordan River's water— deepened the rift between Israel and Lebanon. Israeli Prime Minister Ariel

Sharon had described the project as a casus belli, arguing that Israel could not allow the project to proceed. A hot conflict between two states was averted through U.S. mediation.[10] Hence, the water dispute in the Jordan basin is a distribution conflict embedded in a protracted political (Arab-Israeli) conflict, displaying all the characteristics of a zero-sum game.

NILE RIVER BASIN

In the late 1920s, under the full control of Britain, colonial water-sharing agreements were concluded throughout the Nile basin. Following the wave of independence in Africa in the 1950s, all upstream riparian states declared those agreements void, including the most important one, the 1929 Nile Water Agreement. This was later replaced by the still legally binding 1959 Agreement for the Full Utilization of the Nile Waters, under which the two riparians agreed to share the water with 75 percent and 25 percent for Egypt and Sudan, respectively.[11] The 1959 agreement has never been accepted by any of the upstream riparians, remaining a cause for recurring tensions. Egypt, so heavily dependent on the Nile waters, has used its military might and hegemonic status to threaten any upper riparian, primarily Ethiopia, from undertaking any projects that would risk Egypt's share of the Nile.[12] Challenging this

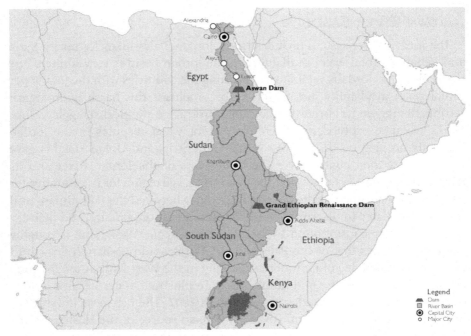

historical status quo, in March 2011, the Ethiopian government announced plans to construct a hydroelectric dam on the Blue Nile, the Grand Ethiopian Renaissance Dam, which is expected to generate approximately 6,000MW of electricity, becoming Africa's largest power plant. Concerns have been raised over the dam's impact on Egypt. Tensions over the dam increased in May 2011 when Ethiopia temporarily diverted the flow of the Blue Nile as part of the construction process. After exchanges of harsh rhetoric between the heads of states, the foreign ministers of Egypt and Ethiopia met and agreed to hold further talks on the construction of the dam in June 2011.[13] The current water dispute in the Nile basin intimately relates to the unfair clauses in the historical bilateral sharing agreements. The increasing ability and desire of the upstream states, namely Ethiopia, to challenge Egypt's status as hydro-hegemon and the overall status quo underpins the current tensions over water.

Euphrates-Tigris Basin

The water question emerged on the regional agenda in the Euphrates-Tigris basin when the three riparians initiated major water and land resource

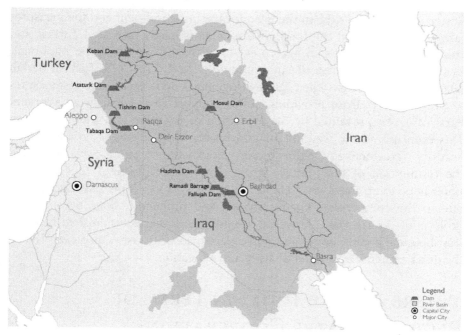

development projects. Only since the 1960s have Turkey and Syria put forward ambitious plans to develop the waters of the Euphrates-Tigris river system for energy and irrigation purposes. At the same time, Iraq also announced new schemes for an extension of its irrigated area.[14] As the national water development ventures progressed, mismatches between water supply and demand occurred throughout the river basin. The ad hoc technical negotiations were unable to prepare the ground for a comprehensive treaty on equitable and effective transboundary water management. Hence, a series of diplomatic crises occurred in the region in the last quarter of the 20th century. Turkey started impounding the Keban Reservoir by February 1974 at the same time that Syria had almost finalized the construction of the Tabaqa Dam. This was a period of severe drought. The impounding of both reservoirs escalated into a crisis in the spring of 1975. Iraq accused Syria of reducing the river's flow to intolerable levels, while Syria placed the blame on Turkey. The Iraqi government was not satisfied with the Syrian response, and the mounting frustration resulted in mutual threats bringing the parties to the brink of armed hostility. A war over water was averted with Saudi mediation, resulting in extra amounts of water being released from Syria to Iraq.[15] In January 1990, Turkey temporarily intervened in the flow of the Euphrates River in order to fill the Atatürk dam reservoir. Even though Turkey had notified its downstream neighbors by November 1989 of the impending event and had sent delegations to Middle Eastern countries to explain the need for the impoundment and the measures taken, the Syrian and the Iraqi governments officially protested Turkey, and consequently called for an agreement to share the waters of the Euphrates, as well as a reduction in the impounding period.[16] In 1998, Turkish-Syrian relations became tense when Turkey threatened Syria with military measures to prevent Syria from providing ample support to the Kurdistan Workers' Party. War was prevented by the mediation of Egyptian and Iranian leaders. This event paved the way for the conclusion of the Turkish-Syrian Ceyhan Security Agreement in October 1998.[17] Shortly after signing, Syria requested the resumption of the Joint Technical Committee meetings to enable the water issue to be considered. Hence, the water dispute in the basin originated due to the competitive, uncoordinated, and unilateral water development projects of the riparians; however, the political linkages established between transboundary water issues and non-riparian security issues also exacerbated the disagreements over water-sharing and allocation.

WHERE ARE WE TODAY IN TERMS OF REGIONAL WATER COOPERATION?

There is no regional institution that is capable of bringing together all the major countries in the region to negotiate and manage economic and political issues. The main intergovernmental regional organization, the Arab League, does not include Ethiopia, Turkey, Iran, and Israel, and the organization itself is beset with internal divisions. Under this non-cooperative regional framework, historically, transboundary rivers in the Middle East have been a source of tension between countries. In this context, although the claim that water was a major cause of the 1967 war is much disputed, there is little doubt that the development of Israel's National Water Carrier in 1964 and subsequent Syrian attempts to divert the headwaters of the Jordan River played a part in the chain of events leading to the war.[18]

With regard to regional water cooperation, there are only rudimentary forms of cooperation and agreements in place. Comprehensive transboundary agreements or treaties that could help regulate potentially inharmonious claims by riparian states are not found. There are a limited number of bilateral, and sometimes outdated, protocols and other arrangements. Hence, the existence of a treaty on a water basin in the MENA region could not be accepted as evidence of cooperation. To illustrate, the volatile relations between the Arabs and Israelis occasionally witnessed attempts at transboundary water cooperation, albeit fruitless.[19] Nonetheless, in the aftermath of the Gulf crisis in 1990, coupled with the end of the Cold War, the rules of engagement in the region drastically changed. With the political scene changed, U.S. President George H.W. Bush was in a position to convene the Madrid Peace Talks in October 1991.[20] In the treaties and agreements signed since then, water has been given utmost attention.[21] In addition to the bilateral nature (Israel-Jordan; Israel-Palestinian Authority) of these agreements, Syria and Lebanon were excluded since they boycotted the Middle East Peace Process altogether. In the peace treaty between Israel and Jordan, Article 6 and Annex II are devoted to water problems. Even though the water stipulations of the treaty are rather balanced in terms of the emphasis on equitable and efficient use of available water resources, the rights of the Palestinians in the West Bank are totally ignored.[22] The treaty did not detail what would happen to the prescribed allocations in a drought. In early 1999, the worst drought on record led to tensions as water deliveries to Jordan fell.[23] On the other front, the Oslo Accords between Israel and the Palestinian Liberation Organization incorporate, in the very detailed Article 40, "the Palestinian water rights in the West Bank," but water rights of the Palestinians from the surface water of the Jordan River are not discussed at all.[24] All in all, these agreements are bilateral and exclude the water rights of pivotal riparians, and they predominantly concern water quantity or border issues while neglecting vital and urgent issues such as drought management.[25]

In 1987 and 1990 two bilateral protocols—acknowledged by all the riparian states as interim agreements—were signed, following a number of high-level meetings of top officials in the Euphrates-Tigris basin. In 1987, the Turkish-Syrian Protocol on Economic Cooperation was the first formal bilateral agreement reached on the Euphrates. Turkey promised a water flow of up to 500 m³ per second, or about 16 km³ per year, at the Turkish-Syrian border, with the intention of reaching an agreement with Syria on security matters.[26] On the other hand, the Syrian-Iraqi water protocol of 1990 designated Syria's share of the Euphrates waters at 42 percent and the remaining 58 percent was allocated to Iraq as a fixed annual total percentage.[27] However, these bilateral accords have failed to include basic components of integrated water resources management, namely the exchange of water and land resources data, water quality management, environmental protection, and stakeholder engagement. Indeed, data and information regarding stream flow, water removal, return flow, present water use, land use, and so forth have been generally incomplete and not regularly exchanged between riparian states. This constitutes a major limitation to proper assessment and management of water and land resources in the basin. Furthermore, both treaties failed to address fluctuations in flow, meaning that they contained no clauses referring to the periods of drought that occur frequently in the basin and cause drastic changes in the flow regime that require urgent adjustment to the use of the rivers.[28] The water-sharing protocols also lack an effective organizational backup, at least in the form of joint monitoring of these agreements.

River basin organizations or technical water committees that might serve as platforms for the accommodation of water conflicts largely do not exist in the MENA region, and, if they do, they are unable to fulfill their mandate. In the early 1980s, the Euphrates-Tigris basin riparians managed to build an institutional framework, namely the Joint Technical Committee (J.T.C.), whose members included participants from all three riparians.[29] Yet, they couldn't succeed to empower the committee with a clear and jointly agreed mandate. Instead, the riparian countries continued unilateral and uncoordinated water and land development ventures. The J.T.C. meetings did not make an effective contribution to the settlement of the transboundary water dispute, and it did not provide a platform for delineating the co-riparians' priorities and needs as a basis for addressing regional water problems. In this respect, water use patterns and the riparians' related legislation and institutional structures never had a chance of being discussed at the J.T.C. meetings. National management and allocation policies were like "black boxes," and water management practices within the various countries simply could not be debated during those negotiations.[30]

On the other hand, there have been considerable cooperative efforts in the Nile River Basin, culminating in the founding of the Nile Basin Initiative (N.B.I.) in 1999.[31] Under the auspices of the N.B.I., there have been many cooperative projects and negotiations to devise a Cooperative Framework Agreement (2010), which has so far been signed by six countries and ratified by three.[32]

So, despite the fact that there remain bilateral disputes over water-sharing (e.g., between Egypt and Ethiopia), there have been credible efforts to reach a joint management scheme for the entire river basin. Even regarding the status of the most controversial project, namely the Grand Ethiopian Renaissance Dam, the three concerned riparians (Egypt, Ethiopia, and Sudan) started consultations in 2011, which culminated in the establishment of the International Panel of Experts (I.P.O.E.) in May 2012. Based on the recommendations of the I.P.O.E., the three countries agreed to carry out selected specialized studies to quantify impacts and support the formulation of dam filling and operation guidelines.[33] Subsequently, the three countries signed the Declaration of Principles (D.o.P.) on March 23, 2015, the core of which involves the agreement by the three countries to formulate and agree on the first dam filling and operation guidelines and rules.[34] Years of deliberations in N.B.I. fora have helped the parties, first, to understand each other's concerns, and, second, to know each other better and thereby more effectively manage the rigor of such negotiations. However, despite the progress achieved by these cooperative institutions, these initiatives could not operationalize the globally agreed principles of customary international law, namely "the equitable reasonable utilization," "the obligation not to cause significant harm," and "the principle of protection and conservation of the river's ecosystem." All these principles have been referred to as the main constituents of cooperative framework agreements and institutions, yet the riparians have not been successful in putting them into practice and replacing the 1959 agreement.

Notwithstanding the failures in interstate water cooperation, as well as the shortcomings and loopholes in existing water agreements, the present overarching challenge in the MENA region is to coordinate water resource management and to establish transboundary water cooperation in the midst of the current state of affairs. That is to say, the turmoil in Syria and instability in Iraq, which have had deep impacts and spill-over effects on their neighbors, demonstrate that, while the genesis of these conflicts have complicated narratives, water is a key part of them. The depletion of lakes and rivers, the lack of clean water to drink, and the loss of livelihood for farmers and fishermen dependent on these water resources are integral parts of these conflicts. With the rising violence and instability in the region, and with no regional coordination and poor security schemes along the rivers themselves, violent non-state actors, namely ISIS, have been able to use water as both a resource and a weapon. Not only have they destroyed water-related infrastructure, such as pipes, sanitation plants, bridges, and cables connected to water installations, but they have also used water as an instrument of violence by deliberately flooding towns, polluting bodies of water, and ruining local economies by disrupting electricity generation and agriculture. To illustrate, in 2014, when the group shut down Fallujah's Nuaimiyah Dam, the subsequent flooding destroyed 77 square miles of Iraqi fields and villages.[35] In June 2015, they closed the Ramadi Barrage in Anbar Province, reducing water flows to the famed Iraqi marshes and forcing the Arabs living there to flee. The Mosul Dam gave ISIS control of nearly 20 percent of Iraq's electricity generation while it was in the group's possession for a few weeks in August 2014.[36] Furthermore, since the civil war erupted in Syria, ISIS has seized the opportunity to control territory in the conflicted region by joining the fight against the Assad regime.[37] By the end of 2012, ISIS controlled all of the country's major dams, including the Tabaqa Dam, a centerpiece of water management in Syria.[38] ISIS lost the Tishrin Dam, located downstream from Tabaqa, in December 2015 after an alliance of rebel forces carried out major operations in the area.[39] Yet, ISIS still controls swathes of territory on the western bank of the Euphrates River from Raqqa to Jarablus on the border with Turkey.[40] At the same time, governments and militaries have used similar tactics to combat ISIS, closing the gates of dams or attacking water infrastructure under their control. But ISIS fighters are not the only ones hurt by these efforts—the surrounding population suffers too. The Syrian government has been repeatedly accused of withholding water, reducing flows, or closing dam gates during its battles against ISIS or rebel groups, and it has used the denial of clean water as a coercive tactic against many suburbs of Damascus thought to be sympathetic to the rebels. Water contamination then becomes widespread, with disastrous results and an increase in deadly water-borne diseases.[41]

WHERE WILL THE REGION BE IN 2030 WITHOUT COOPERATION?

Water is not just about providing a resource to people, it is also about security on the individual, national, and international levels. Water insecurity will increase in the MENA region if the current situation of minimal water cooperation persists under the disabling conditions of political volatility, economic disintegration, institutional failure, and environmental degradation. A lack of cooperation will precipitate economic decline and worsen the negative impacts of climate change on water resources and socio-economic development.

Despite the recent history of political turbulence, MENA has yet to witness a full-scale war over water, but the danger of such a confrontation is only mounting. So far, Middle Eastern leaders have acted carefully when it has come to taking the risk of waging a war over water, despite strong rhetoric to the contrary. However, this historical pattern might not hold if leaders fail to establish sustainable cooperation over water. That is to say, water has recently become a weapon in sub-state level conflicts in the pivotal transboundary river basins of the region, namely the Euphrates-Tigris river basin. The ongoing spread of ISIS across the basin has led to "violent non-state actors" seizing control of water resources in Syria and Iraq.[42] Continuation of the current situation means prolonged water shortages, causing severe problems for urban and rural people and generating serious agricultural and economic decline. Syria's water crisis has already deepened alongside the civil war; water availability is about half what it was before the crisis began in 2011.[43] In conflict-affected areas, the availability of water per person has decreased to one-third of pre-crisis levels, from 75 to 25 liters per person per day. Treatment of sewage has decreased nationally from 70 percent before the crisis to 35 percent today.[44] Ongoing violence and heavy clashes have caused severe damage to pipelines and other water infrastructure.[45] The International Committee of the Red Cross reporting from Aleppo revealed that water routinely gets cut in both government and rebel-held areas and that different sides continue to exchange blame over who is responsible for the lack of water. A similar situation exists in Damascus, where cutting the water supply has been used as a tactic by warring parties to exert pressure on the other.[46] Water shortages have also been a factor leading to displacement within and migration from the country. Since the eruption of civil war, 4.8 million Syrians have been forced to leave the country, and 6.5 million are internally displaced, making Syria the largest displacement crisis globally.[47]

Economic integration and coherence among MENA states remains weak.[48] This phenomenon has direct reflection in domestic and transboundary water resources management. To illustrate, the riparian states of the Euphrates-Tigris river basin have adopted competitive economic development policies for food and energy security. Water and land resource development projects (i.e., the Southeastern Anatolia Project and the Euphrates Valley Project of Turkey and Syria, respectively) were carried out unilaterally and mainly with a development focus with insufficient care for ecosystem protection. If these actors continue these unilateral, uncoordinated, and competitive water-based economic development projects, their actions will aggravate tensions in the region and lead to prolonged, unsustainable use and management of resources and a loss of ecosystems.[49]

Accessible water resources are unevenly distributed across the globe, with per capita resources particularly low in MENA. Within the region there are significant variations in water availability. Inequality within and between countries, communities, and households means that many people continue to have inadequate access to water. If MENA countries continue to pursue uncoordinated water-based development policies, the depletion of water resources will continue in the region, and by 2030-2040, the region may face severe food shortages.[50]

On the other hand, the studies on climate change show that the surface temperature of the Middle East will increase by 2.5 to 5.5°C in the years to come, causing a 20 percent decrease in precipitation in the region.[51] Water security in terms of accessing enough clean water and sanitation, as well as benefitting from water for economic, social, and cultural development, is in jeopardy due to human-induced climatic changes in MENA. There will be less water available for irrigation, energy production, and domestic and industrial use. Less water in the rivers will also increase the stress on the ecosystems along the rivers. Such events, which could be more frequent and intense in the future, could threaten water availability and food security and may cause further conflicts in the region.

The severe drought in the Euphrates-Tigris basin conveys important messages about what might happen in the MENA region in the future. Policy analysts have previously suggested that the drought played a role in the Syrian unrest, and scientific researchers addressed this as well, saying the drought had a catalytic effect.[52] The uprising in Syria was, in fact, triggered by a series of contextual factors, including, growing poverty caused by rapid economic liberalization and the cancellation of state subsidies after 2005, a growing rural-urban divide, widespread corruption, rising unemployment, the effects of a severe drought between 2006 and 2010, and a lack of political freedom. All these elements are connected and have mutually influenced each other, making it difficult to untangle the importance of different "triggers" or to identify any single one as the definitive cause.[53] With all its complex reasons, the civil war in Syria has caused one of the largest refugee crises in recent world history. There is no doubt that increased efforts are needed to address not only the pressing humanitarian situation, but also the root causes of the refugee crisis. An important number of these causes are found in the nexus between climate change, water scarcity, poor governance, and conflict. Water scarcity, or stress, is not the only driver of migration, but there is, without question, an indirect correlation between climate change, drought, and migration. If unattended by the concerned regional authorities, climate change will aggravate existing social tensions and political instability and will likely add additional pressures on the states and regions that are already fragile and conflict-prone, as in the Syria case.

THE BENEFITS OF REGIONAL COOPERATION

There is an obvious and urgent need for regional water cooperation in the MENA region. In designing such a regional water cooperation framework in the Middle East, it is useful and inspiring to draw lessons from historical and contemporary models that exist in the world, which demonstrate that water and its sustainable management can be an excellent source of cooperation. Many countries around the world have proved that building strong institutions that effectively govern transboundary water resources in a collaborative manner is an effective tool to manage any natural calamity as well as to prevent conflicts based on other factors.[54]

Water issues usually formed an important part of historical peace agreements in Europe. To recall, the Congress of Vienna (1815) established the regime for the Rhine River and the Central Commission for the Navigation of the Rhine.[55] Likewise, the 1856 Paris Agreement established the European Commission on the Danube. Both commissions exist today in their modernized forms and are among the elements of European stability.[56] These historical examples show that there is a close relationship between peace and water cooperation and vice versa.

Contemporary models of regional water cooperation demonstrate that the relationship between water and peace is not only a matter of post-conflict arrangements. Water management is an important instrument for the prevention of conflict. The establishment in 2010 of the Commission on the Administration of the River Uruguay, following the peaceful resolution of a bitter dispute between Argentina and Uruguay, is an example of the political necessity of administrating environmental matters in an effective, preventive manner.[57] Moreover, there exist other initiatives that lay down the foundations for long-term regional cooperation and stability. The Senegal River Basin Organization is probably the most far-reaching arrangement today. The organization controls the water assets in Mali, Senegal, Mauritania, and Guinea and manages them as a "regional common," transcending national interests.[58]

Water cooperation between countries sharing transboundary water resources is directly correlated with the security of nations involved in such cooperation and with peace in the continent or subcontinent to which they belong. The examples of the European Union, which used steel and coal to begin its process of cooperation, and the Southern African Development Community (S.A.D.C.), which used broad economic development as its starting point, clearly indicate that a regional approach is essential. Africans have learned from the European example and expanded on the S.A.D.C. to incorporate a number of other vital aspects, including a common water region for all member countries, even though some of them, such as Madagascar and Malawi, do not share common water resources.[59] These countries have found value in a shared policy framework and use that framework as the basis for negotiating basin-specific agreements. The wisdom demonstrated by countries in Europe and southern Africa can be relevant for those in the Middle East and elsewhere.

Examples of active water cooperation mechanisms indicate that it is not the size and nature of a country or its economy, or its recent history or political markup, but its political will and commitment at the highest level that are the keys to success. There is also no all-encompassing set of formulae for such institutions and mechanisms. Over time, countries and regions have devised their own success stories. Yet, if we look closely, we realize that countries that engage in active water cooperation, which also includes cooperation concerning energy, environment, and other development factors, tend to move beyond their differences on other issues.

In this respect, one productive approach to the cooperative development of transboundary waters in the Middle East should be to take a regional view of the benefits to be derived from the river basins. When negotiations focus solely on water-sharing, upstream and downstream differences will be exacerbated, thereby giving greater prominence to water gains and losses. Taking a broader view of regional benefits has regularly required the riparian states to see water as more than just a commodity to be divided—a zero-sum, rights-based view—and to develop a positive-sum, integrative approach that ensures the equitable allocation not of the water, but of the benefits derived from it. Adding development opportunities in other sectors may enlarge the area of possible agreement and make implementation more manageable. Inter-sectorial linkages may offer more opportunities for the generation of creative solutions, allowing for greater economic efficiency through a "basket of benefits."[60]

There is a possible scope for increasing water cooperation from quantity or quality issues to a broader set of issues and for moving from "sharing water" (i.e. allocating water resources among riparian states) to "sharing the benefits of water" (i.e. managing water resources to achieve the maximum benefit and then allocating those benefits among riparian states, including through compensation mechanisms).[61] There is even greater scope for increasing cooperation by moving from "sharing the benefits of water" to "realizing the broader benefits of water cooperation," such as greater economic integration in the region. Those benefits can be realized by accelerating economic growth, increasing human wellbeing, enhancing environmental sustainability, and contributing to political stability and peace.

One of the factors often hindering better regional water cooperation is the lack of recognition of the benefits of cooperation. Countries generally cooperate when the net benefits of cooperation are perceived to be greater than the net benefits of non-cooperation, as well as when the distribution of these net benefits is perceived to be fair. The decision-makers in the ministries responsible for the environment, water resources, economics, and foreign affairs should realize the potential of regional water cooperation by providing an overview of the full set of benefits that can be exploited, an introduction to how the specific benefits can be assessed, as well as a guide on how the assessment of such benefits can be integrated into policymaking processes. A holistic approach to transboundary water cooperation should be adopted by looking at the environmental, social, and economic implications of water use.

Regional water cooperation, through improved water management, generates a range of economic, social, and environmental benefits. Although comprehensive identification, assessment, and implementation remains a challenge, most of those benefits are well-known in the water policy community, such as developing hydropower, producing food by irrigated agriculture, supplying water to urban and rural communities, as well as flood control and drought management. Below, Table 1 demonstrates the diversity of economic, social, and environmental benefits that can be derived from improved water management under a regional water cooperation framework. Moreover, it also displays how regional water cooperation could foster regional economic integration and generate peace and security benefits from enhanced trust.

TABLE 1. POTENTIAL BENEFITS OF REGIONAL WATER COOPERATION

	ON ECONOMIC ACTIVITIES	BEYOND ECONOMIC ACTIVITIES
FROM IMPROVED WATER MANAGEMENT	ECONOMIC BENEFITS EXPANDED ACTIVITY AND PRODUCTIVITY IN ECONOMIC SECTORS (IRRIGATED AGRICULTURE, ENERGY GENERATION, INDUSTRIAL PRODUCTION) REDUCED COST OF CARRYING OUT PRODUCTIVE ACTIVITIES REDUCED ECONOMIC IMPACTS OF WATER-RELATED HAZARDS (FLOODS, DROUGHTS)	SOCIAL AND ENVIRONMENTAL BENEFITS HEALTH IMPACTS FROM IMPROVED WATER QUALITY AND REDUCED RISK OF WATER-RELATED DISASTERS. EMPLOYMENT AND REDUCED POVERTY IMPACTS IMPROVED ACCESS TO SERVICES (SUCH AS ELECTRICITY AND WATER SUPPLY) AVOIDED HABITAT DEGRADATION AND BIODIVERSITY LOSS
FROM ENHANCED TRUST	REGIONAL ECONOMIC INTEGRATION BENEFITS DEVELOPMENT OF REGIONAL MARKETS FOR GOODS, SERVICES, AND LABOR INCREASE IN CROSS-BORDER INVESTMENTS DEVELOPMENT OF TRANSNATIONAL INFRASTRUCTURE NETWORKS	PEACE AND SECURITY BENEFITS ABILITY TO AVOID COSTS OF MILITARY CONFLICTS SAVINGS FROM REDUCED MILITARY SPENDING OTHER GEO-POLITICAL BENEFITS

SOURCE: "COUNTING OUR GAINS: SHARING EXPERIENCES ON IDENTIFYING, ASSESSING AND COMMUNICATING THE BENEFITS OF TRANSBOUNDARY WATER COOPERATION," POLICY GUIDANCE NOTE, 2014, ACCESSED AUGUST 29, 2016, HTTP://WWW.UNECE.ORG/ENV/WATER/WORKSHOP_BENEFITS_COOPERATION_2014.HTML#/

WHERE COULD THE REGION BE IN 2030 IN A SCENARIO INVOLVING SIGNIFICANT REGIONAL WATER COOPERATION?

In order to design a modus operandi for a mechanism for regional water cooperation in the MENA region, one simply has to look back at the recent past. In 2010, in a historic series of meetings, proactive leaders of four countries in the Middle East, (Turkey, Syria, Jordan, and Lebanon) came together and forged ties for the creation of a future economic regional community. They had a vision to create a European Union for the Middle East and call it "Shamgen," named after Syria's historical name "al-Sham," which stretched from Mesopotamia to the Eastern Mediterranean. Their vision would cover trade and transport, oversee banking and business laws, eliminate visa constraints, allow for the free movement of goods, and provide a new future for the people in the region. The international community lauded their efforts and was eager to aid in these endeavors. There was talk that the community and union could further expand in the future to cover other aspects of governance and life, such as water resource management, and could continue to grow in the future. The leaders of the four countries intricately connected by common history, people, and resources also invited Iraq to join in their journey. This invitation was born out of a realization that Iraq was closely linked to three of the countries in the "Shamgen zone." It was expected that Iraq would join once it solved its internal constitutional constraints.

While, in view of the political volatility since 2011, such cooperation may appear to be a dream; the situation was different in the second half of 2010. The decision taken by the leaders in June 2010 to promote regional integration was promptly implemented through various policy measures, mechanisms, and arrangements within a few months. The countries' leaders called for region-wide cooperation on transport, banking, trade, and other sectors and could have laid the foundation for further agreements on the distribution of regional natural resources like water. Though ambitious, the ideas and sentiments behind the proposals had the power to transform that pivotal MENA sub-region.

No matter how bleak the future might look, the "Shamgen" experiment of 2010 clearly demonstrates that cooperation is possible. As soon as the next window of opportunity opens, the five countries, including Iraq, will have to demonstrate the same vision and foresight so as to create new means of cooperation. In fact, there is no alternative to cooperation.

Another attempt for cooperation over water resources is still in the process in the Nile basin. Egypt and Ethiopia, who had been locked in a bitter war of words over Ethiopia's Grand Renaissance Dam project, managed to sign a deal (D.o.P.) in 2015 that paved the way for a joint approach to regional water supplies. The agreement included giving priority to downstream countries for electricity generated by the dam, a mechanism for resolving conflicts, and the provision of compensation for damages. Signatories also pledged to protect the interests of downstream countries when the dam's reservoir is filled. The deal is important because it appears to mark a move away from Egypt's historical insistence on maintaining colonial-era agreements on water rights.[62] The Ethiopians also argue that the dam will transform their country, where only around one-third of the population has access to electricity, into a major electricity exporter to East Africa—raising living standards, spurring economic growth, and moving beyond a history of drought and famine.[63] Yet, still, the overarching management challenges in the Nile basin are poverty, water scarcity, and variability on the one hand, and weak relations between and political instability within many of the riparian states on the other. Since 1999, the N.B.I. has operated in the basin to manage basin activities, such as planning transboundary water projects that have the potential to transform food, water, and energy security. In order to reach a sustainable, efficient, and equitable water future in this vast sub-region of the MENA region, its members should clearly empower the N.B.I. to become a forum for joint planning, management, and development of the transboundary water resources.

In the Jordan River basin, where transboundary water relations have always been a bone of contention, a cooperative spirit has emerged recently through creative ideas on innovative joint water development and management. Israel, Jordan, and the Palestinian Authority have been moving ahead, in a cooperative mood, with a plan to build a water-carrying canal from the Red Sea to the Dead Sea, which will rehabilitate the shrinking Dead Sea and supply drinking water to Israelis, Jordanians and Palestinians.[64] Yet, the project is not without problems. The Friends of the Earth Middle East (F.o.E.M.E.), a leading N.G.O. in the region, and other environmental groups have countered that the mega-project was fatally flawed from the outset. They argue that the only sustainable solution is to tackle the source of the problem by rehabilitating the Jordan River, which, since time immemorial, has fed the Dead Sea with fresh water. Such freshwater is now singularly lacking because of massive diversions in the form of dams, canals, and pumping stations constructed by Israel, Syria, Jordan, and the Palestinian Authority alike.[65] On the other hand, F.o.E.M.E. commissioned an interesting scientific proposal, which evidently demonstrated that Israelis and Palestinians can reach an agreement over the use of water resources even before they solve other thorny issues and can, thus, create a precedent for cooperation on a contentious matter. According to this proposal, new bilateral committees (instead of the problematic Joint Water Committee created by the

Oslo Accords) would determine water allocation not by fixed quotas, as is the case now, but rather according to guidelines designed to protect the ecosystem and to benefit all. It would make key decisions on rates of pumping and transport of water based on advice from a subsidiary scientific body, which would operate under the auspices of the Palestinian Authority and Israel. A mediation board would deal with any complaints by groups opposing the decisions made by the new bodies. The proposal's main goal is to provide water to all parties and to secure efficient, equitable, and sustainable management of shared resources over the long term. The proposal serves interests on both sides, because it will ensure that the Palestinians receive more water and that the water used by Israel will be of good quality.[66]

The MENA region, in fact, represents a diverse set of sub-regions, such as the Gulf. The natural features and climates of the Gulf states are similar, with each state having extremely arid climates with negligible precipitation. Natural water sources are scarce, and arable land is extremely limited. Human factors, such as high population growth, rapid urbanization, and gigantic industrial and agricultural projects exacerbate the pressure on already strained water-supply systems. The Gulf states have had little choice but to secure alternative (un-conventional) water supplies. The most important of these alternatives are the desalination plants in the Gulf, which, as of 2014, accounted for some 70 percent of the world's desalinated water output. However, dependence on desalination has placed a severe strain on the national budgets of the Gulf states and has caused irreparable damage to local and regional ecosystems.[67] What Gulf countries need is a broad strategy for addressing water security that does not simply rely on energy export revenues to finance short-term solutions to the problem. They should strive to create a more conscientious society through environmental and social awareness campaigns and education programs. Investment in water recycling for irrigation and municipal use presents a great opportunity for reducing the demand for desalinated water. Furthermore, research and development in renewable energy for desalinization may provide sustainable, long-term fixes. Other creative solutions include the construction of dams that would improve rain capture and groundwater recharge and the use of cloud seeding to enhance rainfall. While there may be no quick fix, a competent strategy to tackle water security from both the supply and demand side is necessary for ensuring that the economic development that has defined this region in the previous decades continues for years to come.[68]

Water cooperation in the MENA region does not develop overnight or even in the space of a few months; it takes time and requires a great deal of trust. The necessary change, involving various cooperative initiatives, is closely and intimately related to the change in overall political relations, with decisions being made at the highest level. However, the recent initiatives and efforts for water cooperation, particularly in the pivotal transboundary river basins of the region, are important steps in the right direction and have the potential to create long-lasting relationships between nations that can expand into other areas. Experiences from around the world demonstrate that countries that have achieved regional water cooperation have prospered together and kept the threat of conflict a remote possibility. It is time for the countries in the Middle East to realize that there is no alternative to sustainable water cooperation and to take the necessary steps to sail together in that direction.

ENDNOTES

1. "Water Sector Brief," The World Bank, September 2010, accessed August 29, 2016, http://siteresources.worldbank.org/INTMNAREGTOPWATRES/Resources/Water_Sector_Brief--Fall2010.pdf.

2. "General Summary Middle East Region," Food and Agriculture Organization of the United Nations, 2009, accessed August 29, 2016, http://www.fao.org/nr/water/aquastat/countries_regions/meast/index.stm#a3.

3. J. S. Pal and E. A. B. Eltahir, "Future Temperature in Southwest Asia Projected to Exceed a Threshold for Human Adaptability," Nature Climate Change 6 (2016): 197–200.

4. P. H. Gleick, "Water, Drought, Climate Change, and Conflict in Syria," Wea. Climate Soc. 6 (2014): 331–340.

5. M. Lowi, Water and Power (Cambridge: Cambridge University Press, 1995).

6. S. Lonergan, "Human Security, Environmental Security and Sustainable Development," in Environment and Security, eds. M. Lowi and B. Shaw (Macmillan Press, 2000).

7. Ibid., 78.

8. Ibid., 79.

9. Human Development Report, United Nations Development Programme (UNDP), 2006.

10. Somini Sengupta, "In Israel and Lebanon, Talk of War Over Water," The New York Times, October 16, 2002, accessed August 29, 2016, http://www.nytimes.com/2002/10/16/world/in-israel-and-lebanon-talk-of-war-over-water.html.

11. J. Waterbury, "Legal and institutional arrangements for managing water resources in the Nile Basin," International Journal of Water Resources Development 3, no. 2 (1987): 92-104.

12. S. Dinar, "Geopolitics of Hydropolitics: Negotiations over Water in the Middle East and North Africa," SAIS Working Paper Series No. WP/01/03 (2003).

13. L. Raus, "Resolving the Egypt-Ethiopia Nile Dispute: Actions for Moving Forward," Egypt Oil and Gas Newspaper 80 (2013).

14. A. Kibaroglu, 2002, Building a Regime for the Waters of the Euphrates-Tigris River Basin (London: Kluwer Law International, 2002).

15. Ibid., 226, 229-230.

16. A. Kibaroglu, "Socioeconomic development and benefit sharing in the Euphrates-Tigris river basin," in eds. Shuval H, Dweik H (Berlin: Springer, 2007): 185-193.

17. W. Scheumann, "The Euphrates Issue in Turkish-Syrian Relations," in Security and Environment in the Mediterranean: Conceptualising Security and Environmental Conflicts, eds. H. G. Brauch, P. H. Liotta, S. Marquina, P. F. Rogers, M. El-Sayed Selim (Berlin: Springer, 2003).

18. J. Selby, "The Geopolitics of Water in the Middle East: Fantasies and Realities," Third World Quarterly 26, no. 2 (2005), 329-49; S. Lonergan, "Human Security, Environmental Security and Sustainable Development," 79; Lowi, Water and Power.

19. In 1953 when Israel started the construction of the National Water Carrier, the project quickly led to armed skirmishes with Syria. President Eisenhower, realizing that the water conflict could develop into a new war, sent a special envoy, Eric Johnston, to the region in 1953 in order to gain the support of the four basin states of the Jordan for one distribution plan. After two years of negotiation, Johnston achieved a compromise (the Unified Plan): the negotiating teams accepted it, but their governments did not. See S. Libiszewski, "Integrating Political and Technical Approaches: Lessons from the Israeli-Jordanian Water Negotiations," in Conflict and the Environment, eds N. Gleditsch et al, (Kluwer Academic Publishers, 1997): 385-402.

20. A. Jagerskog, "Why States Cooperate over Shared Water," Unpublished Doctoral Dissertation, Linköping University, 2003.

21. For a critique of the Oslo Process, see J. Selby, "Dressing-up domination as cooperation: The Case of Israeli-Palestinian Water Relations," Review of International Studies 29, no. 1 (2003): 121-38.

22. H. Donkers, "Fresh Water as a Source of International Conflicts," 155.

23. Human Development Report, United Nations Development Programme (UNDP), 2006.

24. Ibid. 156.

25. J. A. Allan, "Hydro-Peace in the Middle East: Why no Water Wars? A Case-study of the Jordan River Basin", SAIS Review 22, no. 2 (2002).

26. "Protocol on Matters Pertaining to Economic Cooperation Between the Republic of Turkey and the Syrian Arab Republic," United Nations Treaty Series 87/12171, July 17, 1987.

27. Law No. 14 of 1990, ratifying the joint minutes concerning the provisional division of the waters of the Euphrates River, accessed August 29, 2016, http://ocid.nacse.org/qml/research / tfdd/toTFDDdocs/257ENG.htm.

28. M. Schiffler, "International Water Agreements: A Comparative View," in Water in the Middle East: Potential for Conflicts and Prospects for Cooperation, eds. W. Scheumann and M. Schiffler (New York: Springer, 1998): 31–45.

29. Turkish Ministry of Foreign Affairs, "Water Issues Between Turkey, Syria and Iraq," Perceptions: Journal of International Affairs 1 (1996).

30. A. Kibaroglu and W. Scheumann, "Evolution of Transboundary Politics in the Euphrates-Tigris River System: New Perspectives and Political Challenges" Global Governance 19, no. 2 (2013): 279-307.

31. "About Us," Nile Basin Initiative, accessed August 29, 2016, http://www.nilebasin.org/.

32. Ibid.

33. "International Panel of Experts for Ethiopian Renaissance Dam Final Report," International Rivers, accessed August 29, 2016, http://www.internationalrivers.org/files/attached-files/international_panel_of_experts_for_ethiopian_renaissance_dam-_final_report_1.pdf.

34. "Full Text of 'Declaration of Principles' signed by Egypt, Sudan and Ethiopia," Ahram Online, March 23, 2015, accessed August 29, 2016, http://english.ahram.org.eg/News/125941.aspx.

35. A. Vishwanath, "The Water Wars Waged by the Islamic State," Global Affairs (2015), accessed August 29, 2016, https://www.stratfor.com/weekly/water-wars-waged-islamic-state.

36. Alex Milner, "Mosul Dam: Why the Battle for Water Matters in Iraq," BBC, August 18, 2014, accessed August 29, 2016, http://www.bbc.com/news/world-middle-east-28772478.

37. A. S. Hashim, "The Islamic State: From al-Qaeda Affiliate to Caliphate," Middle East Policy (2014).

38. W. Hussein, "How IS uses water as weapon of war," Al Monitor, May 11, 2015, accessed August 29, 2016, http://www.al-monitor.com/pulse/en/originals/2015/05/arab-world-water-conflict-isis-control-war.html.

39. Simon Tomlinson, "Bomb us if you dare: Senior ISIS militants are holed up inside Syria's largest dam with high-value prisoners knowing air strikes would unleash apocalyptic flood," Daily Mail, January 22, 2016, accessed August 29, 2016, http://www.dailymail.co.uk/news/article-3412205/Bomb-dare-Senior-ISIS-militants-holed-Syria-s-largest-dam-high-value-prisoners-knowing-air-strikes-unleash-apocalyptic-flood.html.

40. T. von Losso, "Water as Weapon: IS on the Euphrates and Tigris" ISN, Center for Security Studies (2016).

41. Vishwanath, "The Water Wars Waged by the Islamic State," Global Affairs.

42. Ibid.

43. "Red Cross: Water Being Used as Weapon of War in Syria," Al Jazeera, September 2, 2015, accessed August 29, 2016, http://www.aljazeera.com/news/2015/09/red-cross-water-weapon-war-syria-150902114347090.html.

44. "Running Dry: Water and Sanitation Crisis Threatens Syrian Children," UNICEF, February 2013, accessed August 29, 2016, http://www.unicef.org/mena/Syria_Crisis_WASH-Syria-Feb-2013-En.pdf.

45. "Severe Water Shortages Compound the Mistery of Millions in War-torn Syria - says UNICEF," UNICEF, August 25, 2015, accessed August 29, 2016, http://www.unicef.org/media/media_82980.html.

46. "Syria: Five years of war. For how much longer?" International Committee of the Red Cross, March 15, 2016, accessed August 29, 2016, https://www.icrc.org/en/document/syria-five-years-war-how-much-longer.

47. "Syrian Arab Republic," United Nations Office for the Coordination of Humanitarian Affairs, accessed August 29, 2016, http://www.unocha.org/syria.

48. S. Kalaycioglu, "Regional Economic Co-operation in the Middle East," Perceptions: Journal of International Affairs 1, no. 3 (1996), accessed August 29, 2016, http://sam.gov.tr/wp-content/uploads/2012/01/7.-REGIONAL-ECONOMIC-COOPERATION-IN-THE-MIDDLE-EAST.pdf.

49. A. Kibaroglu and S. I. Gursoy, "Water–energy–food nexus in a transboundary context: the Euphrates–Tigris river basin as a case study,"

Water International 40 (2015): 5-6.

50. "The state of food and agriculture, Food systems for better nutrition," Food and Agriculture Organization of the United Nations, 2013, accessed August 29, 2016.

51. M. Collins, et al., "Long-term Climate Change: Projections, Commitments and Irreversibility," in: Climate Change 2013: The Physical Science Basis. Contribution of Working Group I to the Fifth Assessment Report of the Intergovernmental Panel on Climate Change, eds. Stocker, et al., (Cambridge: Cambridge University Press, 2013), accessed August 29, 2016, http://www.climatechange2013.org/images/report/WG1AR5_Chapter12_FINAL.pdf.

52. P. Gleick, "Water, Drought, Climate Change, and Conflict in Syria," Weather, Climate and Society 6 (2014): 331–340.

53. F. de Châtel, "The Role of Drought and Climate Change in the Syrian Uprising: Untangling the Triggers of the Revolution," Middle Eastern Studies 50, no. 4 (2014): 521-35.

54. A. Vishwanath, A. Kibaroglu and Y. Ahmmad, "The Blue Peace: Achieving Peace and Security though Water Cooperation," Insight Turkey 17, no. 1 (2015): 41-49.

55. "Organisation," Central Commission for the Navigation of the Rhine, accessed August 29, 2016, http://www.ccr-zkr.org/.

56. "About Us," International Commission for the Protection of the Danube, accessed August 29, 2016, https://www.icpdr.org/main/icpdr/about-us ; "Welcome," International Commission for the Protection of the Rhine," accessed August 29, 2016, http://www.iksr.org/en/index.html.

57. "Home" Commission on the Administration of the River Uruguay, accessed August 29, 2016, http://www.caru.org.uy/web/.

58. D. Turk, "Global High Level Panel on Water and Peace Statement," Chairman of the Panel November 15-16, 2015, Geneva, Switzerland, on file with the author.

59. "About SADC," Southern aFrican Development Community, accessed August 29, 2016, http://www.sadc.int/.

60. A. T. Wolf, "Criteria for equitable allocations: The heart of international water conflict," Natural Resources Forum 23, no. 1 (1999): 3-30.

61. C. W. Sadoff and D. Grey, "Beyond the river: benefits of cooperation on international rivers," Water Policy 4 (2002): 389-403.

62. "Egypt, Ethiopia, Sudan sign new deal on Nile dam," Al Jazeera, December 30, 2015, accessed August 29, 2016, http://www.aljazeera.com/news/2015/12/egypt-ethiopia-sudan-sign-deal-nile-dam-151230105650388.html.

63. C. MacDiarmid, "Hydro-diplomacy on the Nile," Al Jazeera, March 10, 2016, accessed August 29, 2016, http://www.aljazeera.com/news/2015/03/hydro-diplomacy-nile-150309092540029.html.

64. The multinational proposal is to build a 180 km pipeline engineered to carry up to two billion cubic meters of seawater per year from the Gulf of Aqaba on the Dead Sea through Jordanian territory to the Red Sea.

65. J. Josephs, "Green Light For Red-Dead Sea Pipeline Project," WaterWorld 28, no. 6 (2015), accessed August 29, 2016, http://www.waterworld.com/articles/wwi/print/volume-28/issue-6/technology-case-studies/water-provision/green-light-for-red-dead-sea-pipeline-project.html.

66. D. B. Brooks and J. Trottier, "An Agreement To Share Water Between Israelies and Palestinians: The FoEME Proposal - Revised Version," EcoPeace/Friends of the Earth Middle East, March 2012, accessed august 29, 2016, http://foeme.org/uploads/13411307571~%5E$%5E~Water_Agreement_FINAL.pdf.

67. T. Al-Farra, "Water Security in the Gulf Region," Al Jazeera Centre for Studies, March 31, 2016, accessed August 29, 2016, http://studies.aljazeera.net/en/dossiers/2015/03/20153318534835257.html.

68. R. El Houry, "The Gulf Countries' Water Crises," Muftah, May 9, 2011, accessed August 29, 2016, http://muftah.org/the-gulf-countries-water-crisis/#.VxEjfZMrIgo.

CHAPTER NINE

MILITARY COOPERATION IN THE MIDDLE EAST:

UNCERTAINTY IN THE FACE OF CHANGING THREATS

ANTHONY H. CORDESMAN

INTRODUCTION

The rhetoric of security cooperation is easy to forge and equally easy to ignore unless there is a common perception of the threat, a willingness to act, and the creation of effective security efforts and forces. Success is dependent on the priorities states give to various threats, the willingness of given regimes to act, the resources they develop and have available, and the level of interoperability between their forces.

In practice, almost all real world security cooperation is based on coalitions of the willing and capable, regardless of whether the cooperation is designed to provide leverage, deter, contain, fight, or reach some form of resolution to a conflict. Cooperation for one set of goals may not mean cooperation for others. For example, opposing the same threat or enemy does not mean the same interests exist in shaping the outcome of a conflict. The uneasy coalitions and efforts at cooperation on all sides of the Syrian and Iraqi conflicts are good cases in point. Iran and Russia may ultimately differ as much over the outcome of the fighting in Syria as the United States and Iran do in Iraq.

Formal agreements and institutions can help create the conditions that make such cooperation possible and effective, but many effective alliances are shaped in response to specific threats and challenges and have meaning only to the degree that partners are capable of given levels of action.

The Gulf Cooperation Council, for example, has made progress over the years, but that progress has been slow and limited. The U.S. and Saudi-led coalition, which was forged in response to Saddam Hussein's invasion of Kuwait, had to be created quickly to deal with a specific contingency and was shaped by the existing politics and military capabilities of the countries involved. Its key elements proved remarkably effective, while less committed nations like Egypt and Syria moved slowly or not at all.

Ambitious efforts like the Baghdad Pact, Arab League, and United Arab Republic all collapsed under the pressure of events, and even initially successful alliances like that of the Egyptian-Syrian invasion of the Sinai and Golan in 1973 collapsed once Egypt and Syria faced different combat priorities and set different goals.

THE CURRENT LEVEL OF REAL WORLD SECURITY COOPERATION

Today, the most important aspects of real world security cooperation in the MENA region are driven by different coalitions fighting on different sides of the conflicts in Syria, Iraq, and Yemen. The Syrian war now involves two separate coalitions that are fighting ISIS and each other. One involves the Assad regime, Iran, Russia, and the Lebanese Hezbollah. The other involves some 40 different Syrian Arab rebel forces, Syrian Kurdish forces, a U.S.-led air coalition with European and Arab participants, Turkey, and a diverse mixture of U.S., European, Saudi, U.A.E., and Qatari ground forces and advisors. Cooperation within each coalition is limited at best: there are no clear common strategic goals on either side, and each actor pursues somewhat different goals and tactics.

Iraq involves even more diverse forms of security cooperation. ISIS is the primary enemy, but the same U.S.-led air coalition that operates against ISIS and Jabhat Fateh al-Sham (formerly Jabhat al-Nusra) in Syria also flies against ISIS in Iraq. The United States and Iran operate in parallel in supporting Iraqi government and militia ground forces while competing for influence over Iraq. Canada and European countries also provide special forces and other "train and assist" elements. Turkey opposes Syria's Kurds—which have strong U.S. backing—but cooperates with Iraqi Kurds. Iraqi forces are deeply divided between central government elements that are largely Shiite and various Kurdish, Shiite, and Sunni militias, with only limited central government coordination. The Arab Gulf states provide some backing to selected Sunni tribal elements. Once again, there are no clear common strategic goals, and every side looks toward future competition for power and influence once (and if) ISIS is defeated.

Two key military powers—Israel and Egypt—stand outside the broader structure of regional cooperation, although both cooperate informally with other regional states. Israel's ties are largely to the United States, its principal source of aid. Egypt is also heavily dependent on U.S. military aid, but is now deeply involved in a struggle to create an authoritarian military regime that can secure its own power against internal resistance and threats.

Regional security cooperation in North Africa is limited at best, although Egypt does play a limited role in aiding Tunisia and seeking to secure its border with Libya. Algeria and Morocco continue to feud over the Western Sahara and Polisario, and North African security cooperation is shaped largely by the role that the United States and Europe play in individually supporting Morocco, Tunisia, and Egypt.

There is no effective security cooperation within North Africa. Israel, Egypt, and Jordan cooperate relatively effectively in securing their border areas and in some aspects of counterterrorism, but there is no overt cooperation in broader military terms among the states in the Levant. Instead, cooperation (and non-cooperation) is heavily shaped by the ties Israel, Egypt, and Jordan have to the United States and by the role of state and non-state actors in the Syrian civil war.

In the case of the Gulf, the G.C.C. remains a relatively weak structure with important divisions between its members, particularly between Saudi Arabia and Oman. The G.C.C. talks about security cooperation, but that is largely a façade with little real world cooperation or effective efforts to create interoperability or common intelligence, reconnaissance, training, and support facilities. U.S. bilateral cooperation with individual Gulf states is generally more critical than the loose security cooperation between G.C.C. states, although Saudi Arabia and the U.A.E. have increasingly emerged as effective partners in dealing with Iran and the war in Yemen.

U.S. forward deployments and power projection capabilities underpin and dominate security cooperation in dealing with Iran, in building up Arab forces and ensuring Israeli military capability, and in developing real world cooperation in counterterrorism—where most regional states will only share limited intelligence data and cooperate largely in terms of border security.

Britain and France still provide arms and power projection capabilities that can aid North African, Levantine, and Gulf states but suffer from a lack of resources. At the same time, trust in the U.S. willingness to stay, and to remain aligned with Arab powers, is uncertain, and Saudi Arabia has sought to reduce its dependence on the United States. Saudi Arabia has focused on developing a close partnership with the U.A.E. and has sought to create a coalition to support its war in support of the government of Yemen against the Houthi rebels and pro-Saleh forces. As of mid-2016, this coalition was largely one of Saudi-U.A.E. forces backed by U.S. intelligence, targeting aid, and naval forces.

Saudi Arabia also began in December 2015 an attempt to create a broader Arab coalition of some 35 of the 57 countries in the Organization of Islamic Cooperation (O.I.C.) to fight terrorism, but this coalition too has remained more a façade than a reality. Like the G.C.C., however, it is far easier to create the façade of common purpose than actual military cooperation in the field or in building an effective level of deterrence. As the G.C.C. has discovered since its founding, words are cheap and easy. Actual force deployments, participation in combat, interoperability, standardization, common support and logistic structures, and integrated operations and battle management are difficult, expensive, and often impossible to achieve.

Iran is seen as the leading military threat by the Arab Gulf states, Israel, and the United States. It currently cooperates with the Syrian government, Hezbollah, and Russia in the war in Syria and with the Iraqi central government and Shiite militias in Iraq. Its Islamic Revolutionary Guards Forces, Al Quds Force, and intelligence services (M.O.I.S.) have been increasingly effective in expanding Iranian security influence and "security cooperation." They play a role in supporting Shiite and Palestinian militant movements in Bahrain, Kuwait, Gaza, and Yemen.

Looking Toward the Future

It is all too easy to develop ambitious plans to change this situation, to try to strengthen the G.C.C. or create broader Arab coalitions, to find ways to avoid reliance on outside powers, or even to suggest security structures that would somehow include Iran and its Arab neighbors. In practice, however, real security cooperation is driven largely by either mutual necessity or the evolution of meaningful political ties. A truly moderate regime in Iran, for example, could dramatically change the nature of regional security cooperation, as could the emergence of a new, ISIS-like threat of a takeover in a state or region. Such developments are always possible. None, however, currently seem predictable or probable.

Even ISIS has failed to generate effective real world cooperation. Saudi Arabia, Jordan, Qatar, the U.A.E., and Kuwait have all dealt with Syrian Arab rebel forces in different ways and have differed over how to deal with the Iraqi government and ISIS in Iraq. Intelligence sharing is limited, and counterterrorism efforts are largely national. Efforts to deal with ideological threats are also largely done by individual states with different priorities. The priorities given to other extremist movements like Jabhat Fateh al-Sham and al-Qaeda in the Arabian Peninsula (A.Q.A.P.) are equally diverse.

In what may be a very long interim, the key questions for the future revolve around how today's real world relations will evolve, and much will depend on the level of change in the threats and the patterns of regional conflict. Several key sets of variables are involved—all of which could substantially change the nature of security cooperation in the region by 2030:

- The evolution of the ongoing conflicts in Syria, Iraq, and Yemen
- How ISIS, Jabhat Fateh al-Sham, A.Q.A.P., and similar violent Islamist extremist movements evolve over time
- The level of continued U.S. strategic and military involvement in the region; U.S. bilateral and multilateral cooperation with given states; and U.S. involvement in supporting Morocco, Tunisia, Egypt, Israel, Lebanon, Jordan, Bahrain, Iraq, Kuwait, Oman, Qatar, Saudi Arabia, the U.A.E., and Yemen
- The extent to which Britain, France, Italy, and other European states will play a real world power projection role in the Mediterranean, North Africa, and the Gulf
- The role Russia will play in Syria, Iran, and other regional states, both in terms of an actual presence and in terms of technology transfer and arms sales
- China's role in technology transfers and arms sales and its interest and capability in playing a role in the Indian Ocean, Gulf region, and Red Sea
- How the civil war in Libya plays out, the future stability of Tunisia, the extent to which tensions between Morocco and Algeria become more serious, and the role Egypt plays in North Africa
- The extent to which Israeli-Palestinian tensions and conflicts reemerge as a major factor affecting the attitudes and behavior of Arab states
- Whether and how an end takes place to the civil war in Syria, the conflict with ISIS in both Syria and Iraq, and Iraq's future alignment with Iran and other powers
- Iran's willingness to accept the terms of the J.C.P.O.A.; its success in gaining strategic influence in Lebanon, Syria, Iraq, and Yemen; its ability to create modern and highly effective ballistic and cruise missile forces with precision strike capability with conventional warheads; and its ability to increase its air asymmetric naval missile threat to maritime traffic in and near the Persian Gulf, the Gulf of Oman, and possibly the Red Sea

> ➤ The success of the Saudi-U.A.E. alliance in the war in Yemen, and the extent to which Yemen does or does not remain a threat to Saudi Arabia and the Gulf states or becomes tied to Iran

All of these variables interact to some extent, but there is little reason to assume that the outcome is going to be more favorable for broad efforts at regional cooperation than in the past. There seems to be little prospect of these factors resulting in any broad regional architecture. External powers beyond the region are likely to play just as critical a role in the future as in the past, and real world security cooperation will be driven largely by events and the need to form "coalitions of the willing" to deal with specific threats.

The three major exceptions would be: a major U.S. withdrawal from its security commitments in the region; either a shift in Iran to political moderation or an escalation to a major level of conflict between Iran and its Arab neighbors; or the emergence of a violent Islamist extremist threat so broad it forced regional states into new patterns of cooperation to counter it. Once again, such developments are possible, but not probable or predictable.

REACTING TO CHANGING THREATS AND PATTERNS OF CONFLICT

There are, however, several, ongoing developments in regional security that may lead to new forms of cooperation at a less ambitious level, or which seem likely to force at least local shifts in security cooperation. These range from the impact of Iran's military efforts on regional balance and cooperation, to changes in the Islamist extremist threat, to the impact of some form of settlement or outcome to the fighting in Libya, Iraq, Syria, and Yemen.

IRAN AND THE ARAB STATES

While the West tends to focus on the threat posed by violent Islamist movements, it is the growing tensions and arms race between Iran and its Arab neighbors that does the most to drive the military build-up in the region. One can argue the extent to which each side drives the tensions on other side and how much Iran is to blame for the rise in tension and force levels.

At the same time, it is important to remember that the United States does see Iran as a rising threat as well and that it is largely the security cooperation between the United States, Saudi Arabia, and the U.A.E.—coupled with British and French power projection and support from Bahrain, Kuwait, Qatar, and Oman—that drives the balance of forces posed to deter or fight Iran, not the Gulf Cooperation Council or regional cooperation per se.

It is equally important to remember that each Arab state sees Iran somewhat differently and takes a different approach to security cooperation. Saudi Arabia and the U.A.E. actively plan both to deter Iran and to fight it. Kuwait, Bahrain, Qatar, and Oman all see Iran as a threat, but rely in part on U.S. power projection, and Qatar and Oman are cautious in their relations with Iran.

Iraq cooperates with Iran without being allied to it. Syria is dependent on Iran, not only for direct support but also because of Iran's support of Hezbollah. Yemen's Houthi rebels have some ties to Iran, but Iran does not play a major security role in the civil war. As for the rest of the Arab states, Jordan has made it clear it fears Iran's regional expansion, Lebanon is forced to accommodate Iran's support of Hezbollah, Egypt has been cautious in identifying Iran as a threat, and the other North African states do not play a meaningful security role.

U.S., European, and Arab security cooperation in dealing with Iran is driven by four different threats.

1. The Nuclear Dimension

The nuclear agreement with Iran, and Iran's initial compliance in reducing its stocks of enriched material and centrifuge and reactor programs, has put the nuclear issue on hold. Iran did, however, reach the point of a nuclear threshold state. A number of Gulf states—including Saudi Arabia and the U.A.E.—talked about nuclear power programs in response that had the potential for weapons development, and the United States raised the possibility of extended deterrence.

Any Iranian return to a program with serious weapons potential would probably trigger a major debate over Arab efforts to acquire nuclear weapons, extended deterrence, and the Non-Proliferation Treaty. It is unclear whether it would build more Arab security cooperation, how the United States would shape a military response, and how much a revived Iranian nuclear program would affect security cooperation in other areas. It seems clear, however, that a "snapback" to pre-J.C.P.O.A. sanctions would not be enough, and there would at least be a major debate over going nuclear and the prospect of extended deterrence.

2. The Conventional Ballistic and Cruise Missile Dimension

Iran has not halted its development of conventionally-armed ballistic and cruise missiles or long range artillery rockets. It is developing solid fuel ballistic missiles, creating mobile systems, shelters, and tunnels, and actively seeking to develop precision strike capabilities that would make ballistic and cruise missiles lethal against many military targets, critical infrastructure, and petroleum facilities.

Some of these Iranian efforts are in response to the massive lead that Arab states and the United States have in advanced air strike and combat capability. Iran has not been able to buy more than a small number of export versions of Russian Su-24 and MiG-29 fighters since the fall of the Shah, and most of its air force consists of obsolete combat aircraft like the F-4. In contrast, the United States is deploying stealth strike aircraft like the F-35, Saudi Arabia has advanced F-15s, the U.A.E. has advanced F-16s, and both the Saudis and the U.A.E. have long-range precision strike missiles like Storm Shadow. On the other hand, Iran has equally obsolescent surface-to-air missile defenses, although Russia began deliveries of the far more advanced S300 system in 2015.

These developments have already led the Arab Gulf states to buy more advanced versions of the Patriot missile (which Saudi Arabia has used to intercept Scud missiles launched from Yemen). For example, Qatar and the U.A.E. have made tentative offers to buy theater missile defense systems like the U.S. Terminal High Altitude Area Defense (THAAD)—a system capable of intercepting endo-atmospheric missiles at long ranges. It has also led the G.C.C. to consider creating a theater missile defense system based on the U.S. Aegis/Standard missile system—although its exo-atmospheric capabilities make it somewhat less suitable than THAAD. The United States has also begun to deploy Aegis missile defense ships into the Gulf.

The end result is likely to be a major shift in at least one aspect of regional defense cooperation. A theater missile defense system is extraordinarily expensive and must be tied to air defense systems that can protect against cruise missiles. Its effectiveness is dependent on access to satellite warning and intercept data that only the United States can provide. It requires integrated warning and battle management, even more than air combat, and would push the Arab Gulf states toward far more integrated defenses than currently exist for both cost and war-fighting reasons.

There is no present way, however, to judge the architecture of any such system, and the Arab Gulf states have so far been remarkably slow in creating real world integrated sensor and battle management capabilities for both air and naval combat, as well as other aspects of tactical intelligence—relying on national capabilities and the United States. There also is no way to judge the level of Iranian response to such missile defenses, Iranian acquisition of countermeasures for its missiles, and the extent to which it could buy more advanced air and missile systems from Russia and China by 2030.

It is also important to note that the Iranian missile program has partly prompted Israel to develop a three-tiered missile and rocket defense system involving the Arrow, endo-atmospheric Arrow-2, and exo-atmospheric Arrow-3 theater missile defense systems, the David's Sling to defend salvos of heavy long-range rockets and short-range ballistic missiles, and the Iron Dome short-range anti-rocket missile defense system. These capabilities are also designed to deal with the steadily growing missile and rocket threat posed by massive Iranian and Syrian rocket missile transfers to Hezbollah in Lebanon, which already include some systems with limited precision strike capability with Syrian 302mm rockets, Iranian half-ton warhead Fatah-110 rockets, and armed drones. Syrian government forces still pose another missile threat that includes Scud B-class ballistic missiles, which can deliver one-ton warheads at ranges of some 300 km (186 miles).

It seems unlikely that any form of cooperation in missile, rocket, and air defense will take place between the Arab Gulf states and Israel, but Israel might provide missile defense coverage of Jordan. It is also important to remember that Israel has nuclear-armed missiles of its own, Saudi Arabia has upgraded the ballistic missiles it bought from China, and cooperation in defense does not necessarily mean cooperation in launching retaliatory/offensive air or missile strikes.

3. Iranian Asymmetric Naval Missile and Air Capabilities to Attack Targets in the Persian Gulf, Gulf of Oman, and Indian Ocean

The third major threat Iran poses is a mix of naval, land, and sea-based anti-ship missiles, air missiles, and maritime reconnaissance capabilities that it can rapidly disperse throughout the Gulf, has already deployed at or near the Strait of Hormuz, and can use in the Gulf of Oman and Indian Ocean. This force includes large numbers of missile patrol boats, fast suicide boats, naval mines and smart mines that virtually any boat or ship can deploy, submarines, submersibles, and long-range land and air-based anti-ship missiles. It presents a major threat both to combat ships and to all forms of commercial maritime traffic, including tankers. Many of the missiles can also be used to strike land targets with some degree of effectiveness.

In theory, this threat should also push the Arab Gulf states toward security cooperation. In practice, many have been remarkably slow in making their own navies effective on a national basis or in tailoring and modernizing their naval forces to meet the threat, as distinguished from buying prestige ships. Progress in creating effective naval-air joint warfare capabilities has been limited. Readiness and modernization have not been integrated, and security cooperation has depended heavily on the U.S. Navy and Air Force to provide both core mission capabilities and support.

Saudi Arabia began to make some progress in changing this situation in 2015 and began to place orders for new ships that it has needed for years, if it is to modernize its navy. However, it is unclear how well any of the Arab Gulf states will respond over time. It is also unclear how effective they would be in dealing with serious threats like Iranian mine and smart mine efforts or in coordinating joint warfare against Iran's complex mix of asymmetric warfare forces in the Gulf, if the United States should withdraw its naval forces. This is an obvious area for security cooperation, but this does not mean that such cooperation will take place or could become effective.

At the same time, Iran cannot come close to matching U.S. air-sea capabilities, and one must remember that Britain and France have naval power projection capabilities. Moreover, Iran faces two critical problems. It cannot 'close the Gulf' and seriously threaten maritime traffic without blocking its own petroleum exports and maritime imports. Furthermore, any major Iranian effort that threatened the export of some 17 million barrels of oil through the Gulf, and the stability of the world economy, would almost certainly trigger a massive U.S. response in striking Iran and in seeking to destroy its military capabilities as quickly as possible.

4. Iran's Expanding Military Role and Influence

The fourth major threat Iran could pose is far harder to predict. Saudi Arabia, the U.A.E., Jordan, and other Arab states have expressed growing concern that the fighting in Syria and Iraq, Iran's support of Hezbollah, and Iran's links to the Houthi and Saleh forces in Yemen give it an increased ability to influence countries outside Iran. They are particularly concerned that Iraq seems to be drifting toward some form of division between an Arab Shiite dominated central government (including the southern oil-producing area and the zone along the Iran border), a marginalized and impoverished Arab Sunni region in the west, and an autonomous Kurdish region in the north. They fear that ethnic and communal tensions will further push the Shiite-dominated Iraqi government toward dependence on Iran. They also, however, see Iranian influence growing in Syria and fear the role Iran could play if it could gain access to Yemen or exploit Sunni-Shiite tensions in other Arab Gulf states like Bahrain.

This prompted Saudi Arabia and other G.C.C. states to improve their security relations with Jordan and to launch what now seems to be a failed and aborted Saudi effort to aid the Lebanese Army to check Hezbollah. It has not, however, led the Arab Gulf states to reach out to Iraq and try to effectively counterbalance Iran. It has resulted in Saudi Arabia and the U.A.E. supporting the Yemeni government against the Houthis in a war that does not yet seem to have any clear end. It also has led the Arab Gulf states to make poorly coordinated efforts to support Arab rebels in Syria and to become even more hostile to the Assad regime.

The key issue that is now totally unpredictable is how the different wars in

Syria, Iraq, and Yemen will proceed over time, how successful Iran will be in maintaining and expanding its influence in each case, and whether Iran's actions will lead to any new form of Arab security cooperation. One critical issue is whether Iraq will emerge from the fight with ISIS as a strong and unified enough state to act independently and deter any Iranian efforts to increase the threat it can pose to other Arab Gulf states—particularly Kuwait. At present, Iraq seems more likely to be weak and divided and a source of tension between Iran and other Arab states.

COUNTERTERRORISM AND COUNTERINSURGENCY

Iran is the key force driving states toward some form of regional cooperation, but all regional states also face some form of threat from violent Islamist extremists and sectarian, ethnic, and tribal divisions. In some cases, this takes the form of actual terrorism by extremists. In others, it takes the form of ethnic and sectarian dissent that may or may not legitimately be labeled as terrorist, and state terrorism or repression may be the response.

A.Q.A.P. is an example of a real terrorist movement, while Shiite dissent in Bahrain is often labeled as terrorist to justify repression. Egypt has moved from labeling the Muslim Brotherhood as a terrorist movement to repression at a broader level with increasingly unclear motives, despite Brotherhood actions at times not going beyond legitimate political dissent. Israeli-Palestinian tensions have reached the point where extremist movements like Hamas and the Palestinian Islamic Jihad do carry out terrorist attacks, but much of the violence is a reflection of the steadily deteriorating relations between Israelis and Palestinians, including violence at a more personal level.

Four regional countries have reached the point where the threat is not terrorism but insurgency or civil war. The fight against ISIS in Syria and Iraq involves terrorism but is primarily a fight against an insurgency, complicated by civil war and explosive struggles between Sunni and Shiite, Arab and Kurd. Libya became both a regional and tribal civil war and a fight against an ISIS enclave. Yemen has been a counterterrorism struggle against A.Q.A.P. and a complex civil war between the Houthi rebels, supporters of former President Ali Abdullah Saleh, and a central government that was driven out of the capital and much of the country.

Each element of these struggles and tensions has involved different approaches to counterterrorism and counterinsurgency as well as different mixes of internal action and outside alliances. None have involved coherent regional cooperation or clear engagement of regional and outside activity. It is equally unlikely that any future mixes of terrorism, insurgency, and repression are likely to be any more consistent or coherent in terms of either regional cooperation or the role of outside states.

There are more coherent forms of cooperation in classic counterterrorism and in dealing with relatively low levels of terrorist activity. U.N. and State Department reporting shows that most countries formally adhere to the U.N. resolutions and other international efforts to cooperate in counterterrorism, and a number of states do cooperate in sharing information on known terrorists in a form that supports control of cross-border movements and financial transactions.[1]

The actual level of enforcement and cooperation differs radically by country; some states support and make use of extremist movements and internal factions, and the level of actual counterterrorism capability varies sharply from country to country. In a number of countries, cooperation with outside powers like the United States, Britain, and France is more real than cooperation with neighbors. There are also no standard methods for training and organizing counterterrorism forces and intelligence efforts, dealing with terrorists and suspects once arrested, and countering ideological extremism and calls for violence.

The various unclassified reports on the subject do indicate that slow progress is being made in cooperation but largely on the basis of specific countries and not by region. It is possible that this situation may change if far more serious threats emerge over time from the successor to ISIS or its existing rivals, but it is equally possible that countries will continue to pursue their own efforts and methods separately. The issues involved are simply too sensitive for countries to cooperate or share sensitive and embarrassing data. Trust is often highly personal or built between specific organizations rather than between countries as a whole.

ISRAELI-EGYPTIAN-JORDANIAN COOPERATION

Almost all of the actual cooperation between states in the Middle East and North Africa (MENA) region is centered on Syria, Iraq, and the Gulf. There is no meaningful security cooperation between Morocco, Algeria, Libya, and Tunisia. For all the rhetoric about Egyptian cooperation with the Gulf, Egypt focuses on its own security. The Arab-Israeli conflict may have narrowed down to formal states of war between Israel and Lebanon and Syria, but the Arab League peace proposal has made virtually no progress and shows little sign of future success.

The long history of violence from the Iranian Revolution to the Iran-Iraq War, the invasion of Kuwait, the Gulf War, the U.S.-led invasion of Iraq, the upheavals in 2011, the civil war in Syria, the rise of ISIS and fighting in Iraq and Syria has, however, to some extent, eased tensions between Israel and its Arab neighbors. Similarly, the level of cooperation between Israel, Egypt, and Jordan that grew out of their respective peace settlements has been reinforced by the fact that Egypt now faces a threat in the Sinai as Israel does in Gaza and Jordan needs security on its border with Israel to the same extent that Israel needs security on its border with Gaza.

Intelligence and counterterrorism cooperation has improved in both cases, as has the level of dialogue between Israel and several Gulf states over Iran, Lebanon, and other security issues that are not directly related to the Palestinians. This does not, however, mean that Arab states will ignore the Palestinian issue or see Israel as an ally; nor does it mean that tensions between Israel and the Palestinians are not increasing or that there exists an "enemy of my enemy is my friend" understanding. While this is often said to be an Arab saying, it actually seems to date back to an ancient Sanskrit book on war called *The Arthashastra*, and history has shown that alliances of convenience can easily revert to the formulation that "the enemy of my enemy is my enemy."

If Israeli-Palestinian tensions turn into real conflict, and the present series of low-level incidents of violence turn into another intifada, Arab and Muslim states could find it very difficult to ignore such a conflict. The same could be true of a new round of fighting in Gaza or between Israel and Hezbollah. Iran and Sunni Islamists would be almost certain to use such conflicts to try to discredit moderate Arab regimes, and the ongoing struggle for the future of Islam would create further challenges if Arab Muslims were seen as becoming "martyrs" by Israel.

OTHER REGIONAL VARIABLES

It is tempting to predict that security cooperation will continue to struggle given the wars in Syria and Iraq, the rivalry between the G.C.C. and Iran, the Israeli-Palestinian conflict, making no real progress in North Africa, and only slow and partial gains in dealing with terrorism and violent extremism. It is important to note, however, that other regional variables are involved:

➤ World Bank and I.M.F. assessments indicate that little progress has been made in dealing with any of the problems in governance, corruption, economic development, the distribution of wealth, and employment flagged by the U.N. Arab Development reports as early as 2002 and that exploded into political upheavals in 2011[2]

➤ In several states—Egypt, Iran, Iraq, Libya, and Yemen—the situation is now much worse than it was in 2011. Moreover, massive 40-60 percent cuts in petroleum export revenues since 2014, cuts in tourism revenues, and sectarian and ethnic instability present new challenges in most other states.

➤ U.N. and U.S. Census Bureau data show that population pressure remains a critical issue, with population increases of five to six times between 1950 and 2015, on a path towards another 50 percent increase by 2050[3]

➤ A major bulge in the number of men and women entering the labor force has created major direct and disguised unemployment problems for young men and women in most countries—often creating high levels of real world unemployment or a critical lack of career opportunities for 20 percent or more of the youth in given MENA countries[4]

➤ Most countries face serious sectarian, ethnic, and tribal divisions, compounded by hyper-urbanization and growing tensions between Sunnis, Shiites, and other sects, that exacerbate the problems created by religious extremism

➤ Security expenditures in most MENA states are a strikingly higher percent of the G.D.P. than those in other regions and place a further burden on the economy

➤ U.S. State Department and other human rights reports warn that many regional states pursue security policies that are so repressive that they alienate significant portions of the population[5]

➤ No major ongoing civil conflict has a clear outcome ending in stability and development

The majority of existing governments may well be able to ride these pressures out and make significant progress by 2030, but assuming that current conditions continue ignores some extraordinarily important trends.

COOPERATION FROM OUTSIDE THE REGION

There is one final aspect of regional security cooperation that also deserves close attention. As previously described, security cooperation is certainly affected by the politics, military forces, and perceived threats within various parts of the MENA region, but at the same time, security cooperation is often dominated by outside nations and the role they play in individual states.

THE U.S. ROLE IN THE REGION

The U.S. military presence in the Mediterranean and the Gulf, U.S. ties to NATO and the power projection forces of Britain, France, and Italy, U.S. rapid deployment capabilities and advisory missions all combine to make the United States the most important single force for security cooperation in the region. Iran and other regional states confront the reality that the regional military balance is only one factor they must consider.

U.S. ability to reinforce allied countries or act unilaterally makes a decisive difference, and the importance of the United States is made clear by its near monopoly on advanced battle management, intelligence, and targeting systems. It is also reinforced by the role its military and contractors play in supporting many regional states in maintaining advanced weapons and providing the support necessary to sustain them in combat. In practice, the United States plays a critical role in security cooperation in Morocco, Egypt, Israel, Syria, Iraq, and the G.C.C.

Regional states can certainly do more to develop their own battle management, intelligence, targeting systems, and capability to maintain and sustain their forces. However, they cannot provide anything similar to the level of technology and practical combat experience possessed by the United States or afford to develop advanced capabilities in areas like satellite intelligence and targeting capability. This is also true of nations like Britain and France that must cope with serious limits on military spending and are also dependent on U.S. systems for advanced technology in battle management.

This makes the present security structure in the region—particularly in the Gulf—critically dependent on the level of U.S. military commitments and support. Real world regional security cooperation cannot provide a substitute for the foreseeable future, and dependence on the United States may grow as regional states move into new and more technically complex areas like missile defense. This does, however, depend on both continued U.S. strategic commitments and U.S. willingness to act. More specifically, it is dependent on U.S. military assistance and aid to critical states like Egypt, Israel, and Jordan, and on the flow of U.S. arms sales and support to the Arab Gulf states.

ARMS SALES AND SECURITY COOPERATION

The overall flow of arms transfers involves broader and equally critical issues for security cooperation. As states like Iran have learned the hard way, smaller and moderately developed states cannot compete in producing modern arms. The technology and manufacturing systems are too costly and complex, the resulting production runs too limited, and the unit costs too high. Real world business models make it brutally clear that not only are these systems high risk and high cost, but they provide few jobs, require massive investment and imports of technology, and have little benefit in terms of creating a technical and manufacturing base that can help development in the civil sector.

This is not a minor aspect of security cooperation, given the cost of existing arms transfers and orders. For example, estimates by the International Institute of Strategic Studies indicate that the G.C.C. as a whole had military expenditures more than seven times those of Iran in 2015, and these are typical of spending levels over the last decade.[6] Many of these expenditures went to arms transfers, and a study by the Congressional Research Service (C.R.S.) using declassified U.S. intelligence estimates indicated that the G.C.C. states ordered nearly 200 times more arms during 2007-2014 than Iran did and took actual delivery on 74 times more arms. This advantage also rose with time. The

Arab Gulf states ordered a total of $135.9 billion in new orders and took $44.2 billion worth of deliveries during 2007-2014—largely from the United States.[7]

Iran has made limited progress in manufacturing its own arms, and the C.R.S. report does not cover the cost of Iran's nuclear and some missile efforts. However, the C.R.S. study shows that Iran only imported $700 million worth of arms in 2007-2010, and imported less than $50 million worth in 2011-2014, for a total of little more than $750 million in 2007-2014. It took delivery on only $500 million worth of arms in 2007-2010 and $100 million in 2011-2014, for a total of $600 million.

The data in the C.R.S. study do not include the arms transfers affecting competition between Iran/Russia and the U.S./Arab states in shaping the civil war in Syria. They do, however, affect the equally serious competition for influence over Iraq—another major petroleum exporter. Although Iraq is subject to considerable Iranian influence, it has also had massive military support from the United States and should be seen as a separate case from the Iran-Arab Gulf arms race. Iraq bought $5.6 billion worth of arms in 2007-2010 and a massive $21.7 billion million in 2011-2014. It took delivery on $2.6 billion worth of arms imports in 2007-2010, but this total rose to $6.1 billion in 2011-2014.

These figures only tell part of the story. As a rough rule of thumb, it costs much more to support, modify, and service a weapons systems during its life cycle than it does to buy it, and these costs rise in direct proportion to its use in combat. They require further imports and often either support contracts with foreign firms or expensive specialized support facilities for a given weapons system. If the G.C.C. or any other regional body had more success in standardization and creating common integrated facilities, some of these costs would be lower. However, it would now take at least a decade to make major progress in such efforts, given the existing mix of different weapons systems and orders for new systems.

THE FUTURE ROLE OF OTHER OUTSIDE POWERS: RUSSIA, CHINA, AND TURKEY

One key issue for the future will be the role that other outside powers play in both providing military support and arms sales—factors that, again, illustrate the limits to regional security cooperation. Russia has already shown how decisive even limited military intervention can be in Syria. It also has shown how critical Russian arms sales can be through its sale of the S300 air defense missile to Iran.

Russia may well see that playing a growing role in the MENA region is a way of putting pressure on NATO and reasserting its status and power on a global level. It would be almost certain to react if the United States leaves a growing power vacuum in the region by reducing its forces and commitments or by an unwillingness to act. China is not yet ready for major power projection efforts in the Gulf or MENA region and is only beginning to acquire the ability to make advanced arms transfers. It is, however, developing port facilities in Pakistan, has acquired some port facilities in Djibouti, and might become more active in the region much sooner if it sees cuts in the U.S. role, or any potential threats to its sources of petroleum.

Turkey has also shown that powers on the borders of the MENA region can play an important role, and there seems to be little prospect that it will not continue to seek its own goals in Syria and in dealing with the different factions of Kurds on its borders.

Living With Complexity and Uncertainty

There is an old joke about the Middle East that "a pessimist is an optimist with experience." If one looks for regional security cooperation as a *deus ex machina* in solving the region's security problems, both experience and the near- to mid-term conditions shaping the future provide every reason to be cautious and doubtful. However, the broader structure and efforts of given regional powers like Saudi Arabia and the U.A.E. in shaping their forces and the overall pattern of cooperation between key regional states and the United States offer a far more promising situation.

Iran is likely to be deterred if the United States continues to play its current regional role, as European states provide their current levels of limited support. International action has reduced the nuclear threat, and ISIS is scarcely winning. A combination of peace efforts and military developments have also limited the scope of any probable form of renewed Arab-Israeli conflict. The MENA region may not be moving toward stability, but there is no clear reason to assume that major new forms of conflict or instability will take place. As the scorpion said to the frog, "this is the nature of the Middle East."

ENDNOTES

1. "Country Reports: Reports by Member States Pursuant to Security Council Resolution 1624," Security Council Counter Terrorism Committee, 2005, accessed August 1, 2016, http://www.un.org/en/sc/ctc/resources/1624. html; "Country Reports on Terrorism 2015," US State Department, accessed August 1, 2016, http://www.state.gov/j/ct/rls/crt/2015/index. htm.

2. Tokhir Mirzoev and Adnan Mazarei, "Four Years After the Spring," Finance and Development, 52, 2 (June 2015), accessed August 1, 2016, http://www.imf.org/external/ pubs/ft/fandd/2015/06/mazarei.htm.

3. "Population Trends and Challenges in the Middle East and North Africa," Population Reference Bureau, accessed August 1, 2016, http://www.prb.org/Publications/ Reports/2001/PopulationTrendsandChallenges intheMiddleEastandNorthAfrica.aspz.

4. "MENA Overview," Worldbank, last updated March 30, 2016, http://www.worldbank.org/ en/region/mena/overview.

5. "Country Reports on Human Rights Practices for 2015," US State Department, accessed August 1, 2016, http://www.state.gov/j/drl/rls/ hrrpt/humanrightsreport/index.htm#wrapper.

6. Based on the country data in the IISS, Military Balance 2016, and previous editions.

7. Catherine A. Theohary, "Conventional Arms Transfers to Developing Nations," 2007-2014, Congressional Research Service, December 21, 2015.

Chapter Ten

Toward Regional Cooperation:

The Internal Security Dimension

Querine Hanlon

Introduction

The paradox of regional cooperation in the Middle East and North Africa is that it is one of the least integrated regions in the world, despite the existence of numerous shared challenges—and even common interests. In no area of potential collaboration is that paradox more evident than in the internal security dimension.

The "internal security dimension" encompasses statutory forces with an internal security mission of public order and law enforcement. It includes the police; militarized police such as the national guard or gendarmes; prison guards; border guards; specialized tactical forces, like counterterrorism or crowd control units; maritime law enforcement fleets; and other law enforcement actors with an internal security function. It also includes the ministries that oversee them, such as the ministry of interior. The internal security sector is a component of the state's security sector, which also includes the functions of national defense (armed forces, ministry of defense), intelligence, justice (ministry of justice, judiciary, prison system) and oversight and governance (parliament and their specialized committees, the executive, civil society).

The security sector is often described as a system, in that each of the component functions are closely interconnected. The function of the security sector is to protect the state—and the lives and livelihoods of its citizens—from both external and internal threats. For the internal security dimension, this includes the provision of public order and crime prevention, a broad category of activities that range from traffic enforcement, making and processing arrests, and collecting evidence to manning Ports of Entry (POE) at borders, protecting national institutions, and preventing acts of terrorism.

In the internal security sector, there is a much greater variation in how these systems are structured and how these duties are carried out across states than is the case for the defense sector. In the latter, the military rank and force structure looks much the same, for example, in Colombia, Jordan or Indonesia. In the internal security sector, however, these can vary widely. Some are civilian led, others are entirely uniformed. Some constabulary forces report to ministries of interior, others to ministries of defense. Prison management also varies widely, as do processes for evidence collection and prosecution. These differences exist even within like polities, exemplified by the differences between the French or Italian system of law enforcement and that of the United Kingdom, the United States, or Canada. Fundamental differences also derive from how law enforcement actors deliver their mission of public service, from models of democratic policing or community policing, which emphasize community engagement and public service, to more authoritarian models, which prioritize regime protection and repression.

Given these fundamental differences, it is not surprising that regional cooperation in the internal security dimension lags behind cooperation in other realms. Nonetheless, there are real benefits that can be derived from bilateral and even multilateral cooperation among law enforcement entities within the internal security sector across the MENA region. Given the goal—put forth by Ross Harrison in his *Defying Gravity: Working Toward a Regional Strategy for a Stable Middle East* chapter of this book—of a more stable and prosperous Middle East by 2030, can regional cooperation among these law enforcement actors and institutions, despite the constraints inherent to the internal security dimension, measurably improve security and stability across the region?[1] Are the pillar countries Harrison identifies—Saudi Arabia, Egypt, Iran and Turkey—the most appropriate stewards of this effort? And what, specifically, can be done to leverage today's nascent regional cooperation in the internal security dimension to realize this goal?

THE CHALLENGES OF COOPERATION IN THE INTERNAL SECURITY DIMENSION

The term "regional cooperation" brings to mind well-established organizations with regional mandates in the economic, political or defense spheres like the E.U., ASEAN, or NATO. But there is no like organization explicitly mandated to address shared issues in the internal security dimension, which is (with the possible exception of intelligence) arguably the least regionally integrated sector worldwide. Security specialists are correct to counter this argument with examples of institutionalized mechanisms like INTERPOL or EUROPOL, which do have an explicit mandate to coordinate information sharing among various law enforcement agencies in member countries. But there is no equivalent "MENAPOL" for the Middle East and North Africa—and certainly no framework for integrating the region's internal security sector like NATO does for the European defense sector.[2]

Among the reasons why regional cooperation in the internal security dimension lags behind cooperation in other realms is simply that the risks of cooperating with other internal security forces and institutions are quite evident, whereas the benefits of doing so are far less apparent. For the authoritarian regimes of the MENA region, most information about the internal security sector, such as the number and types of forces, budgets, and rules of engagement, are classified as "state secrets." Formal high-level cooperation, which often requires binding agreements, intrusive information sharing, and changes to domestic law, risks exposing this information to regional adversaries—and to their own populations.

Cooperation also presents risks for the region's small states. Exposing their capacity gaps in the internal security sector through cooperation with other states in the region raises the risk that these vulnerabilities could be exploited. The fear that cooperation could make these states less secure is even more acute for the region's transitioning democracies, where democratic practices are still being institutionalized and where the risk of reversion to the status quo ante is always present. This reticence to share even basic information is not a MENA-only phenomenon. A U.N. report on crime and justice statistics for European countries highlights "the disturbing observation" that calls for data often go unanswered by "countries that are known to possess the required data but do not respond."[3]

There is another reason for the lack of cooperation in the internal security dimension that applies not only to the MENA region but also to assessing the prospects for cooperation among law enforcement entities more generally. The nature of law enforcement itself—and its largely internal mission of security as opposed to an external mission of defense—does not intrinsically lend itself to cooperation with other law enforcement entities. Much of what law enforcement does day-to-day, such as processing traffic infractions, dealing with domestic disturbances, monitoring public demonstrations, securing large scale sporting events, or even responding to violent crime, is largely an internal or domestic activity (although this is changing as organized criminal actors like gangs increasingly operate internationally). Where regional cooperation could prove valuable, however, is in those law enforcement activities that come close to the dividing line between external defense and internal law enforcement. Thus, we do see cooperation in the internal security dimension among gendarmerie or national guard forces that protect land and maritime borders, or for Special Weapons and Tactics (SWAT) units that have a counterterrorism or specialized protection mission. Their ability to deliver these missions and to capture and prosecute perpetrators can be meaningfully enhanced by cooperating and sharing information with counterparts across borders.

However, there is an even more fundamental reason for the lower level of cooperation in the internal security dimension worldwide. Cooperation among national police forces, for example, to share information about specific criminal actors or crimes could impinge on citizen rights or violate due process. This is why there are restrictive legal frameworks for sharing evidence or police intelligence (as opposed to information) outside of established legal processes and for the burden of proof that these require, both of which fundamentally derive from democratic norms and the rule of law. Further complications arise from democratic standards of transparency and accountability. These deliberative processes serve to make law enforcement cooperation inherently difficult, if not burdensome and unwieldy, even among states that otherwise cooperate closely on matters of defense or trade.

In the MENA region, the prospects for regional cooperation have been further complicated by the events of the Arab Spring. Prior to the Arab Spring, the region's security forces cooperated, mostly in a bilateral fashion, to counter threats to their regimes and to repress internal dissent. For example, although there were important tensions among Tunis, Algiers, Tripoli, and Cairo, there was also a surprising degree of coordination among internal security forces along their shared borders, including coordinated operations and intelligence sharing.[4] Even across the closed border between Morocco and Algeria, security forces engaged in limited cooperation to repatriate wayward shepherds or to counter smugglers.[5] This cooperation was largely founded on shared interests—among which regime protection and even survival were among the most important. But in the aftermath of the collapse and overthrow of the regimes in Tunisia, Libya and Egypt, this cooperation largely ceased—not only because those shared interests had disappeared, but also because, in the case of Libya, there was no regime to cooperate with. As one senior border security officer in Tunisia explained, "On the border with Libya, we are doing the work of two. We have no counterpart across the border."[6]

Whereas the pre-Arab Spring regimes were authoritarian states that used their defense and internal security forces to protect the regime and repress dissent, the democratic-aspirant regimes that replaced them initially expressed a commitment to meeting the demands of the Arab Spring, including the creation of democratically accountable internal security sectors that could effectively protect these new states, meet the security needs of their citizens, and adhere to the rule of law. In the immediate post-Arab Spring, newly elected regimes began to take steps that could have fundamentally overturned the security apparatus of the old order. Although few of these reforms were successfully initiated—and even fewer implemented—the Arab Spring presented a serious, if not existential, threat to the many countries in the region who feared the diffusion of these democratic aspirations among their own citizens. The shared interests upon which regional cooperation had been built disintegrated, to be replaced by distrust, fear, and even active measures to undermine these nascent transitioning democracies.

In the years since 2011, however, the pattern of cooperation—mostly on a bilateral basis, but with some interesting regional initiatives, and focused mostly "on the ground" through operational, tactical or technical coordination—has carefully resumed, even with some of the post-Arab Spring countries. For example, within 24 hours of Tunisia's Ennahda-led regime stepping down in favor of the "technocrat" government, relations between Algiers and Tunis were reestablished, and their security forces began coordinating to counter the terrorist threat along their shared border. These initiatives, and others like them, suggest that there is a modicum of regional cooperation and a more significant level of bilateral cooperation upon which future efforts can be built.

DEFINING A STRATEGIC PURPOSE FOR REGIONAL COOPERATION

There is an implicit assumption that regional cooperation in the internal security dimension can further the goal of a stable Middle East—if not in the near-term, then at least a generation hence. But is it really in the interests of the international community to promote cooperation among security forces and institutions that, at best, struggle to meet the security needs of their governments and populations and, at worst, operate with impunity, violate human rights, and even torture their own citizens? Are all of the pillar countries Harrison identifies—Saudi Arabia, Turkey, Egypt and Iran—the best stewards for this effort? And given that the dysfunctions in the internal security dimension are exactly that—internal dysfunctions—how can regional cooperation address those internal dysfunctions?

A NEAR-TERM APPROACH: NARROW TECHNICAL OR FUNCTIONAL COOPERATION

One approach is to ignore these larger political issues—or at least defer them in the near-term—by focusing on continuing, and building on, technical regional cooperation, limited information sharing, and force professionalization efforts. Such an approach would promote cooperation among states in critical subregions with shared security challenges. Efforts would likely focus on purely tactical or technical cooperation, perhaps with limited operational coordination to counter a specific threat; enhancing the professionalism of the region's internal security forces; or promoting coordination among security sector officials on critical shared threats, such as counterterrorism cooperation. This is currently taking place among some states, in a very limited form, in North Africa and the Sahel, as various ISIS and al-Qaeda affiliates expand their operations. Many of these examples involve exercises, simulations, or scenario-driven engagements drawn from real world challenges "on the ground." Most of this cooperation is highly technical. Bigger political issues are strictly "off-limits."

Another example of a broader, but still limited cooperation, is found in the activities of the Global Counterterrorism Forum (G.C.T.F.), which was created in September 2011 to serve as an "informal, multilateral counterterrorism (C.T.) platform" to enhance global counterterrorism cooperation by identifying "critical civilian C.T. needs and mobilizing the necessary expertise and resources to address such needs."[7] With 30 members (29 countries and the E.U.), the forum operates internationally to convene C.T. policymakers and practitioners through six thematic and regional working groups with the United States and Turkey serving as co-chairs in 2015 (and the Netherlands and Morocco in 2016).[8] There are also "G.C.T.F.-inspired institutions," including the Hedayah Center of Excellence in Abu Dhabi and the International Institute for Justice and the Rule of Law in Valletta, Malta, which offer training to internal security sector officials and operational forces across the MENA region.[9] Although the focus of the G.C.T.F. is on promoting global counterterrorism cooperation, the activities of the working group, including the development of various "best practices" documents, also address broader law enforcement capacity issues. Such a platform could serve as a useful starting point for building deeper and wider regional cooperation in the internal security dimension.

Other potentially promising initiatives for promoting regional cooperation in the internal security dimension predate the Arab Spring. Notable among these are the efforts by countries like Morocco, Jordan, the U.A.E., and Turkey to promote training of more effective police forces in the region—

initiatives that build trust and the operational capacity of the region's internal security forces to more effectively counter threats to the regions' regimes and citizens. For example, with support from the U.N. Office of Drugs and Crime (U.N.O.D.C.), the Dubai police anti-narcotics unit has trained counterparts from Iraq, Egypt, Syria, Lebanon, Qatar, Jordan, Morocco, Yemen and the Palestinian Territories to combat drug smuggling and abuse in the region at the Hemaya International Training Center.[10] Another initiative is the Arab Interior Ministers Council (AIM). Established in 1982, AIM was created to "develop and strengthen cooperation and coordination efforts" among Arab countries in the field of internal security and the fight against crime."[11] It coordinates with INTERPOL to host regular meetings of member states' INTERPOL heads, as well as holding annual meetings of its members.[12] It also includes subsidiary organizations and institutions, including the Naif Arab University for Security Sciences (NAUSS), which offers training programs, and subsidiary offices with an internal security focus, including the Arab Office for Civil Protection and Rescue, the Arab Office for Crime Prevention, the Arab Criminal Police Office, and the Arab Office on Drug Affairs.[13]

Established coordination mechanisms like the G.C.T.F. and AIM suggest that regional cooperation in the internal security dimension is possible, that such cooperation is likely best focused on shared threats or challenges, and that efforts to promote cooperation favor technical and functional over political issues. Given their established relationships with international organizations like INTERPOL and the United Nations, these platforms could also serve as potential entry points for the international community to promote wider or deeper cooperation in the region in the future.

The benefit of such an approach is that it could potentially help stabilize critical subregions and potentially help participating regimes manage their growing security challenges. Additionally, the benefits of such narrow technical or functional cooperation, which would not require deeper information sharing or even legislative changes, would also likely exceed the potential risks; enhancing the likelihood that states would be willing to cooperate. But the potential benefits, even in the longer term, would likely be at the margins. It is unlikely that such narrowly defined cooperation alone would contribute to greater stability across the MENA region. But it would create an entry point for engagement that could, in turn, provide the basis for wider or deeper cooperation in the long-term.

A LONG-TERM APPROACH: SECURITY SECTOR REFORM

A more promising approach is to promote cooperation, in accordance with the principles of Security Sector Reform (S.S.R.), to reform and improve the delivery of internal security across the region. Such an approach could create a stable and more secure environment for ordinary citizens and their governments. It could also pave the way for the further advancement and development of the region across the other sectors profiled in this series of studies on regional cooperation.

S.S.R. is a conceptual approach to strengthening, reforming, or (re) constructing the human and institutional capabilities and capacities of the security sector to provide security, maintain the state's monopoly of force, and operate in accordance with democratic principles and the rule of law.[14] The S.S.R. approach is a broad one. It focuses on the security sector as a whole. Its aim is to promote effective and accountable security sector forces and institutions. In other words, its purpose is to improve how the security sector is governed—and how and for what purpose its forces and institutions operate.

S.S.R., as it has been practiced since the late 1990s, is largely a national endeavor. Within the MENA region alone, there is tremendous diversity of national contexts and S.S.R. challenges. For example, at one end of the spectrum is Libya; a post-conflict state in which there is no monopoly of force and the S.S.R. challenge is not reform, but (re)construction. At the other end of the spectrum are states such as Israel, Iran, Saudi Arabia, and Turkey, with robust security sectors that are wielded in fundamentally different ways and for different purposes. Further variation derives from vastly different legal and constitutional frameworks across the region's states.

Given varied regional contexts and legal frameworks, serious political challenges, and the inherent limitations of cooperating in the internal security dimension, regional S.S.R. will be more narrowly constrained than the national variant. What a regional S.S.R. approach can do is build the human capital so essential for the transformation of the region's internal security dimension.

At a practical level, S.S.R. is a framework "through which national and international actors can structure an interlinked series of activities designed to buttress stability in a given state."[15] The central objective of this process is to "create a secure environment…conducive to development, poverty reduction, and democracy."[16] For international donors, like the United States and its allies, S.S.R. can frame and prioritize foreign assistance beyond merely providing training and equipment to support the goals of S.S.R. For MENA governments seeking to strengthen, reform, or (re) construct security sector forces and institutions, S.S.R. provides a "conceptual roadmap" for how to do so.

The story of S.S.R. in the MENA region has not been a positive one.[17] Efforts to promote S.S.R., some of which pre-date the Arab Spring, have been attempted to a greater or lesser extent in Algeria, Bahrain, Egypt, Iraq, Libya, Morocco, the Palestinian Authority, Syria, Tunisia, and Yemen. None of these efforts have produced a "durable consensus" among the leading political actors, or society more generally, about the role of the security sector or how it should be governed.[18]

The hurdles are many and appear almost insurmountable. Authoritarian and patronage-based practices are deeply embedded; public institutions are dysfunctional; and both elites and populations are threatened either by the loss of their privileged status or by the increasing social disorder, rising crime, and the growing threat of terrorism and violent extremism. In the security sector, there are real challenges to divesting institutions like the ministries of defense and interior from the economic, security, and intelligence functions that serve as their power base. These institutions have also served to employ significant portions of the population. Divesting these institutions of those functions risks exacerbating already severe unemployment and social discontent. As these S.S.R. efforts have proceeded, faltered, or failed, populations who once demanded reform are increasingly prioritizing stability over democracy, rule of law, or human rights.[19] Within the security sector, the response has been to return to practices of coercion and repression. These "faltering, halfhearted attempts at security sector reform" have prompted some to conclude that "Western models of security sector reform cannot adequately resolve the dilemmas revealed by Arab states in transition and can do no more than alter these sectors superficially."[20]

If not S.S.R., then what is the alternative?

Without an S.S.R. framework to provide a long-term strategic objective for U.S. and allied efforts in the region, such efforts will likely continue to be largely focused on leveraging narrow openings created by gaps in regional states' technical or operational proficiency. Breaking the "vicious cycle of dysfunction" to achieve a more stable and secure Middle East, as Harrison argues, will require addressing the fundamental dysfunctions of the region's internal security sector. Until these can be addressed, stability and prosperity for the broader region will remain aspirational.

Six S.S.R. Principles

There are six guiding principles for S.S.R.[21] These provide the outline of a "roadmap" for promoting more effective and responsive internal security sectors that ultimately can provide a foundation for a more stable and prosperous Middle East. These also suggest some entry points for promoting greater regional cooperation in the internal security dimension across the MENA region.

1. S.S.R. should be locally owned and the region's governments should have a stake in its successful outcome. Local ownership—that the reform process is shaped and driven by local actors—is a foundational principle of the S.S.R. concept.[22] Without it, no reform is possible. Ultimately, the agent of change in S.S.R. is the host nation government. Assistance provided under

an S.S.R. framework can only support that reform, provide technical guidance, shore up needed resources, and encourage efforts to implement change.

2. The purpose of S.S.R. should be to enhance the effectiveness, accountability, and transparency of security sector oversight institutions and security forces. Each of these must guide how S.S.R. is designed and implemented. Effectiveness is measured by the capacity and capability of institutions and operational forces to provide security in accordance with human rights standards and the rule of law. Institutional effectiveness means that the institutions that exercise oversight over security forces—such as the ministry of interior, but also the executive and parliamentary committees—have the capacity and capability to oversee, lead, manage, provision, train and control them. Accountability refers to a system of checks and balances through which security institutions and forces are held responsible for their actions to the chain of command, their civilian leadership, and ultimately to the populations they serve. Finally, transparency refers to the open and accessible operation of security sector institutions and forces.[23] Together, enhancing the effectiveness, transparency, and accountability of security institutions and forces strengthens democratic institutions and governance.

3. S.S.R. should promote the rule of law. The rule of law requires that all citizens and institutions, including the state itself, are accountable to the law. Furthermore, these laws must be "publically promulgated, equally enforced, and independently adjudicated."[24] Legal frameworks must be fairly and impartially applied to all citizens, including minorities and other vulnerable groups. Within the S.S.R. framework, promotion of the rule of law means that judiciaries are independent and impartial, and the police do not act with impunity and uphold the law.

4. S.S.R. should foster and promote the consolidation of democratic practices, placing the security sector under civilian control. The core S.S.R. concept includes a strong normative commitment to democratization and to the principles of human rights and good governance.[25] The strong emphasis on norms has generated criticism that S.S.R. is "misleadingly optimistic" or that it is "too…prescriptive and ethnocentric."[26] But, S.S.R. without a commitment to promoting democratic principles and practices is not really S.S.R. If the purpose of S.S.R. is to enhance the effectiveness, transparency, and accountability of security institutions and forces, then doing so requires adopting democratic practices to bring the forces and their oversight institutions under civilian supervision. This does not mean that S.S.R. aims at democratic government; it aims at the consolidation of democratic practices. This distinction is an important one. There will

be countries that are not democracies, electoral democracies that are not liberal democracies, and others in transition where democratic government remains a long-term goal rather than a current reality. Promoting democratic practices and civilian control will increase the likelihood that the purpose of S.S.R.—effective, accountable and transparent security sector institutions and forces—will be realized.

5. S.S.R. should be employed to strengthen the state's monopoly of legitimate force. The monopoly of violence is a foundational concept of the modern, Westphalian state system and the S.S.R. concept.[27] In its S.S.R. variant, this is achieved by bringing the forces and institutions of the security sector under civilian democratic control. In practice, what this means is that all forces that operate within the territorial confines of the state (over which its writ legally extends) should be statutory forces—they are sanctioned by law, and they are led, managed, provisioned, trained, and deployed by the state (ministries of defense or interior, the executive authority, and ultimately, the people they serve). Although somewhat more controversial, this category of legitimate security providers can also include various private security actors provided the state permits them to wield force, but ultimately retains "the sole right to use [or authorize the use of] physical violence."[28] The critical issue here is that the privatization of security is "top down"—it is state sanctioned.[29]

6. S.S.R. should be holistic in its design, although reform activities may not occur simultaneously. Holistic design is another foundational principle of S.S.R. It requires that any reform program should include "activities with multi-sector strategies, based upon a broad assessment of the range of security and justice needs of the people and the state."[30] Although the approach is laudable, it is neither realistic nor practical.[31] A more pragmatic and realistic approach is to require that the conceptualization and design of S.S.R. be holistic, but that the delivery or implementation of reform is prioritized and sequenced to address the most critical security sector dysfunctions first.

S.S.R. is a tall order. At its roots, it is less about technical improvements and changes in Standard Operating Procedures (SOPs) and more fundamentally about renegotiating the social contract between state and citizen. What is the role of government? What are its obligations toward citizens? What role should the security sector play in the provision of public order? And what, in turn, are the obligations of citizens toward their governments?

It is not surprising, given the enormity of the task, that little progress has been made in the few years since S.S.R. efforts began in the region. Nor should there be an expectation that any subsequent renewal of these efforts will produce rapid results. Timeframes for S.S.R. are measured in decades, if not generations. S.S.R does not require that the entire security sector be dismantled and reconstituted at once. Initially small, incremental steps toward the long-term goal of improving the delivery of public services in the security sector can gradually improve how internal security is delivered; thus contributing to the creation of stability so essential to achieving the goals of prosperity and security across the region.

A Roadmap for Change

The value of S.S.R. is that it can serve as a framework both for how the international community can promote the goal of building a more stable and secure environment across the region and how regional states can achieve greater security and stability for their governments and citizens. S.S.R. offers both a strategic objective for that regional coordination—improving the delivery of internal security—and a possible roadmap for how to build on existing technical and functional cooperation for the long-term. The following are some recommendations for how to do so:

Recommendation 1:

Create a regional S.S.R. network of security sector officials, senior operational commanders, parliamentarians, civil society organizations, and regional S.S.R. experts to identify, develop, and disseminate security sector best practices.

A useful starting point for implementing Recommendation 1 is to build on recent and ongoing efforts to promote the sharing of best practices across the region. For example, the U.S. Institute of Peace and the Carnegie Endowment for International Peace have both implemented regional S.S.R. initiatives in the aftermath of the Arab Spring.[32] The Organization for Security and Cooperation in Europe has similarly focused on S.S.R. for its Mediterranean partners and recently completed new guidance for Security Sector Governance. The G.C.T.F. platform and its regional and thematic working groups offer another good starting point for building such a network, and its C.T. law enforcement good practices documents also offer valuable guidance for S.S.R. best practices.[33]

These networks could serve numerous S.S.R. purposes—including identifying the "change agents" in Recommendation 3 (below) and promoting relationship-building among senior security sector officials and commanders from some of the Arab Spring countries where such engagement was previously discouraged or even prohibited. Numerous officials that have attended such events have recognized the value of engagement for overcoming their sense of isolation. "This engagement is so valuable to me," one beleaguered Yemeni security official explained, "because now I know that I am not alone. My regional counterparts are facing the same challenges I am."[34]

Such a network can also be used to raise awareness among those responsible for promoting or implementing S.S.R. about how to do so holistically. Although the focus here is on the internal security dimension, strengthening the capacity of the police will have implications for other segments of the security sector, such as justice and defense. For example, improving police methods for evidence collection will not improve security if the laws and court processes for handling evidence are not also addressed. Such a network also provides a venue for disseminating best practices for promoting democratic processes, strengthening the monopoly of force (in accordance with S.S.R. principles), and enhancing effectiveness, accountability and oversight.

RECOMMENDATION 2:

Through the auspices of the S.S.R. network, other existing platforms disseminate knowledge of S.S.R. best practices through regional workshops and other skill-building activities.

Throughout the region, there are significant knowledge gaps about S.S.R. best practices. After the Arab Spring, many of the new leaders of police units and ministries of interior sought guidance on how to reform their practices. Recommendation 2 suggests addressing those knowledge gaps through targeted skills and building on specific internal security sector functions, such as: appropriate use of force policies; how to create and implement a new mission for the police; best practices for engaging citizens; guidelines for community policing and other policing models; developing new standards for policing and embedding those in recruitment, training, promotion, and sanction policies. The selection of topics can be informed by the activities of network members and should be focused on providing participants with practical guidelines to help inform the design and implementation of new national policies.

In accordance with the principle of local ownership, international efforts to implement Recommendations 1 and 2 should aim at providing a venue and opportunity for engagement, but should defer the content, frequency, and hosting to regional states to ensure that the network serves the interests of its participants. Over the long-term, such a network could be institutionalized, possibly under the auspices of a regional organization.

RECOMMENDATION 3:

Identify "change agents" within the region's security sector institutions and forces, and empower them with targeted assistance and capacity building activities.

Throughout the region, there are individuals—or groups of individuals—in key ministries or security units who are interested in, or committed to, improving how their internal security sector functions. Implementing Recommendation 3 should be weighed against the potential risks of "empowering" these actors. Where conditions are appropriate for implementing Recommendation 3, there are a few ways these individuals or units can be "empowered." One way is to include them in the aforementioned network. A second way is to provide S.S.R. training to likeminded colleagues to build a larger network of change agents in the same institution or unit. A third way is to leverage the provision of assistance to enhance the prominence or influence of the individual or unit vis-à-vis detractors (with the important caveat that such assistance could potentially put those change agents at risk). Over time, and under the appropriate conditions, such efforts could seed small centers of reform in key ministries that could promote change from within.

RECOMMENDATION 4:

Support and expand nascent regional cooperation efforts in the technical and operational spheres to promote wider and deeper regional cooperation.

Recommendation 4 suggests building on regional initiatives, much of which pre-date the Arab Spring, for promoting greater professionalism and building the operational and technical capacity of regional police and other specialized internal security forces. These efforts, led by countries like Jordan, Morocco, the U.A.E. and Turkey, have not garnered high-level attention, but have nonetheless impacted hundreds of thousands of internal security forces in the region. In Jordan, for example, this training takes place at the Jordan International Police Training Center, which has welcomed police from Iraq, Lebanon, and the Palestinian Territories. Dubai's efforts have focused on training police to combat drug smuggling. Morocco has promoted the professionalization of security forces across the African continent.

There are numerous technical and functional areas where such efforts could focus. For example, drug smuggling, human trafficking, and antiquities smuggling are important law enforcement challenges that countries across the region have a shared interest in countering and for which platforms like AIM might be well-suited. Other issues where wider and deeper cooperation would be useful include efforts to counter the growing threat of al-Qaeda and ISIS, foreign terrorist fighter (F.T.F.) recruitment and return, and weapons smuggling. In accordance with the principle of local ownership, there is tremendous value in having these efforts delivered by security organizations within the region (often with the support of international donors). Nascent efforts in the region also suggest that, in place of some of the pillar countries Harrison identifies, there might be other countries, like Morocco and Jordan, better suited to initiating such efforts and, given the political complexities of the region, to securing the participation of some of the internal security organizations from pillar countries, like Saudi Arabia and Egypt, and other important regional states like Algeria. Such efforts also have the benefit of strengthening the capacity of the host organization. In the near- and mid-term, these efforts would likely require funding and support from the United States, its allies, and international organizations like the United Nations.

RECOMMENDATION 5:

Explicitly design and deliver regional capacity building activities for operational forces that enhance both their effectiveness and accountability.

The United States and its allies are engaged throughout the region to build the capacity of key partner security forces and institutions. With some important exceptions, the majority of this engagement is bilateral and much of it is focused on enhancing the operational effectiveness of forces, often through the provision of equipment and the training to go with it. Accountability is often viewed as a by-product of force professionalization. Recommendation 5 suggests elevating accountability to an explicit goal of security force training and embedding it in all aspects of operational training. Doing so in a regional context can usefully highlight the progress of national forces that have further advanced the agenda of professionalizing their units and can also serve as another avenue through which to identify the regional "change agents" in Recommendation 3.

RECOMMENDATION 6:

Promote the reform and modernization of security force academy curricula through regional workshops on academic management, curricular content, and pedagogy.

Recommendation 6 focuses on another entry point, one that is more likely to be embraced by more risk averse regional governments. The reform and modernization of security force academies is a long-term and costly initiative, which many in the region have deferred in order to address more immediate security threats and challenges. But it is one of the most promising entry points for S.S.R. due to its potential to shape the next generation of security officers region-wide.

Because the institutional and capacity gaps are so urgent, there will likely be interest on the part of the leadership of these academies to engage in workshops that address how to manage security force academies (human capital, assessment of student learning, strategic planning), improve content (modules and courses, teaching materials, classroom technologies), and adapt/adopt new pedagogical tools (instructional methods). Doing so in a regional context provides MENA governments that have made strides in academy reforms, such as Saudi Arabia, Oman, Algeria, and Jordan, with the opportunity to share their achievements and provides resource-constrained governments in the region with valuable tools and curricular content.

RECOMMENDATION 7:

Foster the sharing of best practices among parliamentarians for oversight and accountability practices in the internal security sector.

Recommendation 7 highlights another area where regional cooperation can prove beneficial and where engagement at the regional level is more likely to be welcomed. This is particularly true for the region's transitioning states, where newly elected parliamentarians are struggling to fulfill their new roles, often with little real experience and few institutional resources to support their vital oversight functions. Here, regional cooperation is likely best approached through general skill-building activities focused on specific parliamentary oversight processes (how to review a ministerial budget, how to review procurement processes, how to incorporate expert testimony, how to manage a parliamentary inquiry) and through activities that build relationships among parliamentarians (both within and across countries).

RECOMMENDATION 8:

Under the auspices of international centers of excellence for S.S.R. and with regional S.S.R. experts, develop a Blueprint for S.S.R. in the MENA Region with specific guidance for how to implement and sequence S.S.R. activities in the transitioning and post-authoritarian context.[35]

Recommendation 8 seeks to address a critical gap in knowledge about how to strengthen, reform or otherwise improve the delivery of internal security in the region. Much has been written about the challenges and roadblocks to S.S.R. in the region, but little comprehensive guidance exists for how to implement such efforts in the challenging context of transitioning and post-authoritarian states. Developing such a blueprint—essentially a "Development Assistance Committee (DAC) Handbook for the MENA region" would help address this critical gap. The regional S.S.R. network can also serve as a useful venue for identifying and including regional experts and for disseminating the guidance.

These recommendations do not address the full range of internal security challenges across the region simply because many of these challenges can only be dealt with through national efforts. These recommendations are meant to provide entry points for building a wider regional consensus about the need for improving the delivery of security, meeting the security needs of citizens across the region, and disseminating best practices for how to do so. Given the broader political constraints across the region and the inherent challenges of cooperating in the internal security dimension, these recommendations center on building the human capital necessary to achieve the long-term goal of a more stable and prosperous Middle East.

Of all the potential spheres in which regional cooperation can be promoted in the MENA region, the internal security dimension is likely to be the last to deliver meaningful results, and success in doing so will most likely hinge on the successful implementation of regional cooperation in the political, defense, and economic sectors. Indeed, greater cooperation in these other spheres may well be prerequisite for wider and deeper cooperation in the internal security dimension. However, as the development experts who first proposed the S.S.R. approach discovered, meaningful and sustainable development is not possible without security. They are inextricably linked. Economies cannot flourish if ordinary citizens cannot safely conduct business or transport their goods between cities. Investment will flounder if impunity persists. Repression cannot overcome regional governments' legitimacy deficits. Stability—not just across the region, but within each society—is essential for the broader advancement of the Middle East and North Africa. And stability cannot be achieved if the dysfunctions of the internal security dimension are not addressed. Although the goal is an ambitious one, the better provision of internal security across the region is a foundational building block for the broader advancement of the region and the achievement of stability and prosperity for the next generation.

ENDNOTES

1. Ross Harrison, "Defying Gravity: Working Toward a Regional Strategy for a Stable Middle East," *Middle East Institute Policy Paper Series*, May 2015, accessed July 13, 2016, http://www.mei.edu/sites/default/files/publications/Harrison%20policy%20paper.pdf.

2. INTERPOL does promote cooperation and information sharing among internal security forces in the MENA region, as do other international organizations, like the World Customs Organization. For example, there is a memorandum of understanding between INTERPOL and the Arab Interior Ministers' Council and other INTERPOL-sponsored activities with INTERPOL chiefs in the MENA region. See www.interpol.int.

3. S. Harrendorf, M. Heiskanen, and S. Malby, "International Statistics on Crime and Justice," Helsinki and Vienna: European Institute for Crime and Prevention Control, Affiliated with the United Nations (HEUNI) and United Nations Office on Drugs and Crime (U.N.O.D.C.), 2010, 5, accessed July 13, 2016, https://www.unodc.org/documents/data-and-analysis/Crime-statistics/International_Statistics_on_Crime_and_Justice.pdf.

4. Interviews with author, Tunisia, Algeria and Morocco, March-November 2014; Querine Hanlon and Matthew Herbert, "Border Security Challenges in the Grand Maghreb," USIP Peaceworks no. 109 (2015).

5. Interviews with author, Tunisia, Algeria and Morocco, March-November 2014.

6. Interviews with author, Tunisia, September 2014.

7. U.S. Department of State, Office of the Spokesperson, "Global Counterterrorism Forum Co-Chairs' Fact Sheet: About G.C.T.F.," September 27, 2015, accessed June 9, 2016, http://www.state.gov/r/pa/prs/ps/2015/09/247369.htm.

8. MENA member states of the G.C.T.F. include: Algeria, Egypt, Jordan, Morocco, Qatar, Saudi Arabia, Turkey, and the UAE. An additional 40 countries have participated in G.C.T.F.-sponsored events. The six G.C.T.F. working groups are: (1) Criminal Justice Sector and the Rule of Law, co-chaired by Egypt and the United States; (2) Countering Violent Extremism (CVE), co-chaired by the UAE and the UK; (3) Detention and Reintegration, co-chaired by Australia and Indonesia; (4) Foreign Terrorist Fighters (F.T.F.), co-chaired by Morocco and the Netherlands; (5) Sahel Region Capacity-Building, co-chaired by Algeria and Canada; and (6) Horn of Africa Region Capacity-Building, co-chaired by the E.U. and Turkey; "The Global Counterterrorism Forum," accessed July 13, 2016, www.thegctf.org.

9. "The Global Counterterrorism Forum," accessed July 13, 2016, www.thegctf.org.

10. Salam Hafex, "Dubai Police Train Regional Drugs Task Force," *The National*, July 30, 2008, accessed July 13, 2016, http://www.thenational.ae/news/uae-news/dubai-police-train-regional-drugs-task-force; "Dubai Police Drug Law Enforcement Capacity Building and Prevention of Drug Abuse among Youth," UNODC, accessed July 13, 2016, https://www.unodc.org/middleeastandnorthafrica/en/project-profiles/xmej21.html.

11. "The Arab Interior Ministers Council," accessed July 13, 2016, http://www.aim-council.org/Pages/default.aspx.

12. "Heads of INTERPOL Bureaus across Middle East and North Africa Address Regional Policing Issues," INTERPOL, September 23, 2014, accessed July 13, 2016, http://www.interpol.int/News-and-media/News/2014/N2014-181.

13. "The Council of Arab Ministers," Naif Arab University for Security Sciences, accessed July 13, 2016, http://www.nauss.edu.sa/En/NationalCooperation/Pages/mjlswzra.aspx.

14. Querine Hanlon and Richard H. Shultz, Jr., eds., *Prioritizing Security Sector Reform: A New U.S. Approach* (Washington, DC: USIP Press, 2016), 8-9.

15. Ibid., 22.

16. Organization for Economic Co-operation and Development (OECD), *Development Assistance Committee (DAC) Guidelines and Reference Series: Security System Reform and Governance* (Paris: OECD, 2005), 16.

17. Querine Hanlon, "Security Sector Reform in Tunisia: A Year after the Jasmine Revolution," USIP Special Report no. 304 (March 2012); Querine Hanlon, "S.S.R. in Tunisia: A Case of Postauthoritarian Transition," in Prioritizing Security Sector Reform, 69-96 (Washington, DC: USIP Press, 2016); Derek Luttberbeck, "Arab Uprisings and Armed Forces: Between Openness and Resistance," S.S.R. Paper 2 (Geneva: Center for the Democratic Control

of the Armed Forces, 2011); Yezid Sayigh, *Dilemmas of Reform: Policing in Arab Transitions* (Washington, DC: Carnegie Middle East Center, March 2016); "Fixing Broken Windows: Security Sector Reform in Palestine, Lebanon and Yemen," Carnegie Papers no. 17 (October 2009); Yezid Sayigh, "Security Sector Reform in the Arab Region: Challenges to Developing an Indigenous Agenda," Arab Reform Initiative Thematic Papers (2007).

18. Yezid Sayigh, *Dilemmas of Reform*, 3.

19. Ibid., 5.

20. Ibid., 1.

21. These principles and the roadmap that follows are drawn from Hanlon and Shultz, *Prioritizing Security Sector Reform*, 15-34, 237-241.

22. OECD, *Security System Reform and Governance* (OECD: DAC Guidelines and Reference Series, 2005), 34; "Securing Peace and Development: The Role of the United Nations in Supporting S.S.R.," Report of the Secretary-General A/62/659-S/2008/39, January 23, 2008, accessed July 13, 2016, http://unssr.unlb. org/Resources/UNDocuments/tabid/255/SMID/498/ItemId/78/Default.aspx.

23. Albrecht Schnabel, "Ideal Requirements versus Real Environments in Security Sector Reform," in *Security Sector Reform in Challenging Environments*, eds. Hans Born and Albrecht Schnabel (Geneva: Center for the Democratic Control of the Armed forces, 2009), 5.

24. Ibid.

25. OECD, *Security System Reform and Governance* (OECD: DAC Guidelines and Reference Series, 2005), 21.

26. Nicole Ball and Dylan Hendrickson, *Trends In Security Sector Reform (S.S.R.): Policy, Practice and Research* (London: King's College Security and Development Group, revised January 27, 2006); Alice Hills, "Learning the Hard Way: Implementing S.S.R. in Africa's Post-Authoritarian States," in *The Future of Security Sector Reform*, ed. Mark Sedra (Ontario: The Center for International Governance Innovation, 2010), 189.

27. Melanne A. Civic and Michael Miklaucic, "Introduction: The State and the Use of Force: Monopoly and Legitimacy," in *Monopoly of Force: The Nexus of DDR and S.S.R.*, eds. Melanne A. Civic and Michael Miklaucic (Washington, DC: National Defense University Press, 2011) xv-xxv; Herbert Wulf, "Challenging the Weberian Concept of the State: The Future of the Monopoly of Violence," *Australian Center for Peace and Conflict Studies Occasional Paper*, no. 9 (December 2007); Martina Fischer and Beatrix Schmelzle, eds., *Building Peace in the Absence of States: Challenging the Discourse on State Failure* (Berlin: Berghof Research Center, 2009).

28. Wulf, "Challenging the Weberian Concept of the State: The Future of the Monopoly of Violence," 10.

29. Ibid., 11.

30. OECD, *DAC Handbook*, 21.

31. For a more detailed discussion of this point see Robert Egnell and Peter Halden "Laudable, Ahistorical and Overambitious: Security Sector Reform Meets State Formation Theory," *Conflict, Security, and Development* (April 2009): 27-54; Mark Sedra, "Towards Second Generation Security Sector Reform," in *The Future of Security Sector Reform*, ed. Mark Sedra (Ontario: The Center for International Governance Innovation, 2010), 102-166.

32. Querine Hanlon and Joyce Kasee, "Regional Security through Inclusive Reform in the Maghreb and the Sahel," USIP Peace Brief, December 23, 2015, accessed July 13, 2016, http://www.usip.org/publications/2015/12/23/regional-security-through-inclusive-reform-in-the-maghreb-and-the-sahel.

33. See for example the G.C.T.F. Rabat Memorandum on Good Practices for Effective Counterterrorism Practice in the Criminal Justice Sector, accessed July 13, https://www.thegctf.org/documents/10162/38299/Rabat+Memorandum-English.

34. Interview with the author, 2014.

35. A good place to begin is Carnegie Endowment for International Peace's Arab Voices of the Challenges of the New Middle East project, accessed July 13, 2016, http://carnegieendowment.org/2016/02/12/arab-voices-on-challenges-of-new-middle-east/itru; and the Geneva-based Democratic Control of the Armed Forces (DCAF) regional programming and publications; In the S.S.R. literature, there are four "contexts" or environments in which S.S.R. can be conducted. These include the post-conflict, post-authoritarian transition

CHAPTER ELEVEN

TOWARD A REGIONAL FRAMEWORK FOR THE MIDDLE EAST:

TAKEAWAYS FROM OTHER REGIONS

ROSS HARRISON

THE ARGUMENT

> *"Here we encounter two conflicting concepts with which we must come to grips in our time: the idea of national solidarity and the idea of international cooperation"* – *Gustav Stresemann, German Foreign Minister of the Weimar Republic, Nobel Peace Prize Acceptance Speech, June 29, 1927.*

Iran, Saudi Arabia, and Turkey, states which in theory have the most to gain from a stable and prosperous Middle East, are locked in destructive proxy wars in Syria, Iraq, and Yemen. While efforts have been mounted to get these regional titans to work cooperatively to bring hostilities to an end, there is little evidence that this will happen any time soon.

Other regions of the world have been racked with equal or even greater levels of violence, but eventually developed institutional frameworks that helped with the transition from protracted conflict to stability. The question this chapter explores is what role a regional institutional architecture could play in moving the major powers in the Middle East away from a zero-sum conflict approach to a point where they act on their common regional economic and security interests.

It would be fanciful to think that the regional powers in the Middle East will now suddenly shift gears and orient their attention toward creating regional institutions, even though it might be in their long-term interests to do so. In fact, the experiences of Europe and Asia instruct us that the window of opportunity for creating regional institutions usually opens only once major conflicts have subsided, something that seems a long way off for the Middle East.

But if we look at the formation of regional institutions as a long-term project and the culmination of a process of regionalization of the Middle East, then there is logic to starting now. Even if there is no immediate window of opportunity for creating a formal institutional structure, the process of building nodes of cooperation that could culminate in a regional architectural framework as we move towards 2020, 2030, and beyond should commence.

We need to be realistic about the obstacles that will be confronted on a pathway toward regionalization. Essentially, regionalization is the process of creating interdependencies between states. This chapter will argue that the idea of interconnectedness through common interests has little purchase in the Middle East today, as the region is one of the least integrated of the world. Of course, all states understand they have something to gain by stabilizing the region, but getting states to cooperate involves more than the acknowledgement of abstract common interests. It involves translating these into a web of tangible benefits that can only be maintained and increased through cooperation.

It will also be argued that even if the problem of common regional interests being too abstract can be overcome, there are challenges at the domestic political level within each state that hinder cooperation. Cooperation on behalf of long-term regional interests—where the political costs and risks are incurred in the short-term, but the payoffs only accrue in the long-term—requires a high-level of government legitimacy and political capital, which is lacking in most of the key states today.[1] As a result, there is a tendency for governments with political capital deficits to focus more on short-term domestic interests and eschew longer term regional common interests.

Drawing insights from Asia, Africa, Europe, and Latin America, this chapter will present possible pathways for regionalization in the Middle East, mechanisms for fostering cooperation, as well as different possible models for how regionalization could mature into a more formal regional architecture. It will be argued that we should proceed along two tracks. One track involves thinking about what kind of regional institutional framework would be the most effective in transitioning the Middle East from conflict to stability in the long-term. A second track is more immediately actionable and entails taking measures that facilitate regionalization. The key to catalyzing regionalization is identifying low-risk, legitimacy-enhancing initiatives around which states can cooperate. The idea behind this is that building political capital in these early low-risk, high-benefit initiatives will give states the capacity to invest later in longer term, more politically risky areas, such as cooperating to create a regional institutional framework.

There will be understandable skepticism about the notion that regionalization and institution building might be a place to look for answers to the problems besetting the Middle East today. Given the immediacy of conflict mitigation and humanitarian relief needs in the Middle East, one might consider expending intellectual capital on what is at best a medium-to-long term project a fool's errand.

But focusing on the more immediate on-the-ground situations in Syria, Iraq, Yemen, and Libya, while thinking ahead as to how the region might eventually transition from chaos to stability are not mutually exclusive endeavors. It would in fact be reckless to address the immediate crises without also peering around the corner and asking what processes and structures might be put in place to handle the needs of post-conflict reconstruction and to protect backsliding once the region returns to stability.

Few today would claim that Jean Monnet or Robert Schuman, credited with being founders of what became the European Union, were reckless when they peered beyond the devastation of post-World War II Europe to envision a regional architecture that would create interdependence and provide mechanisms to prevent Europe from plunging back into chaos and violence.[2]

Lessons from Other Regions

The only advantage of the Middle East being one of the least integrated regions of the world is that it is still tabula rasa. While every region's experience is unique, we can nevertheless find clues from the historical circumstances of other areas of the world as to how the Middle East could start the process of regionalization and develop regional institutions that facilitate cooperation.

The European Union (E.U.)

Back story

The story of the European Union is the evolution of regionalization in stages. After World War II, Jean Monnet and Robert Schuman believed that reconstruction and integration weren't taking place fast enough and that cooperative efforts between the European powers needed to accelerate. The first phase of this started with the Treaty of Paris, which in 1951 established the European Coal and Steel Community (E.C.S.C.). The theory was that if the production of coal and steel for France, Germany, Italy, Netherlands, and Luxembourg would be placed under a central authority, the probability of war between these countries would be greatly diminished. The treaty converted what was merely an abstract idea of states sharing an interest in regional stability into something more tangible. States would be constrained by the fact that their coal and steel industries would be under a supranational authority, but also by the specter of mutually assured economic destruction if war broke out. The E.C.S.C. was followed in 1958 with the establishment of the European Economic Community (E.E.C.), and in 1992 with the Treaty on European Union (Maastricht Treaty), which established the European Union we know today.[3]

MODEL OF COOPERATION

The E.C.S.C. created the first strand of interdependence in what was an atomized post-World War II Europe. Over time, integration of the coal and steel industries stimulated interdependence and cooperation on other economic and political matters, eventually culminating in cooperation to create the European Union.

The mechanism for cooperation once the E.U. was established was a body of laws, which developed over time with the negotiation, agreement, and ratification of treaties. The culmination of this was the Treaty of Lisbon of 2007, which created a President of the European Council and new procedures for rendering the E.U. a unified actor on the global scene.

Because the E.U. is underpinned by a body of law enshrined in formal treaties, cooperation is more institutionalized and less ad hoc than in Asia, Latin America and Africa. While bilateral cooperation among members is necessary, the ceding of authority and sovereignty to Brussels on many issues is a unique feature of the European Union. There is, however, the principle of subsidiarity, which means that outside the domains where the E.U. has exclusive powers, there is a preference for state-level decision-making. What this means is that in addition to formal multilateral relations, there is the need for more informal bilateral bargaining between states. For example, monetary policy related to the euro is the purview of the European Central Bank, while fiscal policy is the responsibility of the 28 national governments, meaning any cooperation that occurs in this area is voluntary and bilateral.[4]

TAKEAWAYS FOR THE MIDDLE EAST

Given the sensitivity to sovereignty issues, the E.U. isn't a model of cooperation that could be imported to the Middle East. But what can be gleaned from the European case is that regionalization can occur in different stages, and that economic interdependence and cooperation can be a wedge for later political coordination. The experience of the E.U. teaches us that early progress towards regionalization can open up pathways to more formalized and elaborate institutions. The question this begs (which will be dealt with later) is whether there is a counterpart in the Middle East to the role steel and coal played in catalyzing the process of regionalization in Europe.

Another insight the Middle East can glean from the E.U. is the importance of timing for the process of regionalization to take hold. The impetus for regionalization in Europe was the end of World War II. The lesson here for the Middle East is that while the early stages of regionalization might be able to begin now, it is unlikely that any window for more formalized institutions will open until the proxy and civil wars have subsided.

Last but not least, the E.U. instructs us as to the indispensability of courageous leaders like Monnet and Schuman who were willing to look beyond the present and see a better future.

THE ASSOCIATION OF SOUTHEAST ASIAN NATIONS (ASEAN)

BACK STORY

In August of 1967, the foreign ministers of Thailand, Indonesia, Singapore, Malaysia, and Philippines met at a Thai resort to hammer out the terms of the ASEAN agreement. The catalyst was the end of the guerrilla war former Indonesian President Sukarno had waged against newly independent Malaysia. With Sukarno's ouster by Major General Suharto in 1967, a pathway to ending these hostilities appeared.

The idea for forming ASEAN was proposed by Thai Foreign Minister Thanat Khoman while conducting peace negotiations between Indonesia and Malaysia. The belief among those taking part in the negotiations was that guerrilla wars like the one just ended, plus the ongoing Vietnam conflict, posed threats to regional stability. What is clear is that a sense of geopolitical vulnerability, plus an awareness that the only pathway to economic prosperity was through regional cooperation, became prevalent enough to muster the political will needed to create ASEAN.[5]

MODEL FOR COOPERATION

There were several key features to the ASEAN model. One was the principle of voluntary compliance, a central tenet of the "ASEAN Way." Given the legacy of Dutch, British, and French colonialism in the region, ASEAN members were averse to formal enforcement mechanisms that could possibly impinge on their sovereignty.[6]

But what was it about the ASEAN Way that fostered cooperation between former adversaries? While there were many factors, the principle of noninterference in the internal affairs of member states was important, as it lowered the political temperature of interstate relations. By taking the kind of meddling Indonesia had perpetrated on Malaysia off the table, the idea of cooperation became less politically threatening.

Also, over time soft power and a shift in political culture were sufficiently strong to facilitate cooperation. An example of cooperation made possible by the deft use of soft power occurred when in 1978 Vietnam breached the borders of Cambodia (both non-ASEAN members at the time). ASEAN was influential in getting its members to censure Vietnam and internationalized the dispute by lobbying the United Nations to intervene.

Getting consensus was no small feat, given the initial inclination of Indonesia and Malaysia to break ranks with other ASEAN members and accommodate Vietnam. But once it was clear that the conflict posed a threat to Thailand, a fellow ASEAN member, they reversed their position. This was difficult as both countries saw China as a bigger threat than Vietnam. But two decades into the experiment, the normative tug from ASEAN was sufficiently strong to tilt members toward cooperation.[7]

But there was an even more sophisticated strategy to how ASEAN fostered cooperation, which involved a focus on improving the domestic political conditions of member states. The theory was that leaders would be more likely to cooperate on regional issues if they weren't plagued by legitimacy crises at home.[8] It was understood that the legitimacy of leaders was hinged to the economic performance of the states. So ASEAN started focusing on investment-driven growth strategies that helped attract foreign investors to the region.[9]

The strategy seemed to work in moving Southeast Asia along the path of regionalization. On economic issues central to regime legitimacy, there was even receptivity to making exceptions to the "ASEAN Way" of never ceding state sovereignty.[10] In fact, ASEAN, through the Asian Economic Community (A.E.C.), is moving toward a single market by 2020 which involves members agreeing to more binding rules. The case shows the potential for regional institutions to improve the domestic political climate of states, increasing the capacity and will to cooperate.[11]

But in addition to meeting the domestic needs of states as a means for securing cooperation, ASEAN nurtured a regional identity by linking the bloc to other areas of Asia and beyond. China's treatment of ASEAN as a single entity affirmed a distinct Southeast Asian identity, reinforcing the process of regionalization.[12] Moreover, while the countries within the bloc were diverse, the common front created for engaging the world reinforced shared interests.

This common front engagement didn't happen automatically. The institutional bridge for engaging with China, South Korea, and Japan was

"ASEAN Plus Three (A.P.T.).[13] ASEAN also created the ASEAN Regional Forum (A.R.F.), which included the United States, Canada, North Korea, Russia, and the European Union, among others. While nothing prevented members from engaging bilaterally, the role that ASEAN played as a representative body to the broader international community reinforced regional interests and strengthened the norm of cooperation.

TAKEAWAYS FOR THE MIDDLE EAST

What does ASEAN have to teach us about both the perils and opportunities of erecting a regional architecture for the Middle East? First, ASEAN should give us some confidence that working toward a regional architecture amidst turmoil isn't necessarily quixotic, despite the current dire state of the Middle East. The following quote is about the formation of ASEAN in 1967, but could just as well pertain to conditions in the Middle East today:

> "What is remarkable about this grouping is the fact that it could be established at all. Relations among the founding members were highly charged in the 1960s, with interstate rivalries expressed in various forms: 1) irredentism, when neighbors laid claim to the territory of other states; 2) assistance provided by one government to secessionist groups in another state; and 3) non-recognition of another state, thus denying legitimacy to its government. These added to the existing vulnerabilities of national governments facing the difficult task of governing domestically divided societies and controlling peripheral parts of the state."[14]

Second, if a regional architecture for the Middle East would not include Iran or Israel, bridge mechanisms like A.P.T. can be effective platforms for forging cooperation with these states. Like ASEAN, whose charter members embraced market economics and developed a pragmatic way to reach out to ideological rivals like China, the Gulf Cooperation Council (G.C.C.), Egypt, and Turkey could reach out to Iran and Israel through a bridge mechanism like A.P.T.

But ASEAN also teaches us that membership in regional institutions can evolve in stages. ASEAN was chartered in 1967 with a core group of members—Thailand, Malaysia, Indonesia, Singapore, and the Philippines—and then expanded in the 1980s and 1990s to include Vietnam, Laos, Myanmar, Brunei, and Cambodia. When ASEAN was created in the 1960s, it would have been unfathomable to its founding members that Communist states like Vietnam and Cambodia would one day be included, much like today it is hard to imagine Saudi Arabia, Turkey, Egypt, Iran, and Israel under a single multilateral umbrella.

A third takeaway is that regional organizations that rely on non-compulsory means can engender cooperation by focusing on issues that build domestic political capital for states. ASEAN's focus on economic matters took into account the domestic political constraints of its members. With legitimacy deficits being a characterizing feature of several Middle Eastern states, a focus on issues that can build the domestic political capital necessary for broader regional cooperation should be part of a strategy.

Last, like with ASEAN, which emerged from the armistice between Indonesia and Malaysia, the political will for creating a regional architecture in the Middle East will likely follow some historic event or new threat. It could possibly be a threat from a non-state actor more disruptive than ISIS. Or perhaps it could come from a sudden moderation of policy in Iran or Saudi Arabia.[15]

FROM THE ORGANIZATION OF AFRICAN UNITY (1963) TO THE AFRICAN UNION (2002)

BACK STORY

The Organization of African Unity (O.A.U.) was founded in Addis Ababa in 1963 under the leadership of Ethiopian Emperor Haile Selassie and Ghanaian President Kwame Nkruma. Its mandate was to shepherd states out from under the yoke of colonialism and then safeguard their territorial integrity following independence. The O.A.U. supported successful liberation movements In Mozambique, Angola, and Guinea Bissau, and continued supporting them after they achieved independence from Portugal in the 1970s.[16]

One of the interesting twists of the O.A.U. in terms of cooperation was that independence entailed dissolving large colonial blocs, such as French Equatorial Africa and French West Africa, into separate countries. Before dismemberment, these blocs were held together through extensive functional cooperation, and their dissolution brought an end to the regionalization glue that enabled this.[17]

By the end of the 20th century, it was clear that Africa needed a new organization with a more ambitious agenda of addressing the overall economic and political health of the region. At the 1999 summit of the O.A.U. in Libya, the late President Muammar Qaddafi spearheaded the drafting of the Sirte Declaration which called for the formation of the African Union (A.U.). If the O.A.U. had been state-centric, charged with delivering Africa out of colonialism, its successor was charged with leading African states further down the road of regionalization.

MODEL FOR COOPERATION

It is easy to disparage the O.A.U.'s track record in forging cooperation, particularly when compared to ASEAN. But it is important to understand that there are active and passive types of cooperation. The O.A.U. was successful in forging passive cooperation, where members were implored "to respect frontiers as existing on their achievement of national independence," but weren't called on to take unified actions.[18] The logic was that states emerging from independence would be fragile and therefore couldn't be expected to work on behalf of regional interests. The O.A.U. saw state fragility as the biggest regional threat, going so far as to deny recognition of the right of self-determination to minority groups that laid claim to the states and challenged their boundaries.[19] Consequently, it was believed that the O.A.U. gave more to the states than they gave back to the organization.[20]

The question for the O.A.U.'s successor organization, the A.U., is whether it will be able to shift from this state-centricity to a broader regionalization mandate and an emphasis on active, not just passive, cooperation. While the jury is still out, the A.U. initiatives that have been launched so far are focused on more active cooperation and the goal of broader regionalization. The Continental Early Warning Systems (CEWS) is a security initiative that scans the horizon for both intra and inter-country threats to regional security, mobilizing the financial and technical resources from A.U. member states.[21] On the economic front, the New Partnership for African Development (NEPAD) is a conduit for connecting E.U. and U.S. donors to economic development needs across communities in Africa. And the A.U. Post-Conflict Reconstruction and Development (P.C.R.D.) policy has been active in reconstruction activities in the Sudan, Sierra Leone, and the Democratic Republic of Congo, an effort which requires active coordination of resource across the membership.

TAKEAWAYS FOR THE MIDDLE EAST

Given the prevalence of state failure in the Middle East today, there are lessons to be learned from the O.A.U. of the 1960s and 1970s. The O.A.U. denial of the right of self-determination to sub-state minority groups, and the emphasis of the primacy of the state, has direct relevance to the Middle East today, given the territorial challenges posed by non-state actors like ISIS and al-Qaeda. One of the principles for any Middle East regional architecture will need to be the sanctity of state boundaries.

But we should be careful not to take this analogy too far, for as bad as the situation in the Middle East is, it has some advantages over Africa. In Africa, even the large states like Nigeria and the Democratic Republic of the Congo have been weakened by internal strife, reducing their capacity for regional leadership. In the Middle East, strong states like Iran, Saudi Arabia, and Turkey don't face an existential threat by sub-state actors, which gives them at least the capacity (if not the will) to assert regional leadership.

Another lesson for the Middle East is that regionalization can occur in stages. In Africa, the O.A.U. can be thought of as the state-centric phase followed by a broader regionalization phase of the A.U. Similarly a regional architecture for the Middle East could start around a state-centric approach for Iraq, Syria, Yemen, and Libya, while a later phase would address broader regional challenges. Tied to this is the importance of having an organization, like NEPAD and P.C.R.D., which for Africa acted as central interfaces with the international community. This has direct parallels with the Middle East, where international involvement in post-conflict reconstruction and economic development efforts of Syria, Iraq, Yemen, and Libya will need to interface with regional institutions to be effective.

LATIN AMERICA

BACK STORY

Latin American regional integration goes back to the early 1800s when Simon Bolivar envisioned unity as the key to security and prosperity for the fledgling states newly independent from Spain. The first successful attempt to form a regional institution, however, was the Pan American Union established in 1890, which created a forum for dialogue between Latin American countries and the United States. Decades later, as the United States confronted the realities of the Cold War, and saw the need for hemispheric-wide defense against what was perceived as a growing Communist threat, this organization gave way to the Organization of American States (O.A.S.) in 1948. In the first few decades the organization was heavily dominated by the United States. Evidence of this was that the United States successfully suspended Cuba from the O.A.S. in the 1960s, despite opposition from Mexico, Brazil, and Argentina, and there was only muted criticism after U.S. interventions in Chile in 1973 and Panama in 1989.

Another example of cooperation in Latin America was MERCOSUR, a common market between Brazil, Argentina, Paraguay, Uruguay, and Venezuela (suspended) established in 1991.

MODEL OF COOPERATION

Regional cooperation in Latin America formed around common threats and opportunities, such as the Pan American Union or the O.A.S., or around economic opportunity such as MERCOSUR. Part of the motivation for MERCOSUR was the desire to transform the relationship between Brazil and Argentina, the two regional economic powerhouses, from a competitive stance to mutually beneficial trade relations, on the premise that this would have positive regional economic spillover effects. [22]

Another impetus to cooperation was threat based—the desire to counterbalance and contain U.S. power in the western hemisphere. In response to pressure from the regional powers, the O.A.S. in 1993 adopted new principles directly aimed at limiting the scope of U.S. political intervention.[23] Outside the O.A.S. there were sub-regional institutional forums purposed with counterbalancing the economic influence of the United States. The Union of

South American Nations (UNASUR) was formed in 2004 in order to integrate MERCOSUR and the Andean Community. But it also represented a repudiation of the neo-liberal Washington Consensus economic development model. While the U.S. government, the I.M.F. and World Bank promoted the notion that redressing income inequality required country-level economic reforms, UNASUR pushed regional integration as a better pathway. Around this view, a "Buenos Aires consensus" developed, promoted by Brazilian President Lula da Silva and Argentinean President Nestor Kirchner, as well as the "red tide" governments of Hugo Chavez in Venezuela and Evo Morales of Bolivia.[24]

Counterbalancing the United States through sub-regional institutions, however, didn't mean sundering the bonds between Latin America and its northern neighbor. When Chavez proposed that the Bolivarian Alliance for the Peoples of Our America (ALBA) should lead to the dismemberment of O.A.S., there was strong opposition from more conservative members. In fact, the relationship with the United States was essential to Latin American regionalization. The need to counterbalance the superpower to the north created the geopolitical and economic raison d'être for regional institutions and the impetus for cooperation for Latin American states.

TAKEAWAYS FOR THE MIDDLE EAST

One of the main lessons for the Middle East is that regional institutions can both counterbalance great power influence and provide a common interface for constructive engagement with them. There are dangers, however, in drawing too many parallels between Latin America and the Middle East. Latin America had to contend with a single power, the United States, while states in the Middle East have to balance relations between the United States, Russia, China and the European Union. Nevertheless, the lesson of Latin America is that regional frameworks can provide an interface with international powers yet preserve the independence of states.

Another lesson for the Middle East from Latin America is the potential for regional institutions to act as a bridge between different ideological blocs. While in Latin America the tensions have been between the leftist "pink tide" approaches of Cuba, Bolivia, Venezuela (enshrined in ALBA), the more conservative approaches of Mexico, Columbia, Peru, and Chile (Pacific Alliance), and the neo-liberal approaches of Brazil and Argentina, in the Middle East the cleavages that regional organizations would need to bridge are likely to be on national (Iranian, Arab, and Turkish) or sectarian (Sunni and Shiite) lines.

TRACK 1: PROJECT REGIONALIZATION

Other regions teach us that the conditions conducive to creating a regional architectural framework arise at critical moments in history. For Europe, it was the end of World War II for ASEAN the armistice between Indonesia and Malaysia, for Africa and Latin America it was independence from colonial Europe.

This may be discouraging for the Middle East given that decisive moments have come and gone, with few leaders taking a transformative approach as a result. In addition, the civil conflicts in Syria, Iraq, Libya, and Yemen might continue on for decades, and when they do wind down, there may never be a formal cessation of hostilities. Moreover, the regional leaders who would need to champion the creation of regional institutions, like Iran, Saudi Arabia and Turkey, seem bent on fueling the civil wars.

While the prospects for creating a regional architecture seem grim now, we shouldn't give up hope for this troubled region. Instead, we should think about the process of building a regional architecture as a long-term project. We can't be blind to the possibility that game-changing events may occur that could create the political will necessary for adversaries like Saudi Arabia and Iran to cooperate. It could be the rise of an armed group even more threatening than ISIS, or the emergence of a new leader in Iran, Turkey or Saudi Arabia who plays the role of Sadat going to Jerusalem or Nixon going to China. Because of these possibilities, regional and international powers should put intellectual energy into thinking about and planning for the eventuality that an opportunity for a regional framework for the Middle East might open up.

But we also need to understand that the creation of formal institutions, like the E.U. and ASEAN, were not discrete events, but rather part of a bigger process of regionalization that unfolded over time. In each of the cases we looked at, formal institutions were created at different points on the regionalization continuum. The regionalization process of post-World War II Europe was sparked by the creation of the E.C.S.C. in 1951, but it didn't culminate in a formal institution like the European Union until 1993. In Southeast Asia, the formal institution of ASEAN came much earlier on the continuum, with the institution itself being the primary catalyst for the regionalization process. In both cases, the emergence of institutions were part of, not separate from, a more important process of regionalization.

The message for the Middle East is that the relationship between regional institutions and the process of regionalization is an important one, but we needn't wait for the former to start the latter. In fact, we should be thinking along the lines of the European model where early efforts at regionalization using economic mechanisms helped build the political will for later institutionalization.

The advantage of a regionalization-first approach is that it can help remove some of the structural obstacles that might prevent the idea of a regional architecture from taking hold in the Middle East. Without regionalization, there are no tangible common interests around which cooperation can take place. And since cooperation is the goal of regional institutions, getting the regionalization piece right is even more important than the timing of establishing the overarching institution itself. Getting regionalization right can help create a pathway toward a regional institutional architecture.

THE REGIONALIZATION CHALLENGE: THE MIDDLE EAST IS CURRENTLY A REGION IN GEOGRAPHY ONLY

"There are no mystical qualities in geographic proximity that make neighboring nations a "unit" in any real sense culturally, politically or economically." – Riggirozzi and Tussie.[25]

Geography alone doesn't qualify the Middle East as a political and economic region. In fact, the Middle East lacks many of the attributes we normally associate with a regional system, such as a modicum of interdependence where all states have a shared interest in regional stability. Of course, we can enumerate the long-term political and economic benefits of peace in the region for Iran, Saudi Arabia, and Turkey, and other states.[26] But these common regional interests are abstract and remote, while the parochial national interests that drove these countries to clash in Syria, Iraq, and Yemen are tangible and more immediate. Without these regional powers believing they have something to lose by sowing regional instability, the idea of shared regional interests is illusory. And without shared regional interests, cooperation, and the prospects for a vibrant regional architecture will remain a pipe dream.

How is it that the Middle East has become a region in name only? The reality is that the regional order in the Middle East has been broken for some time. But the more recent hollowing out of the Arab world, brought about by civil wars, the proliferation of fragile states, and challenges from transnational threats like ISIS, has been the coup de grace in creating an atomized region. Concurrent with the collapse of the old Arab order was the rise of Turkey and the emboldening of Iran.

Out of the ashes of the old regional order emerged a new Middle East, dominated by Saudi Arabia, Turkey, and Iran, states that are the least susceptible to succumbing existentially to the disorder, have the greatest capacity to stabilize the region, and are essential to creating any kind of durable regional architecture.

But this new region is a conflict system. The civil wars have drawn Saudi

Arabia, Iran, and Turkey into their vortex, further destroying the Arab political order as well as the social fabric of many of its constituent societies. Within this new system, even if there is an abstract, theoretical notion of common interests, the fog of war makes it difficult to calculate the costs, risks or benefits of acting on those interests.

PROJECT REGIONALIZATION

Given the fact that today any potential common regional interests are completely overshadowed by the realities of the conflict system the Middle East has become, our efforts on the ground should be oriented to starting the process of regionalization, which is a sine qua non for eventual regional institution building.

We should think of regionalization as a process by which a geographic area becomes a system of interdependencies, where all states have a concrete stake in the stability and prosperity of the region. The goals of regionalization for the Middle East should be two-fold. The first should be to take the abstract notion of common regional interests and convert it into a set of tangible benefits for all states. The second goal should be state-centric, that is focusing on measures that mitigate the domestic constraints on regionalization. The challenge is that states that have domestic legitimacy issues will have difficulty incurring the risks and costs of acting on regional interests when the potential benefits accrue only in the long-term. In other words, states need significant political capital to invest in regional cooperation. The goal of regionalization efforts should be to help bridge the gap, by either absorbing some of the costs or focusing on projects that mitigate the legitimacy issues.

A MIDDLE EAST COUNTERPART TO THE EUROPEAN COAL AND STEEL COMMUNITY?

We should take our cues from ASEAN, which used economic cooperation as a legitimacy enhancer for states, and Europe which focused on particular industries, coal and steel, to build a platform of interdependence between erstwhile adversaries. [27]

The question for the Middle East is whether there is a counterpart to European steel and coal that could be a catalyst for regionalization? One area that has potential is water management. If there is any good news to the water shortage problems that plague the Middle East, it is that do-it-alone approaches are unlikely to be successful given the systemic nature of this environmental problem. Since 50 percent of the region's population depends on water that flows from another state, this is truly a problem that begs for a region-wide effort.[28] Moreover, the problem isn't limited to poor and fragile states. Both Iran and Saudi Arabia, strong countries whose cooperation could positively shape the dynamics of the entire region, are facing the dire effects of water shortages, increasing average temperatures, desertification, and potential food supply problems. Also, ISIS has used water as a weapon, threatening key infrastructure points, which could affect the well-being and security of all states in the region.[29] Projections are that without interventions, per capita availability of water will be cut by 50 percent by 2050.[30]

Additionally, water represents an opportunity for mitigating the domestic political constraints on cooperation. Water resource management is essential to the legitimacy of all regimes in the Middle East, including Iran and Saudi Arabia, with the incentives for cooperation outweighing the political risks.[31] The risks of inaction for states are high, as droughts create conditions for domestic unrest and challenges to regime legitimacy, as was evidenced in Syria after the drought of 2006-10.[32] Positive signals have come from Iran on this issue. On the sidelines of the U.N. General Assembly annual meeting in September, the deputy head of Iran's Department of Environment stated that his country was willing to cooperate to restore dried wetlands and reduce greenhouse gas emissions.[33]

There is the potential for initiatives on water to have positive spill-over effects on security, health and trade—all areas that states should care about in terms of building legitimacy. But right now there is no region-wide approach to water. There have been modest efforts by the Arab League and by Jordan, Israel, and the Palestinian Authority, but these are disconnected efforts and haven't made a dent in the regional problem. Efforts should be made to leverage water as one springboard for broader regionalization. Common initiatives such as water sharing and attracting investment in technologies for dealing with this critical issue could be a seminal step. Israel has made advances in water technology, such as advanced irrigation techniques and low-water use toilets, which ultimately could be integrated into a broader regional strategy.[34]

THE ROLE OF THE INTERNATIONAL COMMUNITY

The biggest boon to regionalization and ultimately the formation of a regional architecture would be a thaw in the relations between Iran and Saudi Arabia. If Russia and the United States continue on the path of treating the Middle East as a zero-sum game, then the probability of cooperation between these two regional powers is low. The international community needs to focus its efforts on repairing this relationship. We should remember that after World War II, the United States was instrumental in repairing relations between erstwhile European adversaries.

What would also improve the probability of success in forming a regional architecture would be an International Middle East Support Group. This is not to suggest that existing alliances between the regional states and the United States, Europe, Russia, and China would ever be abrogated. It is likely that the

United States and its allies will continue to back the Gulf Arab states and Russia will still back Iran and Syria. But perched above these bilateral relationships could be a high-level international support group focused on areas of potential cooperation in the Middle East. The P5+1 approach used during the nuclear talks with Iran, or the International Syria Support Group (I.S.S.G.), could be models. But this would need to be less ad hoc and more overarching than these earlier efforts.[35]

BACKDOOR APPROACHES

There are other initiatives that might be less impactful and immediate as a water project, but could contribute to a slow build toward regionalization. As we saw with ASEAN, it was a focus on economic initiatives that burnished the legitimacy of leaders, freeing them up domestically to cooperate on other economic regional issues. In another essay in this series, economist Bernard Hoekman argues that in the current toxic environment in the Middle East, where bilateral trade initiatives have little chance of gaining traction, the sweet spot may be a bottom-up approach, focusing on business-to-business activities.[36] His argument is that businesses have an interest in lower trade barriers, and could be the spearhead of a trade liberalization trend.

Further down the road, another possible backdoor area for advancing the process of regionalization could be the economic opportunities provided by the post-conflict reconstruction needs in Syria, Iraq, and Yemen. Hedi Larbi, another author in this series, argues that cross-border cooperation will be essential to meet the overwhelming logistical and resource demands of these endeavors. Iraq will present opportunities for Iran and Turkey, and once Syria is stabilized, reconstruction business opportunities will exist for Jordan, Lebanon, Turkey, Iran, and G.C.C. states.[37] While these will have to wait for an end to hostilities, there are voices suggesting that the planning for this be done now.[38] These kinds of low-key initiatives could pay regionalization dividends tomorrow.

TRACK 2: BUILDING A REGIONAL ARCHITECTURE—THREE MODELS

> "Devolution is the most powerful political force of our age. But devolution has an important counterpart: aggregation. The smaller our political units get, the more they must fuse into larger commonwealths of shared resources in order to survive." – Parag Khanna, author of Connectography: Mapping the Future of Global Civilization

The establishment of regional institutions is an important milestone on the continuum of regionalization. Without regional institutions to cement and sustain the progress and stability created, regionalization remains vulnerable.

This section will look at three different possible models for what an architectural framework might look like. While they are presented as discrete options, they could also be thought of as different phases of regionalization, much like how pioneering efforts to form regional institutions in Latin America, Europe, Africa, and Asia, were opening gambits that later led to more complex institutional schemes.

As witnessed in our review of other regions, regional frameworks need to embody a set of principles that member states subscribe to. All models presented here presuppose the principle of the sanctity of sovereignty. The colonial legacy in the Middle East has created sensitivity to challenges to state sovereignty. Due to this history and the legitimacy challenges of many states in the region, it would be political suicide for leaders to cede sovereignty to an E.U.-like institution.

Paul Salem has suggested that a number of principles, such as respect for the national security of each state, de-escalation of conflict through diplomacy, and the elimination of armed non-state actors, need to be part of a core set of agreed principles. Salem argues that more ambitious principles, which could be adopted as conditions permit, might also include: strengthening bilateral and regional economic relations, cessation of sectarian propagandizing, as well as commitment to establishment of a structured regional framework.[39]

MODEL 1—AN ARAB CENTRIC MODEL: ANACHRONISM OR THE FUTURE?

What the Arab Spring taught us is that there is a common set of norms, expectations, and shared historical experiences that allowed uprisings to spread across the Arab expanse. And it is clear that what we have been witnessing with the civil wars and the rise of ISIS have been quite specifically Arab phenomena. The Arab-centric model is built on recognition that while the entire Middle East is in turmoil, the core of the problem resides in the collapse of the Arab order. It is also built on the assumption that there has to be an Arab institutional solution to this distinctly Arab problem.

While the Middle East overall may be the least integrated regions of the world, the Arab world has had experience with regional institutions, such as the League of Arab States, the Gulf Cooperation Council (G.C.C.), and the Arab Maghreb Union. Whether integrating these into a broader framework would mean subsuming them under a new umbrella organization or merely tying the missions of these existing institutions together through agreements, there is already machinery in place to facilitate cooperative behavior. The Arab League's intention to create a still unrealized joint military force reflects movement in this area already.[40] Because of these existing institutions, this model could happen earlier on the continuum of regionalization.

Pros: The legacy of existing institutions and the fact that they have at least made efforts in the direction of this model already are plusses. Another plus is that cooperation will be necessary to tackle the reconstruction efforts in Syria, Iraq, Yemen, and Libya. While Turkey and Iran are likely to have a stake in these activities, cooperation among the Arab countries will be at the center of reconstruction efforts. Also, ISIS is an insurgency movement against the Arab order and it will need a distinct Arab response.

Last, in the spirit of Parag Khanna's "devolution before aggregation," this model should be seen as a building block of a regional framework that extends beyond the Arab world. No regional integration project should be built on a premise that traditional identity politics will weaken, but instead should assume that different national identities will be functionally integrated into the whole.[41]

Cons: As mentioned before, the region has become transformed by Arab state failure and the rise of Turkey and Iran. An Arab-centric framework doesn't really address this emerging dynamic. Moreover, it assumes that there are common political and economic interests across the Arab world, whereas we can actually think about the Arab world as having been split in two by the civil wars, with the eastern part of the Arab world actively engaged in these conflicts, while the countries of the Maghreb are more remote from the regional maelstrom. Also, while cooperation may be necessary across the Arab world, further consolidation could be perceived as a threat by Turkey and Iran, reinforcing the patterns of conflict and moving the region further away from cooperation.

Viability: This could work under two conditions. One is that there are mechanisms for outreach to the non-Arab countries of Iran, Turkey, and Israel. Similar to the mechanisms for ASEAN for reaching out to South Korea, China, and Japan, an Arab-centric system would need to create a bridge to the non-Arab Middle East. The second is if sub-regional integration takes place as a first step toward broader integration with Turkey, Iran, and Israel, then this might be viable. But as a long-term model, it would likely be an anachronism at best and a pathway to further conflict at worst.

Model 2: The Arab-Turkish Model

This model would involve an Arab-Turkish axis, which could be thought of as the Arab-centric model plus. In other words, formalized cooperation within the Arab community outlined in the previous model would run parallel to the inclusion of Turkey. One approach would be that Turkey, the Arab League, and the G.C.C would be subsumed under a single umbrella organization. Another could be less formal with agreements binding the Arab institutions and Turkey together. Under either of these arrangements Turkey could act as an informal bridge to Iran. Or the bridge to Iran (and eventually Israel) could be a formal institution, much like how ASEAN developed the A.P.T. as a functional bridge to South Korea, China, and Japan.

Pros: From where we sit today, the obstacles to a region-wide framework including both Saudi Arabia and Iran may be insuperable. Tensions between Saudi Arabia and Turkey, however, are less fraught than the Saudi-Iranian relationship. And while there are tensions between Turkey and Iran over Syria, there remain strong trade relations between them on natural gas. Turkey, thus, would be in a good position to manage tensions between the Saudis and Iranians, and reduce some of the political risks associated with compromise. Countries like Egypt, Oman, and Qatar, slightly more neutral in their views of Iran, could also become part of the bridge. It will be important that the Arab League be an instrument of this model, as broader Arab membership (particularly with Egypt's involvement) is likely to be less threatening to Iran than a Saudi-G.C.C dominated model.

Cons: It is possible that the bridge will fail and that an Arab-Turkish axis will heighten rather than ameliorate tensions with Iran. There is also the potential for Turkish-Arab tensions to undermine this model, particularly with the mercurial Turkish President Recep Tayyip Erdogan's neo-Ottoman lens onto the Arab world. Also, this model could become a new status quo, letting both Tehran and Riyadh off the hook for some form of direct collaboration.

Viability: This could work under conditions where it is impossible to bring Iran and Israel under one tent, but it isn't perfect. It could also work as a transition to a broader framework that includes all major stakeholders, reflecting the power dynamics of the new Middle East.

MODEL 3: THE ALL-INCLUSIVE MODEL

This model accurately reflects the new Middle East and includes at a minimum the G.C.C. countries, Egypt, Turkey, and Iran; at a maximum, of course, it would also include Israel. There are several scenarios as to how it might unfold. It could evolve from successful cooperative efforts of the previous Turkish bridge model. Or it could emerge out of collaboration between international and regional actors on post-conflict reconstruction of Syria and Iraq. Another is that it could develop as a result of a shift in leadership in either Tehran or Riyadh.

Pros: This model would more accurately reflect the new regional power map, and could provide the best forum for seriously ending proxy wars as well as jointly engaging the international community on region-wide issues. This model would also allow for the greatest coordination of resources for post-conflict reconstruction efforts in Syria and Yemen. It would provide a region-wide platform for tackling the problems that are threats to regional security and to the political legitimacy of states, such as climate change, and water shortages.

Cons: This is almost impossible to start now given the intensity of the existing conflicts. This model would also heavily depend on international powers, and with the current deterioration in relations between the United States and Russia, and the election of Donald Trump to the U.S. presidency, it might be still-born. In this vein, the potential for international tensions to undermine this fragile regional system would be quite high. The model would be a high stakes game where failure could lead to an intensification of proxy conflict.

Viability: In any of the models presented, the balance of power between the major states of Saudi Arabia, Turkey, and Iran will be an important determinant of success. But with this model where all of these states fall under an overarching regional institution, this becomes even more delicate. Conditions that would be most conducive for cooperation would be a balance of power system, where states only win through cooperation, not one-upmanship. But maintaining that balance over time, as regional conditions evolve, will be difficult. If done judiciously, an international support group could help correct for imbalances in power, as long as the principle of the sanctity of state sovereignty isn't violated. If this model becomes a reality at all, it will likely be later on the regionalization continuum.

Conclusion

The challenges of regionalization of the Middle East are formidable. The notion of common interests seems a mirage given the upending of the regional order that has taken place. Moreover, states that have legitimacy problems are either unable or unwilling to spend political capital on long-term projects for creating regional security and prosperity. There are also no obvious leaders today with the vision and courage to advance the Middle East toward regional integration as Schuman and Monnet did for Europe.

By these indications, it might be premature to aim for a regional institutional architecture. But if we look at regional institutional formation as one point on the continuum of regionalization, there are opportunities. What is more important than the timing of a regional architecture is that the process of turning a negative regional order in the Middle East into a positive system of interdependencies begins soon. Jump-starting the process of regionalization by focusing on economic opportunities and addressing the region-wide water problems could advance the process of converting abstract interests into shared benefits.

As we have chronicled, there will be headwinds encountered in the march toward regionalization and even greater obstacles in trying to erect a formal regional architecture. However, there are some positive developments that could augur well for this process. The resilience of the Iran nuclear deal could bode well for the international community working together on issues related to the Middle East, which could be a boon to regional cooperation. Also, global trends toward regionalization could be a positive factor, as the emergence of trading blocs elsewhere could make regional cooperation the only way for the Middle East to be competitive. China's One-Belt, One Road program, for example, can be a spur toward greater regionalization across Asia and into the Middle East.[42]

It is important to start regionalization efforts now, even though gratification of seeing a regional architecture materialize will likely not come in the short-term. Early steps require international powers to use their influence to convene, cajole and send signals to regional powers like Iran, Saudi Arabia, and Turkey that the only behavior that will be supported will be cooperation.

Like Rome, a regional architecture can't be built overnight. But as the experiences of Asia, Latin America, Africa, and Europe instruct us, it will never be built unless the early steps toward regionalization are taken. As we saw with our three different models for the Middle East, there are opportunities at different points on the regionalization continuum for different forms of a regional architecture. The stakes for the Middle East and the rest of the world are too high not to aim for a regional architecture that, over the coming years and decades, transforms the Middle East from simply a geographic region into an integrated, stable, and prosperous regional system.

ENDNOTES

1. See Michael C. Hudson, Arab Politics: The Search for Legitimacy, (New Haven: Yale University Press: September 10th, 1979) for one of the better treatments of the legitimacy problems holding back the region.

2. See Francois Duchene, Jean Monnet: The First Statesman of Interdependence,(NY, NY: W.W. Norton and Company: January 1, 1980)

3. See "The European Union Explained: The Founding Fathers of the E.U.", European Commission, Brussels, 2012

4. See "The European Union Explained" How the European Union Works", European Commission, Brussels 2014

5. Yuen Foong Khong and Helen E.S. Nesadurai in Amitav Acharya and Alastair Iain Johnston (editors), Crafting Cooperation; Regional International Institutions in Comparative Perspective (New York, NY: Cambridge University Press: 2007), chapter 2, p. 40 and footnote 13 on same page. Also, see the History section of the ASEAN website. http://asean.org/asean/about-asean/history/

6. Yuen Foong Khong and Helen E.S. Nesadurai in Amitav Acharya and Alastair Iain Johnston (editors), chapter 2, p. 34.

7. ibid, chapter 2, pp. 40-43. Also, letter dated 30th October, 1991 from the Permanent representatives of France and Indonesia to the United Nations addressed to the Secretary General

8. Farrell, Mary, Hettne, Björn, Van Langenhove, Luk, Global Politics of Regionalism, Theory and Practice, Pluto Press, August 2005, chapter 10

9. Yuen Foong Khong and Helen E.S. Nesadurai in Amitav Acharya and Alastair Iain Johnston (editors), Crafting Cooperation; Regional International Institutions in Comparative Perspective (New York, NY: Cambridge University Press: 2007), chapter 2, p. 540

10. Ibid, chapter 2, pp.35-6. Also, see Simon Tay, "The Future of ASEAN: An Assessment of Democracy , Economies and Institutions in Southeast Asia, Southeast Asia, Winter 2001

11. Ibid. page 364

12. Alice D. Ba, "China and ASEAN: Renavigating relations for a 21st Century Asia", Asian Survey, 43:4, 2003, pp. 622-647

13. Yuen Foong Khong and Helen E.S. Nesadurai in Amitav Acharya and Alastair Iain Johnston (editors), Crafting Cooperation; Regional International Institutions in Comparative Perspective (New York, NY: Cambridge University Press: 2007), chapter 2, p. 32

14. Yuen Foong Khong and Helen E.S. Nesadurai in Amitav Acharya and Alastair Iain Johnston (editors), Crafting Cooperation; Regional International Institutions in Comparative Perspective (New York, NY: Cambridge University Press: 2007), chapter 2, p. 39

15. See Anthony H. Cordesman, "Military Cooperation in MENA: Uncertainty in the Face of Changing Threats", Middle East Institute Policy Paper 2016-7, August 2016, p. 5

16. Victor Osaro Edo and Michael Abiodun Olanrewaju, "An Assessment of the Transformation of the Organization of African Unity (O.A.U.) to the African Union (A.U.), 1963-2007", Journal of the Historical Society of Nigeria (Vol. 21 (20120, pp. 44

17. Jeffrey Herbst in Amitav Acharya and Alastair Iain Johnston (editors), Crafting Cooperation; Regional International Institutions in Comparative Perspective

(New York, NY: Cambridge University Press: 2007), chapter 4 pages 131-2

18. Organization of African Unity, "O.A.U. Resolution on Border Disputes, 1964", reprinted in Ian Brownie (ed) Basic Documents on African Affairs (Oxford: Clarendon Press, 1971), p. 361

19. Jeffrey Herbst in Amitav Acharya and Alastair Iain Johnston (editors), Crafting Cooperation; Regional International Institutions in Comparative Perspective (New York, NY: Cambridge University Press: 2007), chapter 4 page 133.

20. Jeffrey Herbst in Amitav Acharya and Alastair Iain Johnston (editors), Crafting Cooperation; Regional International Institutions in Comparative Perspective (New York, NY: Cambridge University Press: 2007), chapter 4 pages 129-130.

21. The Continental Early Warning System (CEWS), African Union Peace and Security. http://www.peaceau.org/en/page/28-continental-early-warning

22. "Mercosur: a brief history" PulsAmerica- The Impartial Latin American News Magazine, July 24th, 2015

23. Jorge I. DomiNguez in Amitav Acharya and Alastair Iain Johnston (editors), Crafting Cooperation; Regional International Institutions in Comparative Perspective (New York, NY: Cambridge University Press: 2007), chapter 3, p. 91. See "Charter of the Organization of American States" (A-41), Principles p. 4. http://www.oas.org/en/sla/dil/inter_american_treaties_A-41_charter_O.A.S..asp

24. Nahuel Arenas-Garcia, "'21st Century Regionalism in South America: UNASUR and the Search for Development Alternatives", eSharp, Issue 18: Challenges of Development (2012), pp. 64-85

25. See Pia Riggirozzi and Diana Tussie, The

Rise of Post-Hegemonic Regionalism in Latin America, , Springer Science and Business Media 2012

26. Shahrokh Fardoust, research Professor at the Institute of the Theory and Practice of International Relations at the College of William and Mary, and former director of strategy and operations, development economics at the World Bank (position held from 2008-2011) estimates that the peace dividend that would accrue to the region should it stabilize would be 2-3% of overall G.D.P. of the region.

27. Karen J. Alter and David Steinberg, "The Theory and Reality of the European Coal and Steel Community" Buffett Center for International and Comparative Studies Working Paper Series, Working Paper No 07-001, January 2007 Working Paper Series

28. Aysegul Kibaroglu, "Natural Cooperation: Facing Water Challenges in the Middle East", (Middle East Institute, MEI Policy Paper 2016-8, p 17 raises the issue of whether water for the Middle East can be the equivalent of what steel and coal was for Europe

29. Aysegul Kibaroglu, "Natural Cooperation: Facing Water Challenges in the Middle East", (Middle East Institute, MEI Policy Paper 2016-8, p 2.

30. John Vidal "Water Supply key to outcome of conflicts in Iraq and Syria, experts warn", Guardian, July 2nd, 2014

31. Aysegul Kibaroglu, "Natural Cooperation: Facing Water Challenges in the Middle East", (Middle East Institute, MEI Policy Paper 2016-8, p 1.

32. Aysegul Kibaroglu, "Natural Cooperation: Facing Water Challenges in the Middle East", (Middle East Institute, MEI Policy Paper 2016-8, p 19.

33. Barbara Slavin, "Environmental Official

says Iran looking for more International Cooperation" Al-Monitor,, September 22nd, 2016

34. Ruth Schuster, "The Secret of Israel's Water Miracle and How it Can Help a Thirsty World", Haaretz, January 25th, 2016

35. See Michael Axworthy and Patrick Milton, "A Westphalian Plan for the Middle East", Foreign Affairs, October 10th 2016

36. Bernard Hoekman, "Intra-Regional Trade: Potential Catalyst for Growth in the Middle East, (Middle East Institute, MEI Policy Paper, 2016-1, April 2016 pp. 21-24

37. Hedi Larbi, "Regional Infrastructure Cooperation: Connecting Countries to Stabilize the Middle East", (Middle East Institute, MEI Policy Paper 2016-4, p 16.

38. "Syria's Reconstruction offers opportunities for Lebanon", The Arab Weekly, September 18th, 2016

39. Paul Salem, "Working Towards a Stable Regional Order", ANNALS, AAPS, November 2016, p. 46

40. Rory Jones and Tamer El-Ghobashy "Arab League Agrees to create Joint Military Force", The New York Times, March 29th, 2015

41. Parag Khanna, Connectography: Mapping the Future of Global Civilization", (New York, NY: Random House: 2016), chapter 4.

42. David Dollar, "China's Rise as a Regional and Global Power: The AIIB and the "One-Belt, One Road", Horizons- Summer 2015, Issue #4.

Made in the USA
Columbia, SC
27 February 2020